FIELD SALES MANAGEMENT

RONALD SERIES ON MARKETING MANAGEMENT

Series Editor: FREDERICK E. WEBSTER, Jr.
*The Amos Tuck School
of Business Administration
Dartmouth College*

Field Sales Management

FREDERICK E. WEBSTER, JR.
The Amos Tuck School
of Business Administration
Dartmouth College

A RONALD PRESS PUBLICATION

JOHN WILEY & SONS

New York · Chichester · Brisbane · Toronto · Singapore

This publication is designed to provide accurate and
authoritative information in regard to the subject
matter covered. It is sold with the understanding that
the publisher is not engaged in rendering legal, accounting,
or other professional service. If legal advice or other
expert assistance is required, the services of a competent
professional person should be sought. *From a Declaration
of Principles jointly adopted by a Committee of the
American Bar Association and a Committee of Publishers.*

Library of Congress Cataloging in Publication Data:

Webster, Frederick E.
   Field sales management.

   (Ronald series on marketing management, ISSN 0275-
875X)

   "A Ronald Press publication."
   Bibliography: p.
   Includes index.
   1. Sales management.   2. Traveling sales personnel.
I. Title.   II. Series.

HF5438.4.W42   1983   658.8'1   83-1388
ISBN 0-471-09224-X

Printed in the United States of America

10 9 8 7 6 5 4 3 2 1

Series Editor's Foreword

As business encounters the challenges of the 1980s, top management is increasingly looking to marketing for sharpened competitive effectiveness. The emphasis on strategy formulation and financial performance at the corporate level that characterized the previous decade is now evolving toward a broader concern for total strategic management. This sharpens the focus on marketing as the prime vehicle for implementing corporate and business strategies.

Marketing management is the most dynamic of the business functions. Marketing must respond to the everchanging marketplace and the constant evolution of customer preference and buying habits, technology, and competition. Marketing management continually grows in sophistication and complexity as developments in management science are applied to the work of the marketing manager.

The books in The Ronald Series on Marketing Management have been written for managers. They combine a concern for management application with an appreciation for the relevance of developments in such areas as behavioral science, financial analysis, and mathematical modeling, as well as the insights gained from analyzing successful experience in the marketplace. The Ronald Series on Marketing Management is thus intended to communicate the state-of-the-art in marketing to managers.

Both marketing practitioners and academic teacher/scholars have contributed to the works in this series which now includes coverage of advertising management, sales promotion, public relations, consumer research, industrial marketing, brand loyalty, financial analysis for marketing decisions, the impact of government regulation, selling and field sales management, new product development, and market planning for new industrial products. As new insights based on research and managerial practice in marketing management are brought forward, this series will continue to offer new entries that convey the state-of-the-art in a manner that permits practicing managers to extend their own experience by using new analytical frameworks, and which acquaint students of marketing with the work of the professional marketing manager.

FREDERICK E. WEBSTER, JR.

Hanover, New Hampshire
September 1982

Preface

The purpose of this book is to examine the duties of field sales managers and the concepts and tools of analysis and decision making that are available to help them fulfill those responsibilities. The results of empirical research on field sales management, as reported in the literature of marketing, management, and management science, will be incorporated where they can help understand the field sales manager's problems and suggest better solutions to those problems.

This text is intended for present and potential managers of field sales representatives and their activities. The emphasis will be on analysis and problem solving, with only minimal description of types and numbers of sales personnel and selling institutions. This is a book *for* sales managers, not *about* selling and management. As a college text, it should serve best in graduate and upper-level undergraduate sales management courses with substantial use of case studies, for which the text can provide helpful conceptual background.

Principal concern will be for the direction and development of field sales personnel. Specific subjects to be discussed include the role of the field sales manager; buyer–sales representative interaction; recruiting; selection; training; organization; motivation, supervision, control, and compensation of sales personnel; sales territory design, and the allocation and deployment of sales effort. Marketing strategy *per se* is assumed to be a given for the sales manager, although one of his or her responsibilities is to contribute to the development of that marketing strategy. Sales force management and deployment strategies will be examined in the context of overall marketing strategy, but little time will be spent on the broader issues of marketing strategy development. The area of marketing strategy to be examined in greatest depth is market segmentation strategy, because it has direct impact on sales force organization, training, deployment, and evaluation.

Compared with other areas of marketing management, sales force management must be much more concerned with management of human resources. This text, therefore, will incorporate and make use of many concepts and research findings from the field of organizational behavior, which draws heavily on the disciplines of psychology, social psychology, and sociology.

This text does have a point of view. It is that the field sales manager and the sales representative are key actors in the implementation of marketing strategy. The field sales manager should be viewed as a manager, responsible for the development and direction of the human resources of the sales organization, not as a supersalesman. The sales representative should be viewed as responsible for managing the relationship with accounts, not as someone whose job is to make people buy. Selling and buying are regarded as interdependent parts of the same process, with the outcome determined by the interaction process itself, not by the characteristics of the individual actors. The field sales manager's major responsibility is to maximize the effectiveness of the sales representatives in their interactions with customers. The field sales manager is a major factor in improving the productivity of any marketing organization.

FREDERICK E. WEBSTER, JR.

Hanover, New Hampshire
June 1983

Acknowledgments

This text was developed over a period of three years in which versions of the material were shared with my students at the Amos Tuck School of Business Administration, Dartmouth College, and with participants in management seminars for Chase Manhattan Bank, E. I. du Pont de Nemours & Company, General Electric Company, IBM, Merrill Lynch, and Norton Company. Each group's reactions to the material provided valuable assistance in its continued development. Special thanks are due to Mr. John E. Taylor, General Sales Manager, Norton Company, for his review of the manuscript in its final form. I am also indebted to representatives of Connecticut General Life Insurance Company, General Foods Corporation, Gould, Inc., Norton Company, the American Marketing Association, the Marketing Science Institute, and Richard D. Irwin, Inc. for permission to reproduce materials used for illustrative purposes in the text.

Dean Richard West of the Amos Tuck School was always supportive of my attempts to find time to work on this project. My secretary, Eunice P. Ballam, professionally and cheerfully typed and organized the multiple drafts of each chapter and kept track of the project details such as illustrations and permissions.

Finally, to my wife, Mary Alice, my thanks for her continued tolerance and understanding, for the past twenty-five years, of the strange schedules and behavior that accompany a writing project.

F.E.W.

Contents

FIELD SALES MANAGEMENT

ONE

The Field Sales Representative

Field selling activities are a primary activity in the economy and a major factor in the productivity of business. The persons who manage such activities have a rich and challenging set of responsibilities, and their management successes and failures are reflected in the sales accomplishments and personal growth of the sales representatives they manage. Field sales managers are a major determinant of the success of the sales organization. This text examines the functions of the field sales manager and the many elements of the field sales management process. It begins by looking at the responsibilities of field sales people and the role of personal selling in the marketing strategy of a business.

Field sales representatives occupy one of the most important positions within a business firm and in the economy at large. These men and women perform the critical function of serving as a communication link between buyers and sellers, representing manufacturers and distributors to their customers, and, equally important, representing the customers' needs and viewpoints back to the manufacturer and distributor.

It is an old cliché, but fundamentally true, that "nothing happens until something is sold." All of the other activities of a business firm depend ultimately upon finding a customer for that firm's product or service and making sure that the customer is satisfied with its performance. The functioning of the economy has at its core a vast number of transactions between buyers and sellers, each likely facilitated by the activities of a sales representative.

"Field" or "outside" sales representatives are those who travel to the buyer's place of business or residence. The other types of sales representatives are clerks in retail stores and "inside" sales personnel in manufacturing and distribution firms who work either at a sales counter or over the telephone. In this book, our concern will be for the field sales representative. According to various government estimates, there were approximately 6,425,000 sales workers in the United States labor force in 1981, roughly 55% male and 45% female. Approximately 2,431,000 of these were retail clerks, and of the retail clerks, over 70% were women. Conversely, women represented about 30% of the salesworkers who were not retail clerks. While the word salesman has often been used as a matter of convenience to describe workers of both sexes, current sensitivities prefer either "salesperson" or "sales representative," to avoid sexism. The author prefers sales representative, shortened to "sales rep" or "rep" for convenience, because "salesperson" traditionally has been used when the specific reference is to a retail sales clerk. To repeat, this text is concerned with the management of the field sales force, those sales reps who travel to the customer's location.

THE ROLE OF THE SALES REP

A sales rep is many things. The rep is usually (but not always!) responsible for obtaining orders. In any given organization, some of the many possible dimensions of the sales rep's functions will be emphasized more than others. A list of typical responsibilities would include the following activities, which clearly are not mutually exclusive:

Obtaining orders.
Providing customer service.
Gathering market information.
Calling on all customers in the assigned geographic territory.
Developing new accounts.
Becoming knowledgeable about customers, products, and competitors.

Selling the full product line.

Installing and maintaining equipment.

Making recommendations about pricing.

Planning sales calls carefully.

Controlling expenses within assigned budgets.

Working with customers and distributors to develop advertising and sales promotion programs for them.

Maintaining displays and adequate inventories at customers' locations.

Completing call reports on time.

Explaining current promotions to customers.

Entertaining customers.

Communicating new product ideas back to the factory.

Obtaining new dealers and distributors.

Training distributors' sales personnel.

Forecasting sales volume in the territory and by account.

Providing information on competitors' activities.

Developing markets for new products.

Conducting seminars for customers and distributors.

Working with applications engineers to solve customer problems.

Expediting orders for the customer.

Training customer personnel in product use.

Demonstrating the product at trade shows.

Each company must develop a specific description of the responsibilities that the sales rep is expected to perform. This job description becomes a critically important management tool for virtually all areas of sales management including recruiting and selection, training, evaluation and compensation, motivation, and supervision. It tells the sales rep how he or she will be evaluated and rewarded and what is expected on a day-to-day basis. Figures 1.1, 1.2, and 1.3 show examples of job descriptions for sales reps in three well-known companies. The differences in job titles are worth noting, as these suggest markedly different emphases in the job definition and in the employer's expectations for three quite different types of sales representative.

TITLE: Sales Representative I

REPORTS TO: Territory Manager

BASIC FUNCTION: To contact retail outlets in order to favorably influence the sales of company's products at the retail level. Responsibility for direct/indirect account contacts may be assigned to the Sales Representative, but would be secondary to the primary retail function.

NATURE AND SCOPE:
The Sales Representative reports directly to the Territory Manager. The Sales Representative concentrates his or her efforts primarily on assigned high-volume retail stores that contribute significantly to the growth of direct accounts in the territory and/or district. The Sales Representative is the foundation of the sales organization. Commensurate with his ability, the Sales Representative will be assigned additional responsibility of headquarter level contacts and is responsible for developing and cultivating mutually beneficial relationships with chain store supervisors.

The Sales Representative must analyze his or her customers, the market and competitive situations, and must develop tactical plans consistent with territory and district objectives that will result in increased volumes and in the strengthening of the division's position. The Sales Representative must be knowledgeable of corporate and division philosophies, policies, procedures, and product knowledge. In addition, he or she must have a firm grasp of both division and district margin, etc., various profit terms, e.g. breakeven, profit margin, etc., various marketing statistical data, CPRs, SAMI, Nielsen, MAJERS, as well as facility with the company's selling method and thorough knowledge of the marketing area or areas in which he or she works.

PRINCIPAL ACCOUNTABILITIES:

I. Retail Conditions. The most critical responsibility of the Sales Representative is the condition of assigned company products in his or her assigned retail stores and involves the following:

Securing and maintaining distribution of assigned products in keeping with division priorities and district standards.

Selling and merchandising in chain and independent retail stores all priority programs and quarterly promotions.

Selling opportunity displays on each retail call.

Assuring adequate inventories will be maintained according to district standards.

Selling media advertising in support of district standards.

Allocating time to conform to the workload.

Developing and maintaining effective proprietary relationships.

II. Retail Sales Analysis and Planning. As a means to accomplish the critical responsibilities established under retail conditions, proper identification of sales needs and adequate planning for their accomplishment must occur, including:

Figure 1.1. A job description for a General Foods sales representative.

4

Obtaining knowledge of all pertinent data related to assigned stores.

Having available all appropriate selling tools and equipment during each retail call.

III. Communications and Reports. The individual must initiate those activities necessary to keep his or her management informed and for the maintenance of appropriate records, including:

Maintenance of a record of activities in his or her assigned area as required by management.

Preparation and submission of all necessary reports.

Reporting on all competitive activities in his or her area.

Submission of recommendations for improving the operations of his or her area.

Initiation and development of intra-territory and intra-district communications with fellow sales personnel which will positively impact on the synergy of the territory and district team.

IV. Account Sales Execution. The Sales Representative must influence direct and indirect buying accounts to purchase, price, promote, and merchandise assigned brands, including:

Sales, securing, and maintenance of direct account distribution at or above division/district standards.

Sale and merchandising of division/district programs and promotions to assigned accounts according to objectives.

Insuring warehouse inventories in keeping with retail store demands.

Managing of assigned accounts to accomplish volume objectives and to develop them to their maximum potential.

Keeping his or her supervisor informed of account activities.

Development and maintenance of appropriate customer records.

Understanding and analysis of the entire operation of his or her accounts.

Development of proprietary relationships with assigned customers.

Management of time in assigned accounts to conform with the structure of the workload.

V. Individual Objectives. The Sales Representative is responsible for planning and accomplishing objectives for his or her assigned position, area, and accounts in conjunction with the objectives of the district by the Management Process:

Personal/business objectives should be developed with the Territory Manager.

VI. Cost Control. Each individual must control activities to insure that sales costs are maintained within operating budgets, including:

Exercise of sound judgment when incurring business expenses.

Exercise of proper care in handling of all company material and equipment.

Figure 1.1. (*Continued*)

JOB TITLE: Sales Engineer

IMMEDIATE SUPERVISOR: Branch Manager

I. Function

    The Sales Engineer is responsible for the coordination of sales activity assigned to him under the supervision of the Branch Manager, consistent with sound sales practice and in accordance with Corporate policies.

II. Objectives

    1. To assist in the achievement of the profit objectives by obtaining technical sales orders for the company.
    2. To initiate and maintain favorable relationships with past, present and future customers through personal visits, oral and written communications.
    3. To promote and sell the facilities of the various works.
    4. To obtain advance information regarding customers' requirements.

III. Responsibility and Authority

    1. Contact customers for sales orders, presenting proposals, soliciting sales or outlining capabilities of manufacturing facilities or engineering services.
    2. Assist, if necessary, the customers' sales, research, engineering, manufacturing, and sales personnel in developing data for product specifications to be enumerated in the quotation.
    3. Establish a customer relationship that may include contact with the president of a smaller company or a vice-president of a larger organization.
    4. Obtain requests for quotation, collect appropriate information, prepare the quotation and deliver to potential customer.
    5. Secure sales orders for both "make-to-print" and "design-and-develop" products.
    6. Coordinate all sales activities with Branch Manager to insure a completely integrated sales effort.
    7. Keep advised of all customer delivery schedules, quality performance and coordination of engineering changes or modifications.
    8. Assist in the planning and coordination of customer visits to company plants or arrange for visits of sales personnel to the customer's offices.
    9. Periodically report on customers' requests, sales problems, and sales results, in both a formal and informal manner, to keep sales management personnel advised of current, future and potential sales activity.

Figure 1.2. A job description for a Gould, Inc. Instruments Divison sales engineer.

10. Maintain active files and sales data on major sales programs with assigned customers or within assigned territory; also current information on company's capabilities, design and development services and related data for sales support.

11. Assist in resolving any quality or delivery problems to the degree that the customer is satisfied that he received prompt attention and equitable treatment.

12. Participate, as appropriate, in the preparation of cost estimates or in furnishing essential data to prepare a cost estimate.

13. Forward information required for sales forecasts or special data on specific projects, customers or sales status.

14. Maintain accurate, up-to-date and complete sales information, including price, delivery time, and other related sales data for use of the customer, or potential customers, if required.

15. Be alert to customers' planning and future developments which may result in business, and also be aware of competition's sales activities, including new products, prices, per cent of penetration of market, and related sales data of major importance to sales planning.

16. Recommend, for consideration, changes in material, design, manufacturing processes, inspection and quality control, to meet a customer's specific problem or to assist field sales personnel.

17. Participate, if requested, in specific test programs or projects, and also in sales meetings.

18. Interpret customers' interests, needs and requirements through direct contacts, conferences, meetings and written reports, and disseminate useful sales information to proper sales personnel.

19. Assume responsibilities common to all members of management.

IV. Relationships and Accountabililty
Within the company

1. Cooperate with other members of the Sales, Marketing, Engineering, and Technical Service Departments in providing a unified sales effort.

2. Communicate with and collaborate with Works personnel to solve problems pertaining to sales, engineering, and manufacturing.

Outside the company

1. Maintain satisfactory relations with customers of products.

V. Qualifications

A college engineering graduate, with an ability to work with company engineering, research, and manufacturing, as well as customer personnel. Requires a minimum of four years' sales office or technical service prior to engaging in field sales activities.

Figure 1.2. (*Continued*)

CONNECTICUT GENERAL LIFE INSURANCE COMPANY
POSITION DESCRIPTION

Title of Position	National Accounts Executive		
Department	Group Insurance Sales—Field	Number in Position	Date
Division	Group Insurance Operations	Report To *(Title)* Manager	

General Purpose: PROMOTES the sale and service of all Group products primarily to large prospective and existing customers through various producers in their particular region. MAINTAINS an assigned book of business of up to $25 million for 25–50 firms by fulfilling ongoing service requirements and persistency and profit objectives. ASSISTS manager in the sales planning and training of the junior sales aand administrative staff.

Responsibilities

Planning (5%)

ASSISTS Field Manager in RECOMMENDING/DEVELOPING plans for production persistency, profit and expenses. ANALYZES/EVALUATES market thrusts (e.g., sales forecast) in an effort to DEVELOP and IMPLEMENT action steps necessary in achieving results which are consistent with all planned objectives.

Account Management (40%)

DETERMINES/FACILITATES appropriate handling of policyholder service needs which entail adherence to service standards set by the Field Manager. IDENTIFIES/ CULTIVATES key policyholder staff/contacts. INTERPRETS and ARTICULATES "complex insurance concepts" to policyholder to SUPPORT renewal action (i.e., method of premium payment, flexibility of funding non-standard plan design, and levels of non-standard benefits.) RESPONSIBLE for successful renewal of an account. ACCOUNTABLE for profitability of business and persistency ratios on assigned complex cases. FOCUSES on addition of new line of coverage and benefit revisions on larger cases. SOLICITS/PRESENTS new/existing benefits to employees and COMPLETES enrollment.

Figure 1.3. A job description for a Connecticut General Life Insurance Company, group insurance sales national accounts executive.

Producer Development (15%)

IDENTIFIES/CULTIVATES producer relationships to ACQUIRE new policyholders and additional business on existing contracts.

Sales Activity—New Accounts (25%)

GATHERS/ANALYZES all pertinent case data. DETERMINES the risk and volume impact of business on corporation. CONSULTS H.O. Underwriting regarding presale underwriting and risk selection and evaluation. DETERMINES/ COMMUNICATES plan design to GAA for proposal preparation. DEVELOPS complex and sophisticated proposal techniques due to multiplicity of benefit options and non-standard plan design (e.g., sales strategy). FOLLOWS UP on proposal presentation and CLOSES sale.

Service (5%)

ACTS as liaison between H.O. and policyholder and in turn PROVIDES service to policyholder. SUPPLIES the data to staff member for case transmission. CONTACTS policyholder/producer in a cancellation situation to DETERMINE the reason for cancellation and FACILITATE appropriate handling of case. COMPLETES proper report form. HANDLES complaints from various sources (e.g., producer, policyholder, employer).

Personnel Training (5%)

ASSISTS Field Manager in the hiring, firing, reviewing, counseling, and rating of service and administrative support personnel. PERFORMS in a supervisory role by PROVIDING counsel, direction and motivation to junior sales staff. ASSISTS in the training of administrative (GAR) personnel. DIRECTS the activities of the Sales Support team.

Self-development (5%)

ENGAGES in activities which foster self-development in conjunction with Field Manager's plans.
Scope data
    Number of employees accountable for 1–9_____ 10–13_____
14_____
    Number of budget dollars accountable for $_____
    Other accountability factors:

_____

Scope data
    Number of employees accountable for 1–9_____ 10–13_____ 14_____
    Number of budget dollars accountable for $_____
    Other accountability factors:

_____

Figure 1.3. (*Continued*)

Stepping back from these detailed descriptions of the sales rep's responsibilities and activities, the role of the field sales representative can be conceptualized in several different ways. Each view sheds a somewhat different light on the nature of field selling responsibilities.

As Part of the Firm's Promotional Activity

From a marketing management viewpoint, the sales rep is part of the *promotional* mix of the firm. Selling is one of several activities including packaging, advertising, catalogues, product displays, sales promotion, publicity, and public relations intended to stimulate demand for the firm's products and services by creating awareness and favorable attitudes. In this view, the rep is primarily a promoter or marketing communicator, delivering selling messages to actual and prospective customers. The sales rep is just one of several sources of these messages for the customer, and the effects of these sources interact with one another. The rep is made more effective by the company's advertising, for example, and is responsible for the effectiveness of other promotional variables such as product displays.

Compared with the other elements of the promotional mix, personal selling has some obvious and essential uniqueness. Most importantly, because the rep is a person, personal selling is *two-way communication*. The rep can listen to the customer's expression of buying needs, preferences, and objections, and can then respond precisely, tailoring the sales presentation to fit that specific buyer. Personal communication is usually much more effective than impersonal (mass) communication in producing a response from the receiver of the message. It is also much more expensive per message delivered.

In Push and Pull Strategies

The nature of the firm's marketing strategy is a major influence on the role of the field sales representative. Promotional strategies that rely primarily on personal selling are characterized as *push* strategies; those that rely primarily on impersonal or mass communications, specifically advertising and sales promotion, are called *pull* strategies. Virtually all promotional strategies have elements of both, so the characterization as push or pull is one of emphasis, as evidenced by the allocation of promotional dollars between personal selling and mass media.

Pull strategies are seen most clearly in consumer packaged goods marketing. Brands of coffee, cigarettes, toothpaste, beer, detergents, soup, and so on are heavily promoted directly to the consumer with massive expenditures for television, radio, magazine, and newspaper advertising combined with sales promotional efforts such as coupons, cents-off labels, free gifts bearing the brand name, and merchandise offers. The manufacturer aims the large portion of promotional expenditures directly at the consumer or end user, in effect "pulling" the product through the channel of distribution from producer through the middlemen in the channel to the consumer. The retailer dosen't "sell" the product on the retail store shelf. (In a real sense, the large supermarket or discount store does not sell products to consumers; it sells shelf space to manufacturers.) Likewise, the retailer must seek out the product from the manufacturer directly or from brokers, wholesalers, and other types of distributors.

Of course, sales reps have a vital part to play within the pull strategy, but it is primarily one of insuring that the stocks and flows of product in the distribution channel are adequate to service the demand created by advertising and sales promotion. This role includes encouraging middlemen to order and stock the product in adequate quantities and making sure that the products and promotional materials are adequately displayed on the retail shelf. In a pull strategy most of the money is spent on mass media, and the sales force facilitates the process of satisfying the consumer demand generated by advertising and sales promotion.

In contrast, push strategies depend upon personal selling as the major promotional variable and are characteristic of industrial products and services as well as certain consumer products and services such as insurance, encyclopediae, and some brands of vacuum cleaners. Personal selling stimulates demand at all levels of the channel of distribution. When a push strategy is used in a consumer products channel, the manufacturer actively sells to the wholesaler, the wholesaler actively solicits orders from the retailer, and the retailer actively sells to the consumer, as illustrated by such products as furniture, shoes, dresses, and suits. Trade margins are generally much higher in push strategies than in pull strategies, 40–50% *vs* 20–25% at the retail level, for example. This reflects the channel members' greater responsibility for stimulating demand and the greater risk involved in stocking merchandise that typically turns over much more slowly than with consumer packaged goods. The markets for push-type products are often smaller and more narrow in terms of buyer characteristics than are the markets for pull-type products, where frequency of purchase is also much greater.

Industrial markets almost always are reached by push strategies. Most industrial marketers spend over 90% of their total promotional funds on personal selling. The primary role of advertising and sales promotion in industrial marketing is to support the efforts of the sales rep by creating awareness of the company and its products, by stimulating sales leads, and by building company reputation and credibility. Compared with consumer markets, industrial markets have many fewer customers, and the customer's buying decision process is much more complex, involves many persons (each of whom has a unique set of buying needs and decision criteria), and takes a much longer time. The industrial sales rep must seek out the many persons involved in the buying decision process and tailor the sales approach to each one. Chapter 3 will look carefully at the nature of the industrial buying process and the implications for the role of the sales rep.

As Part of the Product Offering

There is another subtlety to the role of the industrial sales rep, which is that the industrial customer often does not simply buy a physical product but rather a total capability of the supplier to help solve a customer problem. The industrial sales rep is often part of that problem-solving capability and, in this very important sense, is therefore part of the "product" being purchased by the customer. In other words, in the industrial push strategy, the sales rep is not only part of the promotional mix; but also part of the product offering. The rep often must help the customer define the problem that must be solved, develop procurement goals and specifications, and then suggest one or more combinations of products and services for solving that problem. This is seen most clearly in such examples as the sales representatives for IBM, Honeywell Information Systems, or Digital Equipment, where the computer hardware and software must be designed to fit into a total information system, and customer service must be provided on an ongoing basis if the computer is to perform its functions effectively. Other examples would include commercial banks, manufacturers of packaging materials and supplies, and air freight forwarders. The sales rep not only sells the service component of the product offering; he or she often delivers that service as well.

The industrial sales rep's responsibilities are often better described as managing the ongoing relationship with the customer rather than simply making the sale. This essential point, made much too briefly here given its importance, will be repeated often in the context of specific issues in sales force management. The sales rep's responsibility for account management and for developing key account selling strategies will be discussed in detail in Chapter 5.

As a Communicator in the Buyer-Seller Dyad

The sales representative was earlier described as a communication link between buyers and sellers, with an emphasis on a two-way flow of communication, and we have just finished consideration of the sales rep as a part of the firm's promotional strategy. Both views clearly involve looking at the rep as a communicator. We will now look more carefully at the sales rep as a communicator, using some concepts from the behavioral sciences.

Personal selling is a form of *interpersonal* communication. Interpersonal communication is two-way communication in which both parties serve as both communicator and receiver. The buyer and the sales rep can also be described as a *dyad,* and their communication can be viewed as dyadic interaction. There is a well-accepted viewpoint in social psychology that, because all communication is by definition social behavior, the smallest unit of analysis appropriate to understanding communication is the dyad, the two-person group.

Traditional views of the selling process tended to be very one-sided, focusing on the sales representative as an influence agent who, if he or she knew the prospect's needs and goals and delivered an optimal sales presentation, could produce the desired response from the prospect in the form of favorable attitudes and buying actions. These traditional views were presented under such labels as *AIDA*

(Attention-Interest-Desire-Action) and as the *stimulus-response* theories of selling. The central notion was one of the sales representative moving the prospect through a series of mental stages, with the various conceptions of those mental states referred to as "hierarchy-of-effects" models. Implicit in all these models was a rather passive role for the prospect.[1]

Gradually the pendulum swung to a view, consistent with the customer-oriented marketing concept, of a prospect who actively participates in the sales interaction. This viewpoint in the analysis of personal selling was consistent with developments in communication theory, which emphasized the "active listener" who not only listens but actively defines the content of the message through the processes of selective exposure and attention, selective perception, and selective retention. Seen in this general framework, the outcome of the sales interaction is determined not only by the words and actions of the sales rep but by the information status and perceptions of the buyer as they interact with those of the sales rep.

Therefore, personal selling can be viewed as interpersonal interaction in which the roles of the sales representative and the buyer are being played by the two actors in the dyad. An essential feature of the process is *person perception,* which is different from the perception of other objects in that, in the words of two authorities in the field, "the perceiver regards the [other person] as having the potential of representation and intentionality."[2] They explain the concept of intentionality as follows:

> Each observes that the other directs himself toward him; each can make known to the other that he is sensitive to the other's direction toward himself. These operations provide the "mutually shared" field in interaction—the prerequisite for all true social processes.[3]

The concept of representations is related to intentionality in the following way:

---

[1] Harold C. Cash and W. J. Crissy, "Ways of Looking at Selling," in William Lazer and Eugene Kelley (eds.), *Managerial Marketing: Perspectives and Viewpoints* (2nd ed.; Homewood, IL: Richard D. Irwin, 1962), pp. 554–559.

[2] Renato Taguiri and Luigi Petrullo (eds.), *Person Perception and Interpersonal Behavior* (Stanford, CA: Stanford University Press, 1958), p. x.

[3] *Ibid.,* p. xi.

Underlying this mode of comprehending human action is the capacity we have to note that the person whose actions we are following has within him a representation of his environment, that his actions are mediated by the representations he forms . . . On this basis we can experience the other person as directing himself to us, with intentions, attitudes, and feelings.[4]

In person perception, which is to say in interpersonal interaction, we do not just observe the person's actions toward us, but we make inferences about the feelings, needs, and viewpoints that underlie and cause those actions. We also make judgments about the impact of our own actions and messages upon those mental states of the other person. *Empathy* is defined as the ability to sense the reaction one produces in the other person, the ability to sense accurately the feedback to one's personal communication, and thereby to adjust one's messages to better achieve the goals that motivate the communication. It is widely believed that empathy is one of the essential characteristics possessed by successful sales representatives.[5] There is disagreement, however, as to whether empathy is an innate characteristic of the personality that can be measured by psychological testing, a skill that can be developed through training, or both.

Many companies follow sales training practices today that emphasize developing the sales rep's ability to listen and to analyze and organize what is heard as the basis for tailoring the sales presentation to the customer in a manner that enhances communication efficiency and effectiveness. Such training practices are consistent with the view of the sales representative as a communicator in dyadic interaction.

An important component of the sales interview as interpersonal communication comes from the fact that both participants occupy *social roles*. Social roles are interesting, real phenomena, defined as social positions occupied by individuals. Roles include the goals of those positions and the behavioral repertoires appropriate to those positions and to the attainment of those goals. Every person occupies many social roles at the same time. Every social role has attached to it a set of *role expectations* about how persons in that role should be-

[4]*Ibid.*

[5]David Mayer and Herbert M. Greenberg, "What Makes a Good Salesman," *Harvard Business Review*, XLII, No. 4 (July-August 1964), pp. 119—125.

have and how other persons should behave toward them. Thus, role expectations are *bi-dimensional*, specifying behaviors for both "self" and "other." In any given interaction, only a small subset of a person's many social roles will be relevant in terms of the behaviors expected for self and other, with the social role occupied by other as a primary influence on the behavioral repertoire appropriate for self.

In the sales interaction, the sales rep and the prospective buyer are not simply two persons interacting for the pure social pleasure of it; they occupy two distinct and more or less well-defined social roles— sales representative and buyer. Role expectations will be determined by many factors, including company policies, job descriptions, professional education and background, and by the "stereotype" of each role. A *stereotype* is simply a consensus of role expectations shared by a large segment of the population or culture. Stereotypes are developed based on repeated interaction with persons in a given social role. Most occupations provide social roles with rather strong and clear stereotypes. It is well known that there is a stereotype of the sales representative role, for example, that describes sales people as "talkative," "easy-going," "competitive," "optimistic," "enthusiastic," "excitable," and so on. Even sales reps describe themselves in these terms.[6]

Viewing the selling situation as role playing helps to understand the pressures on the sales representative as well as the complex set of factors that determine behavior in the sales interaction and the outcome of the sales call. A strong research tradition has developed in recent years using role theory as the basis for examining personal selling in a rigorous framework. The results of this research, which will be examined in more detail in Chapter 3, have interesting implications for the development of selling strategy and for the training and supervision of sales personnel. Much of this research has focused on role conflict, the tension created by conflicting role expectations held by the sales rep and the buyer, or by the sales rep and his or her manager, or indeed by any "relevant others" such as spouse, peers, friends, professional colleagues, and so on.

---

[6]Wayne K. Kirchner and Marvin D. Dunnette, "How Salesmen and Technical Men Differ in Describing Themselves," *Personnel Journal*, XXXVII, No. 11 (April 1959), pp. 418–419.

Models of the selling process as two-person communication are among the most significant forces driving research on sales management, and provide an important link with the study of buyer behavior, a field that has also shown heightened interest and substantial development in recent years. Concepts and findings from these areas of inquiry will be integrated into the discussion throughout the text.

As a "Boundary Role" Person

A somewhat different but obviously related view of the sales representative's role focuses on the fact that the rep occupies a "boundary role" in the organization, one that exists at the interface of the firm with the external environment. One of the unique dimensions of field sales management comes from the very basic fact that sales reps travel; are not located at a fixed place of work; are physically isolated from their peers, colleagues, and supervisors; and spend much of their time in non-selling activities. Further complexity comes from the fact that the sales rep brings the viewpoint of outsiders, most notably customers, distributors, and competitors, back into the organization. Quite often these viewpoints represent a challenge to the *status quo*, and provide problems and criticisms for other members of the organization to worry about. The sales rep, therefore, can be perceived as the cause of conflict and controversy. Not only does the rep become the focal point for criticism, complaints, and unsolved problems from the customer, but he or she is also likely to encounter negative responses from his or her own organization.

Therefore, the boundary role person is likely to feel a psychological as well as a physical distance from the organization. Policies and procedures for sales force monitoring, reporting, and control can be viewed as attempts to deal with both types of distance—physical and psychological—to keep the sales rep in the fold.[7]

As a boundary spanning person the sales rep is responsible for representing his or her firm to the customer and for representing the cus-

[7]Robert E. Spekman, "Organizational Boundary Behavior: A Conceptual Framework for Investigating the Industrial Salesperson," in Richard P. Bagozzi (ed.), *Sales Management: New Developments from Behavioral and Decision Model Research*, Report No. 79–107 (Cambridge, MA: Marketing Science Institute, 1979), pp. 133–144, esp. 134–135.

tomer back to the firm, another way of viewing the two-way communication responsibility. As noted, this can be a source of role conflict. It has also been observed, however, that the sales rep can gain power within the firm by means of controlling the flow of information back to the firm as well as by protecting himself or herself from the consequences of poor performance through the manipulation of information about the external environment.[8]

Viewing the sales rep as a boundary spanning person also emphasizes, consistent with the basic tenet of the marketing concept, the rep's responsibility for making the firm responsive to the customer's needs. The rep must represent the customer's viewpoint in discussions with product engineering, production scheduling, credit, transportation, and so on, and in general must stand against those whose viewpoint emphasizes the protection of the internal organization. The theoretical construct of boundary spanning provides support for the practical notion that the sales rep can be an important source of market information for making both short-term operating decisions and long-term strategic choices.[9]

Perhaps the major benefit of this view of the sales rep's role comes from its contribution to an understanding of the major source of role conflict for the sales rep. There is a problem for both the sales rep and the field sales manager to resolve: to make the appropriate tradeoff between the sales rep's need for autonomy as necessary to react intelligently to the customer and to the competitive environment as opposed to the need to maintain close communication and policy enforcement with the rep's own firm. Likewise, there is a tradeoff to be judged between sales force autonomy, giving maximum freedom and flexibility to react to the dynamic external environment, and the need to reduce role conflict and ambiguity to tolerable levels. As autonomy increases, so does the potential role conflict and ambiguity. This is one of the fundamental dilemmas faced by the field sales manager, and it will become an issue in virtually every area of sales management including selection, training, organization, supervision, motivation, deployment, evaluation, control, and compensation.

[8]*Ibid.*, p. 135.
[9]Frederick E. Webster, Jr., "The Industrial Salesman as a Source of Market Information," *Business Horizons*, Vol. 8, No. 1 (Spring 1965), pp. 77–82.

We have examined several different but non-competing views of the role of the field sales representative—as part of promotional strategy, as an element in the product/service offering, as a communicator in dyadic interaction, and as a boundary role person. Each view highlights some of the important aspects of management of the field sales force.

DETERMINANTS OF SALES REP PERFORMANCE

The foregoing review of several different conceptions of the role of the field sales representative has established two minimum conditions for an examination of the area of field sales management. First, the sales representative must be seen as part of the firm and as an element of its marketing strategy. Second, the rep must be viewed not in isolation but in interaction with representatives of the customer's organization. If we then analyze more completely the myriad of factors on both sides of the buyer-seller relationship, and in the external environment within which that interaction takes place, we can begin to appreciate the number and complexity of forces that must be considered as influences on the performance of the sales representative. The broad dimensions of such an analysis are outlined in Figure 1.4. This figure also suggests the factors to be examined more completely in the chapters that follow. (With some minor shifts in emphasis, this figure could also be used to explicate the determinants of the buyer's effectiveness as well.)

Individual Characteristics

The individual characteristics of the sales representative should never be overlooked as a prime cause of his or her effectiveness. Sound health and a modicum of physical stamina are prerequisites to a successful sales career. Such basic personality factors as intelligence, ambition, aggressiveness, sociability, and the need for achievement are enduring characteristics that influence all aspects of the individual's behavior and can have a significant impact on performance in the sales job. These characteristics are not likely to be influenced significantly as the result of training and supervision. They represent the

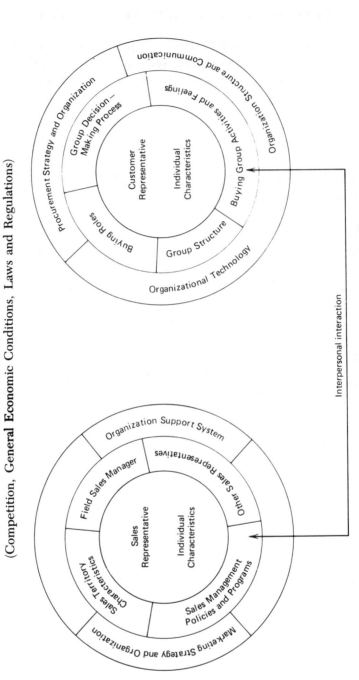

Environmental Factors
(Competition, General Economic Conditions, Laws and Regulations)

Figure 1.4. Determinants of sales representative effectiveness.

accumulated interactions of the inborn traits of the individual with his or her environment over a lifetime. Such basic factors can be assessed during the selection process, through the use of psychological tests, in personal interviews, by examination of the record of past accomplishments, through careful interpretation of letters of reference, by talking with past employers and teachers, and so on.

Education and experience provide a second set of individual characteristics that influence performance. These factors are especially important as determinants of the sales rep's knowledge level and ability to learn, in formal and informal training and from future experiences. Relevant education and experience include knowledge of products, markets, customers, competition, industry, and selling–salesmanship. The ability to analyze problem situations and to develop effective solutions is a complex combination of basic intellectual abilities, formal education and training, and relevant experience. The ability to express oneself effectively, orally and in writing, is an essential skill in the whole process of developing solutions to customer problems. Experience, education, and problem-solving ability can be inferred from careful reading of a well-designed job application form, from the quality of the applicant's resume, and from written reports of various kinds that might be requested by the potential employer.

There is no question that individual, personal characteristics can be a major influence on the sales representative's role performance. There is a long-standing tendency in sales management, however, to overstate the contribution of these personal traits to the final sales result, to see "personality" as the major ingredient in successful selling performance. This tendency leads to a heavy reliance on psychological testing in the sales personnel selection process, in order to locate those traits that correlate, supposedly, with selling success. This viewpoint overlooks the complexity of the selling-buying situation and tends to view selling as something the sales rep does to the buyer, rather than as social interaction. To repeat, the individual characteristics of the sales representative should never be overlooked as a prime cause of his or her effectiveness, but neither should they be regarded as the only determinants of sales success.

Before moving on to look at other factors that determine the sales rep's effectiveness, it must be emphasized that the selling process is, at its base, an interpersonal process. Individuals represent the business to its customers. Within the buying firm individuals—not the organization—make buying decisions. There will be a temptation to overlook this fundamental truth as we examine the nuances of policy, organization, and strategy when we will, of analytical necessity, take the individual sales representative as a "given," a non-varying quantity. Especially when examining the results of research based on sophisticated quantitative and behavioral modeling, it is essential to remember that all of the factors of environment, organization, policy, strategy, and management style have their impact when interacting with the individual person in the role of sales representative. It is this notion that we have attempted to portray in Figure 1.4, by showing the sales representative surrounded by all the aforementioned factors, each of which is discussed next.

Sales Territory Characteristics

A sales territory is defined simply as a collection of assigned accounts, both active and inactive. It may be defined by geographic boundaries, often a set of counties or states, or it may be defined by other, non-geographic dimensions such as customer industry affiliation (SIC—Standard Industrial Classification—code), or by some combination of geographic and non-geographic variables. In industrial selling, territories often consist of a few large customers or perhaps even a single customer, office building, or plant location.

Sales territories represent opportunity and challenge for the sales rep. Because no two territories are similar in all respects, sales reps within the same organization are likely to be given significantly different opportunities and challenges. Furthermore, the nature of the opportunity represented by a territory for an individual will be determined by the interaction of those territory characteristics with the characteristics of the individual. Stated differently, each possible sales rep-account pairing represents a unique set of opportunities and challenges. The so-called "assignment problem" in sales management is concerned with creating optimal pairings of sales reps and accounts, taking into consideration the characteristics of each.[10]

---

[10]See, for example, Leonard M. Lodish, "Assigning Salesmen to Accounts to Maximize Profit," *Journal of Marketing Research*, Vol. 12, No. 4 (November 1976), pp. 440–444.

Territories can be defined by a number of important quantitative dimensions: sales potential, number of accounts, geographic area to be covered and distance to be traveled, population, the distribution of accounts by size of account, and so on. These characteristics, which are measurable, have an impact on the sales rep in terms of workload and opportunity for sales volume—leading to earnings—and are the basis for setting quotas and expense budgets. Quotas are targets for total sales volume, new accounts, sales broken down by product line, sales calls, and other measures of activity and results against which the sales rep's performance will subsequently be evaluated.

One study of sales force performance in three companies found strong empirical evidence of relationships between sales representatives' performance and such measures of territory characteristics as level of competitive activity, market potential, concentration of potential in relatively large accounts, and the geographic concentration of accounts. Also found to be significant were variables that described the marketing firm's policies, programs, and organization characteristics specific to a given territory, including level of promotional expenditures, recent levels of sales volume and market share, and the number of sales reps reporting to the field sales manager. Each had a significant impact on the individual rep's sales performance.[11]

Optimal deployment strategy and fair assessment of the performance of sales personnel depend heavily on having accurate and reliable measures of territory characteristics. Clearly, the characteristics of assigned accounts and geographic territories are major influences on the performance of the field sales representative.

The Field Sales Manager

Every field sales representative reports to a manager, and the title Field Sales Manager is used as a general label for all such managers, regardless of their level within the sales organization. Larger sales forces may have four or five levels of field sales management, with

---

[11]Adrian B. Ryans and Charles B. Weinberg, "Determinants of Salesforce Performance: A Multiple Company Study," in Richard P. Bagozzi (ed.), *Sales Management: New Developments from Behavioral and Decision Model Research* (Cambridge, MA: Marketing Science Institute, 1979), Report No. 79–107, pp. 92–129.

titles such as (from lowest to highest level) Sales Supervisor, Branch Manager, District Manager, Regional Sales Manager, and Sales Vice President or National Sales Manager. The following comments, although they apply in a general sense to all levels of field sales management, focus specifically on the first-level supervisor, the person with day-to-day management responsibility for supervision, direction, and control of field sales representatives.

The field sales manager has direct responsibility for supervising the sales representative, and serves as a communication link between the rep and higher levels of sales management. The manager is also responsible for interpreting and enforcing organization policies and operating procedures. The sales rep's performance is influenced directly by the field sales manager's communication and direction and by his or her perceptions of the manager's expectations.

The field sales manager's job is made more complex, in comparison with other types of supervisory positions, by the fact that the manager is physically separated from those persons who have to be supervised. It is common for field sales managers to spend much of their time traveling with the sales reps, observing their performances and guiding them where appropriate, as well as bringing a management presence to the customer. The manager is responsible for the continued personal development of the people assigned to him or her, as well as for their current sales performance.

The role of the field sales manager will be examined in greater depth in Chapter 2.

Sales Management Policies and Programs

Sales management develops policies and programs to guide and stimulate sales force performance. These policies and programs are implemented under the direction of the field sales manager. Policies are reasonably permanent rules which place limits on individual behavior. Some of the most important policy areas in field sales management relate to pricing (where there is a danger that a sales rep's pricing moves, if allowed, would create the risk of violating the antitrust laws), credit and delivery terms, expense accounts, use of company cars and other property, and what can and cannot be said about competitors' products and service.

The sales rep's communication with other members of the organization as a boundary role person is likely to be guided and constrained by a number of policies relating to such matters as proscribed channels of communication, who can make commitments to customers, how funds spent to solve customer problems can be allocated to departments or charged to the customer, the extent of product modification permitted, and so on. Most policies have the underlying objective of controlling expenses or ensuring the smooth functioning of the organization. In many instances, policies will be perceived as hindrances to sales force performance and to getting effective response to the customer's needs.

Sales management programs can be any coordinated set of actions designed to accomplish some specific objective. They often are of the one-time, special-purpose variety and have such objectives as stimulating sales volume, moving a specific quantity of merchandise, obtaining new accounts, introducing a new product, overcoming a particular competitive threat, or strengthening ties with the distributor organization. Programs often take the form of contests to stimulate interest and to provide excitement. Programs typically involve several tangible dimensions including specially printed materials, price offers, direct mailings to customers and distributors, and other special efforts in the area of advertising and sales promotion.

Such programs can be an important element in the emotional climate of the field sales organization, and obviously are intended to have a direct effect on the performance of sales representatives. There is always an unanswered question, however, when sales programs have been used: What would performance have been if there were no special programs?

Other Sales Representatives

The individual sales rep's performance is influenced directly and indirectly by his or her peers. As individuals, the other sales reps provide information and support. In some sales organizations, there are sales representatives with assigned responsibility to provide special competence relating to particular products or customer industries. A computer sales organization may have a banking specialist in the district office, for example, to assist sales representatives who have banking customers in their territories. In a more general sense, the sales rep's peers provide friendly advice when the rep wants to talk about particular customer problems or other work-related issues. Experienced sales reps often take on the role of mentor for one or more of their junior colleagues, providing advice and counsel and becoming a kind of role model for the young rep, who must develop a set of role expectations and a behavioral repertoire for playing the role of sales representative. Such mentoring may support the supervisory efforts of the field sales manager or it may hinder them.

The sales rep's peers must also be seen as a group, a set of individuals interacting in face-to-face communication, with shared norms and values that have a direct influence on the behavior of individual members of the group. Like formal organizational policies, informal group norms and values guide and constrain the individual's actions. Once again there can be both conflict and consistency between organizational policies and group norms. Where there is conflict, the sales rep will feel role tension and may spend a large amount of time and energy seeking to reconcile conflicting role expectations.

One of the most common types of group norms relates to the amount of effort to be expended. Sales reps who exceed the norms may be viewed as trying to impress the manager while those who fall below the norms may be seen as not doing their fair share. In either case, it is almost certain that the rep will feel pressure from peers to adjust performance. Failure to get in line may result in being shut out of the normal interactions of the group or may even bring mild threats of retaliatory behavior.

Many sales management policies and programs, especially in the compensation and supervision area, are intended to influence group norms and behavior to be consistent with organization objectives and policies. Compensation bonuses based on total district sales volume, for example, may be designed to encourage the sales reps to cooperate with one another and to put a mild amount of group pressure on each individual to achieve his or her individual sales quota. Weekly sales meetings at the branch or district level provide an opportunity for the sales reps to get together and feel the support of their colleagues as well as for the manager to share information with them that will help to make group norms consistent with the interests of management.

The astute sales manager never forgets that the sales rep's peers, both individually and as a group, are a major influence on the performance of the individual sales representative.

So far, we have looked at four sets of variables that have a relatively immediate and direct influence on the performance of the sales representative—the individual's personal characteristics and abilities, the field sales manager, sales management policies and programs, and other sales representatives. At this level, the sales management problem involves essentially tactical and administrative decision making in such areas as territory definition, supervisory practices, compensation planning, and performance evaluation. Stated simply, at this level of analysis, the question is, "Are the sales representatives and their field sales managers doing things correctly?"

At a higher level, one step removed from the day-to-day concerns of the sales rep and field sales manager, are two other sets of factors that also have a pervasive influence on the performance of the individual sales rep and on the sales organization as a whole. This is the strategic level of analysis and decision making where the concern is, "Are we doing the correct things?" Strategically, the need is to assess the resources and capabilities of the organization (as these change over time), and to match them up with the changing pattern of opportunities in the competitive marketplace.

Marketing Strategy and Organization

Every business strategy is predominantly a marketing strategy in that its core elements are a definition of markets to be served and products to be offered. These product/market combinations define a "business" and provide answers to that most basic of all questions for all firms— "What business are we in?" The definition of business strategy translates into a market segmentation strategy that defines the types of customers with which the firm wishes to do business. In this very basic sense, the market segmentation strategy determines the effectiveness of the sales representative by specifying the customers to be called upon.

Of course, the business strategy as implemented through a segmentation strategy does not normally delineate specific customers (although it might). The sales rep typically has responsibility for seeking out customers within well-established guidelines. If these guidelines are weak and inadequate, however, the sales rep may have too much discretion and, depending upon his or her own preferences and abilities, may seek out customers whose needs and wants are inconsistent with the capabilities and strategies of the organization. This can lead to a kind of *ad hoc* segmentation strategy, designed by the sales rep, and can be inconsistent with the other parts of the overall marketing strategy. Conversely, a clear segmentation can markedly assist the individual sales rep by focusing his or her attention on the relevant set of potential customers and by creating a clearly defined set of role expectations. The field sales manager is responsible for directing the sales representatives in a manner that implements the basic segmentation strategy. We will return to this problem in Chapter 4.

In addition to segmentation, the other elements of marketing strategy include product, price, promotion, and distribution. An early section of this chapter looked at the sales representative as part of the promotional strategy, and we considered briefly how the sales rep's effectiveness is influenced by the other elements of promotion. An even more basic determinant of the rep's effectiveness is the product offering, including product, price, and related services. Of course, how the sales rep presents that product offering and to whom it is presented are not unimportant! But many case histories have been written about deteriorating business situations where the problem has been improperly defined as an ineffective sales force when the true problems were obsolete products and unrealistic prices.

Likewise, the sales rep's performance may be intertwined on a day-to-day basis with the performance of one or more distributors. In fact, the sales rep's primary responsibility may be one of working with and supporting a distributor's sales force. Whether or not the type of distribution being used is the correct one is an issue of marketing strategy. Whether the best distributor firms of that type are available to the company is also a function of many factors beyond the control of the sales rep. The effectiveness of the sales rep in working with assigned distributors is also influenced by policies, procedures, and support systems that are reflections of overall marketing strategy. Clearly, all these factors relating to distribution have a significant impact on the rep's performance.

As just one element of marketing strategy, albeit the one with principal responsibility for implementation, the success of the sales rep depends heavily on the quality of the total marketing strategy. There is no way to separate clearly the effectiveness of that strategy from the effectiveness of implementation, however, so the sales force will virtually always be looked at as a cause of deteriorating market share.

Organization Support Systems

Finally, one must consider the influence of the sales rep's performance on all other aspects of the organization that get involved in finding solutions to customer problems and satisfying customer needs. These are lumped together in Figure 1.4 under the very imprecise label of "organization support systems." They include such functions as product design, applications engineering, production scheduling, credit, transportation, packaging, and advertising (where the firm does cooperative advertising with its customers). The organization support systems include four interacting sets of variables: technology; organization structure (with subsystems of communication, authority, status, rewards, and work flow); people; and tasks.[12]

The difficulties involved in the sales rep's interactions with these organization support systems were suggested in our consideration of the sales rep as a boundary role person. The bottom line in this area of concern for the sales manager is the extent to which the total organization is responsive to the customer's needs. This is not a one-way street, as the boundary spanning role concept makes clear. The sales rep cannot just make demands on the support systems; he or she must use the same skills of interpersonal influence in these intraorganizational contacts as are relied upon in dealing with the customer.

The rep must also be mindful of the capabilities of, demands upon, and constraints upon these systems. While representing the customer's needs and problems to the organization, the sales rep must also represent the needs and capabilities of the firm back to the customer. Problems can develop if the rep feels closer to the customer organization than to his or her own—that is, if the psychological distance separating him or her from the employer is too great. One of the func-

---

[12]Harold J. Leavitt, "Applied Organization Change in Industry: Structural, Technical, and Human Approaches," in William W. Cooper, Harold J. Leavitt, and Maynard W. Shelly II, *New Perspectives in Organization Research* (New York: John Wiley & Sons, 1964), pp. 55–71.

tions of the field sales manager is to help the sales reps manage their interactions with the organization's support systems.

The Buyer and the Buying Organization

Referring again to Figure 1.4, we still have not analyzed the right-hand half of that diagram. A whole chapter, Chapter 3, will be devoted to that task. For now it will suffice to note that the selling process is, at its core, dyadic interaction between a sales representative and a representative of the customer organization. It is also important to observe the basic similarities between the influences on both actors, the sales rep and the buyer. Both are individuals motivated by their own needs and perceptions. Both occupy boundary role positions. Both interact with managers and peers in the context of a formal organization that is guided and constrained by strategies, policies, and capabilities. The welfare of each actor depends in varying degree upon securing some response from the other and from the other's organization.

A whole set of factors that determines the effectiveness of the sales representative is therefore beyond the control of the rep and the rep's organization. The rep can attempt to influence these factors to his or her advantage, however. To have any success in these influence attempts, the sales rep must have a good understanding of these factors. That understanding is part of the rep's responsibility and is something for which he or she can be trained, supervised, and held accountable. "Know your customer" is the basic dictum of selling and sales force management.

SUMMARY

In this chapter, the work of field sales management (or what might be called "the sales management problem") has been defined by focusing on the role of the field sales representative. It is the field sales manager's responsibility to develop an effective field sales organization and to maximize the performance and professional development of the field sales representatives. Alternative, but consistent, views of the sales rep's role were examined—as part of the promotional strategy, as part of the product offering, as a communicator in the buyer-seller dyad, and as a boundary role person. Each view highlighted certain aspects of the sales rep's functioning.

Next, several sets of factors influencing the sales rep's effectiveness were identified, and each will be the subject of further analysis in later chapters. The sales representative's individual characteristics will be considered more carefully in the discussion of recruitment, selection, and training in Chapter 4. The impact of sales territory characteristics is an important part of the analysis of Chapter 5, Deploying the Sales Force. The influence of the field sales manager is the focus of Chapter 2, The Field Sales Manager, and Chapter 6, Sales Force Motivation and Supervision. Sales management policies and programs are considered throughout the text but are the exclusive subject of Chapter 7, Evaluation, Compensation, and Control. The influence of other sales reps will be examined in the discussions of motivation and supervision, organization, and compensation. Marketing strategy and organization and related organization support systems will not be examined in depth but will be background for Chapter 5, as well as for Chapter 3, The Buying Process and Buyer-Seller Interaction, which will consider the customer's influence in detail.

TWO

The Field Sales Manager

The field sales manager is a person responsible for management of a firm's field sales operations. He or she may be a first-line supervisor, directly responsible for the day-to-day management of field sales representatives, or the manager may be positioned at a higher level in the management hierarchy, responsible for directing the activities of other managers. In either case, the manager has two types of responsibilities—for achieving or exceeding sales goals established for performance in the current period and for developing the people reporting to him or her. Each set of responsibilities includes a number of more specific functions and activities.

In the first chapter it was observed that the field sales manager is a major source of influence on the field sales representative. The field sales manager often has personal responsibility for accounts and sales volume as well, thus functioning as a field sales representative also. Even where this selling responsibility is not defined formally, the field sales manager may still spend a significant amount of time calling on accounts that are the assigned responsibility of sales reps. There is a potential conflict here, between achieving short-term operating results and developing the sales organization in order to enhance the opportunities for long-term success. The dimensions of this conflict will be examined throughout this chapter.

DUTIES OF THE FIELD SALES MANAGER

A field sales manager faces a number of competing demands for his or her time. There is a real challenge in finding the right allocation of effort among these various duties. The nature of these duties is indicated in Figures 2.1, 2.2, and 2.3, which illustrate three different companies' descriptions of a field sales manager's responsibilities. These are the same firms whose sales representatives' job descriptions were presented in Chapter 1, and this permits a consideration of the relationships between the two levels of the organization. For purposes of analysis, the duties of the field sales manager can be grouped under five headings: supervising sales representatives, developing the sales organization, selling and managing key accounts, administering the office, and representing the company to the local community.[1]

Supervision

The field sales manager's major responsibility is to supervise the field sales representatives assigned to him or her. In many important respects, the field sales manager's function is similar to that of a foreman in a production facility, involving responsibility for directing and controlling the activities of personnel in order to achieve an expected level of production output. As a first-line supervisor, the field sales manager—like the foreman—is the communication link between workers and management, and experiences pressure of various kinds from both directions. The field sales manager's job is complicated, however, by the fact that most of the time those persons being supervised are physically separated from the supervisor and from one another. As previously noted, there is both physical and psychological distance between the sales representative and the field sales manager. It generally is believed that sales representatives as a result are much more susceptible to emotional ups and downs due to their day-to-day successes and failures than are workers in other parts of the firm.

Supervision is the process of overseeing, directing, and controlling the work of others. It involves assigning tasks to be performed, monitoring performance on a continuous basis, and evaluating that performance against standards, redirecting effort as necessary to

---

[1]With minor modifications, this listing of duties originally was presented in Robert T. Davis, *Performance and Development of Field Sales Managers* (Boston: Harvard Business School, Division of Research, 1957).

TITLE: Territory Manager

RESPONSIBLE TO: District Manager

BASIC FUNCTION:
To direct the total territory's effort toward the achievement of district goals/ objectives within the assigned area. This will include supervising and coordinating the selection, development and execution of the Division's activities by assigned personnel. The Territory Manager will be responsible for manpower as well as personal assignment of key accounts. The position fills the need for effective management of a considerable portion of the district's volume. It is the primary resource of the District Manager for planning strategy, executing programs and evaluating results for a complete unit of work (manpower/accounts).

KNOWLEDGE REQUIRED:

Division philosophies, policies, procedures and product knowledge.

District/region standards of performance.

Profit term workshop concepts useful in retail/headquarters selling, e.g., break-even, profit margin, etc.

Marketing statistical data which can be an aid in selling Division products, e.g., CPR's, SAMI's, ERD's.

OB/GQ selling method.

Account policies, procedures and personnel.

Policies, procedures, human relation skills and leadership techniques required to employ, train, counsel, appraise, compensate and develop personnel.

Thorough knowledge of marketing area(s) in which he or she operates to include account policies, procedures and personnel.

CRITICAL RESPONSIBILITIES:
The Territory Manager is totally responsible for the actions of his or her unit in all areas of established accountability. The performance of the unit should meet or exceed all district standards.

I. Retail Conditions. The Territory Manager has complete responsibility for the overall condition of retail stores assigned to the unit. This responsibility includes the maintenance and/or accomplishment of district standards in all retail outlets of the unit. Additionally, when retail outlets are assigned to the Territory Manager, the responsibilities and standards are the same as those established for Sales Representative and Account Manager.

II. Sales Analysis and Planning. The Territory Manager should insure that proper sales analysis and planning techniques are conducted by assigned personnel in accordance with district standards.

Figure 2.1 A job description for a General Foods Corporation field sales manager.

III. Communications and Records. The Territory Manager should insure that all assigned personnel maintain proper records as required. These should include documents which provide analysis of performance from which action plans may be developed. The Territory Manager is responsible for establishing a satisfactory communications network between subordinates, other Territory Managers and the district office. Specific responsibilities outlined for Sales Representative and Account Manager are also applicable.

IV. Account Sales Execution. The Territory Manager has responsibility for the development of a high level of trade franchise with all accounts within his unit. This includes the responsibility that all accounts of the unit meet or exceed standards of performance. When the Territory Manager has headquarters responsibility, the performance expectations are the same as those for the Sales Representative and Account Manager.

V. Cost Controls. The Territory manager must insure that all controllable sales costs of the unit are kept within reasonable limits according to Division policy.

VI. Supervision. The Territory Manager is responsible for all activities that contribute to the hiring and maintaining of qualified personnel. This function includes the training and development, motivation, direction and evaluation of assigned personnel.

Responsibility

1. Recruits and selects new Sales Representatives and Account Managers within parameters established by the District Manager.

Standards

1–A. The Territory Manager will interview and hire to accommodate district needs (proper balance of career/move-throughs).

1–B. Hiring practices will reflect Division/Corporation guidelines pertaining to minority placements.

Responsibility

2. New personnel will be trained to accomplish the responsibilities outlined under each job function.

Standards

2–A. There is evidence that the Territory Manager exposes and effectively trains all assigned personnel to the skills/knowledge required to establish and maintain performance standands.

2–B. The district training program will be utilized to train all new personnel.

Figure 2.1. *(Continued)*

2–C. Continuous training programs should be implemented and reflect current needs of the individual.

Responsibility

3. The Territory Manager and his subordinates will mutually establish objectives designed to improve individual performance against present assignment and, if applicable, design developmental programs in order to prepare subordinates for greater responsibilities.

   Standards

   3–A. The Territory Manager will formally evaluate each individual's performance annually. This will be the basis for establishing new objectives for the upcoming year.

   3–B. An informal review of the individual's progress toward accomplishing objectives will occur on-goingly.

   3–C. The Territory Manager will determine and document to DSM, ERA status for each subordinate formally once a year. However, changes in ERA status should be documented as they occur.

   3–D. The Territory Manager in conjunction with subordinates (when applicable) will develop programs for the individual which will prepare him/her for greater responsibilities.

Responsibility

4. The Territory Manager is responsible for developing and maintaining intra-unit rapport which accomplishes team unity.

   Standards

   4–A. The Territory Manager must exercise personnel management skills which result in a highly motivated sales force.

   4–B. There is evidence that interaction among individuals results in team unity.

Responsibility

5. The Territory Manager will develop a salary administration program in accordance with Division procedures.

   Standards

   5–A. The Territory Manager must annually recommend a salary action program which is in accordance with operating and financial policies.

   5–B. The Territory Manager will adhere to the salary plan except when adjustments are approved by the District Manager.

Figure 2.1. (*Continued*)

5–C. Each individual's salary adjustment will reflect level of performance in relation to critical responsibilities.

Responsibility

6. Effectively communicates both verbally and in writing all instructions and directions to all individuals under his supervision.

    Standards

    6–A. There is evidence that all District Manager directives are understood and disseminated to territory personnel.

    6–B. All Sales Representative Activities are co-ordinated with customer/district sales plans to insure achievement of goals.

    6–C. That all personnel are kept fully informed in regard to all business matters.

Responsibility

7. Maintains a high level of field involvement.

    Standards

    7–A. The Territory manager must properly allocate his time between accounts and people so as to accomplish district performance standards.

    7–B. The Territory Manager must provide the individual a minimum of *two formal work-withs and two formal work reviews per quarter*.

    7–C. Each formal work-with and work review will evaluate the performance of an individual in relation to the critical responsibilities of that position. These formal documents are included with the individual's evaluation.

Figure 2.1. (*Continued*)

JOB TITLE: Branch Manager

IMMEDIATE SUPERVISOR: Regional Sales Manager

   I. Function. Under the general supervision of the Regional Sales Manager is responsible for establishing and maintaining branch sales operation.

  II. Responsibility and Authority. In the district: selects and changes methods of distribution; contacts key accounts; arranges customer and representative training programs; keeps abreast of market conditions and information on competitive products, prices and activities; selects, hires, trains and develops the sales personnel.

Figure 2.2. A job description for a Gould, Inc. Instruments Division field sales manager.

Plan and execute complex work involving new or constantly changing conditions for sales.

Considerable monetary responsibility, since sales in the district may appreciably affect operating profits.

Repeated contact with sales persons in the district; necessitating a high degree of sales and supervisory ability.

III. Education and Experience. Technical degree or equivalent experience; possessing conversational knowledge of the various disciplines in which the Division deals.

3–5 years' experience in technical product sales.

Figure 2.2. *(Continued)*

CONNECTICUT GENERAL LIFE INSURANCE COMPANY
POSITION DESCRIPTION

Title of Position	Manager		
Department	Group Insurance Sales—Field	Number in Position	Date
Division	GIO	Report To *(Title)* Regional Vice President	

General Purpose IS ACCOUNTABLE for the production, conservation and servicing of all Group Insurance products in an assigned territory, in accordance with the Company's standards and policies. PROMOTES the sale and service of group products to prospective and existing customers through various producers. DIRECTS staff in the sale and service of Group business in order to meet production, persistency and profit objectives.

Responsibilities

Operations Management (20%)

DETERMINES marketing direction and thrusts of all Group insurance products through continuous involvement/contact with sales team, policyholders and producers. DIRECTS the marketing of group products through Sales Representatives. MARKETS products to attain the desired amount of new business. IMPLEMENTS action steps to achieve plans. DETERMINES and IMPLEMENTS service standards for each functional level.

Figure 2.3. A job description for a Connecticut General Life Insurance Company group insurance sales manager.

UTILIZES people resources properly through the recognition of individual potential and consequent development of those skills. DEVELOPS plans for sales, persistency, profitability, staffing and expenses. PROVIDES Regional Vice President with forecasts of expected sales activity and results for an assigned territory. ACHIEVES planned results within an overall expense budget.

Sales/Service (15%)

HAS RESPONSIBILITY for the sale and retention of various group products. IDENTIFIES/CULTIVATES producer relationships to acquire new policyholders and additional business on existing contracts. DETERMINES/FACILITATES appropriate handling of policyholder needs. GATHERS/ANALYZES all pertinent case data. CONSULTS H.O. Underwriting regarding risk selection and evaluation. COMMUNICATES plan design to administrative staff and DEVELOPS proposal techniques, presentation, and CLOSES sale.

Sales Support (15%)

SUPPORTS and DIRECTS staff in key policyholder and producer situations. MAINTAINS contact with and ASCERTAINS that staff members are establishing and maintaining favorable relationships with policyholders, agents and brokers. COORDINATES staff and H.O. efforts and DISSEMINATES information to other local line-of-business personnel.

Management Information System (10%)

ANALYZES and UTILIZES data from H.O. produced reports involving production, persistency, profitability and renewals. SUBMITS required periodic reports such as progress review information, large account conservation status, etc.

Sales Personnel Activity/Ongoing Personnel Needs (20%)

IS RESPONSIBLE for the hiring, firing, reviewing, counseling, promotion, rating and training of office personnel. TAKES action to support Company practices and procedures (e.g., EEO goals). HAS RESPONSIBILITY TO PROVIDE necessary physical equipment to properly support staff (e.g. office equipment.)

Sales Training (10%)

DIRECTS and DEVELOPS sales personnel through assistance and instruction. PROVIDES on-site support to sales staff on larger, more complicated sales situations.

Figure 2.3. (*Continued*)

Sales Promotion Activity (5%)

CONDUCTS staff contests and limited external promotion.

Self-development (5%)

DEVELOPS in coordination with Regional Vice President plans to engage in activities which foster self-development.

Scope data
    Number of employees accountable for 1–9_____ 10–13_____ 14_____
    Number of budget dollars accountable for $_____
    Other accountability factors:

Figure 2.3. (*Continued*)

bring performance into line with objectives. Supervision is not synonymous with *motivation,* which is best thought of as a psychological state of the worker being supervised, not something the manager does to the worker. Strictly speaking, managers do not motivate workers; rather, they provide incentives, direction, and support that have effects on the worker's motivational state. In daily usage, of course, it is said that supervisors motivate their employees, by which is meant that they provide incentives to the employees to perform in certain ways.

There are several components to the supervisory function of the field sales manager. These include creating the work environment, establishing standards of performance, developing manpower, acting as a communication link, and interpreting and enforcing policy. Each of these supervisory functions will now be examined more carefully.

Creating the Work Environment.   The work environment, or "organizational climate," within which the sales representative works is very much influenced by the activities of the field sales manager. That work environment is characterized by role expectations for the sales rep, the characteristics of the company as an employer, the nature of the selling job, opportunities for promotion and advancement, and other important characteristics of the company, its products, and the nature of relationships with other personnel with whom the sales rep has contact. There are really three distinct concepts here. First is the *objective characteristics* of the work environment. Second is the sales rep's perceptions of the work environment, which can be described as *organizational climate*. Third is the sales rep's attitude toward and feelings about these perceived characteristics, which we can call the worker's level of *job satisfaction*. Hoping to achieve some clarity and consistency, we will try to use the words objective characteristics, organizational climate, and job satisfaction in this fashion.[2] The work environment includes all three levels of concepts.

The field sales manager can influence the work environment at all three levels—objective characteristics, sales reps' perception of those characteristics, and feelings about them. The manager has this influence through his or her everyday activities, by communicating with the reps in writing, in group meetings, and face to face. The manager structures the work environment by assigning goals, tasks, and working and reporting relationships, most especially by making work assignments, monitoring performance, and evaluating that performance against previously developed standards. He or she reports to the sales reps on activities and outcomes within the organization and in the marketplace and explains their significance, thus influencing the perceptions of the reps and their attitude toward their work.

Establishing Standards of Performance.   The field sales manager sets standards of performance for the sales representatives, both formally and informally. In a formal sense, the manager sets objectives to guide the activities and time allocation of the sales representatives. This goal-setting may take place as part of a formal system of periodic performance appraisal and setting of objectives, often referred to as management by objectives (MBO). A major part of this process may be the negotiation of quotas for sales volume, new accounts, and other measures of sales performance. Targets may also be established for the control of travel and entertainment expenses, expenditures for sales promotion, and other types of spending controlled by the sales representative.

Equally significant but more subtle are the performance standards set indirectly by the manager through the influence of his or her own

[2]Gilbert A. Churchill, Neil M. Ford, and Orville C. Walker, Jr., "Organizational Climate and Job Satisfaction," *Journal of Marketing Research*, Vol. XIII (November 1976), pp. 323–332.

behavior and example. The field sales manager sets the pace for the rest of the organization.[3] Through a variety of informal cues, the field sales manager communicates a set of role expectations for the sales reps. To a degree, the field sales manager may provide a role model for the reps on which they will pattern their own behavior in such matters as hours worked, modes of speech and dress, and work habits concerning planning and making sales calls. The field sales manager will give cues, through actions and words, about his or her own attitudes toward the work environment (and especially toward the company), and these may be adopted by the sales reps.

Developing Human Resources. As a supervisor, the field sales manager is responsible for the continued development of the persons assigned to his or her charge. Through the day-to-day contacts that are part of the supervisory process, the manager has the possibility of improving the knowledge, skills, and attitudes of the sales rep. In this very important sense, the field sales manager is a teacher, or at least has the opportunity to be a teacher. Whether that opportunity is captured depends upon how the field sales manager perceives his or her role as supervisor. If the supervisor's role is seen as one of telling the sales reps what to do, making sure they do it, and doing it for them when they cannot or will not do it themselves, very little learning occurs and the sales reps tend to become dependent upon the manager for their achievement of performance goals. This dependence can be mistakenly perceived as trust, friendship, and support for the field sales manager. The sales reps can actually be made weaker as a result.

A truly effective supervisor views every interaction with a subordinate as an opportunity to make that person stronger. Instead of correcting an error for the subordinate, the supervisor takes the time to teach the subordinate how to avoid the error in the future. Often teaching takes longer than simply doing. A field sales manager, feeling time pressure and the need to achieve current performance goals, can find it much easier to do things for the sales reps that they should be able to do themselves, such as developing careful routing plans, gathering data on accounts, developing key account strategies, and so

[3]Davis, *op. cit.*, p. 5.

on. While this may be more efficient in the short run, in the long run it means that the sales reps become more dependent on the manager, problems recur, and the manager must spend more time correcting problems that could have been avoided if only an effort had been made to develop the people in the sales force.

The objective of every interaction between the field sales manager and the sales representative should be to reduce the need for direct supervision, to make the rep independent of the manager, and to strengthen the rep's ability to achieve performance results without help. To accomplish this the field sales manager must be willing to let the reps try new approaches, take risks, and do things they haven't done before, all of which creates the possibility of failure. As many have observed, we learn much more from our failures than from our successes. That learning potential is reduced significantly if the supervisor takes over and corrects the problem rather than coaches the sales rep as necessary to teach him or her how to correct it.

At this point, we are talking about the field sales manager's ongoing, day-to-day responsibility for developing sales reps, in a supervisory role that can best be described as coaching. The next section of this chapter will look at the manager's responsibility for developing the sales organization, including recruiting, selecting, and training sales representatives. Thus we make a rather arbitrary distinction between the supervisory responsibility for developing present personnel on an ongoing, informal basis and for developing new personnel through more formal programs.

In large field sales operations, the local manager may delegate some of the coaching responsibilities to a sales supervisor or a sales trainer. Numbers of sales reps and time pressure to perform the other duties of a field sales manager may make this necessary. In this case, the supervisor or trainer may be thought of as the first-line management person, but with more narrowly defined responsibilities. The field sales manager, even after delegating a part of the supervisory duties, still retains ultimate responsibility for them.

Acting as a Communication Link.   The field sales manager is the communication link between the field sales force and sales and marketing management. The manager must maintain a two-way flow of communication, keeping the sales force informed about marketing and sales plans, programs, policies, and objectives and keeping management informed about performance and conditions in the marketplace. The sales rep, as the link between the customer and the company, often does not communicate with sales, marketing, and operations directly but rather through the field sales manager, who is responsible for coordinating and consolidating information from the field before passing it on to management. The sheer number of sales representatives in many organizations makes direct communication a virtual impossibility.

The field sales manager must keep upper levels of sales management informed about the work environment, organizational climate, and sales reps' job satisfaction. Such information is vital to the improvement of sales management policies and practice and the continuous adjustment of the organization to changes in the marketplace.

Communication from management to the sales force is a crucial element in the coordination of company activities. Sales programs to be implemented on a national or international basis must be coordinated by field sales managers at the local level. The development of such programs, on the other hand, must be based on the best possible information about local market conditions. Providing that information is a key role for the field sales manager, who should be the person in the organization most knowledgeable about local market conditions. Data provided by the sales reps as well as from the manager's own exposure to customers and competition must be collated, summarized, and interpreted by the field sales manager before it is presented to management.

Interpreting and Enforcing Policy.   Although not really distinct from the dimensions of supervision already described, this responsibility deserves emphasis because of its importance. Policies are thought of as standing answers to recurring questions or problems and as constraints on the actions and discretion of individuals within the organization. Policies of importance to the sales force relate, for example, to pricing, granting of credit terms, promises for delivery dates, extent of product adjustment and modification, use of company automobiles, reporting of customer entertainment and travel-related expenses, use of free merchandise, discussion of competitors' products or selling practices, and so on.

Sales reps may find frequent need to seek out the supervisor's interpretation of the applicability of a policy in a particular situation. The manager needs the authority to use discretion in those instances where the applicability of a policy is unclear, because no formal policy statement can be so detailed as to anticipate every possible combination of circumstances within which the policy must be applied. The field sales manager needs to feel confident that upper levels of sales management will support his or her interpretation of policy at the local level.

However, a policy with more than a modicum of flexibility in its interpretation is no policy at all. By definition, policies must be interpreted and enforced in a reasonably firm manner, otherwise they no longer serve as "standing answers to recurring questions." Policies have little flexibility; if bent more than a little, they break. For the field sales manager, this means that effective implementation of this supervisory responsibility requires the strength to say "no" when exceptions to policy are requested. As obvious as this may appear, it is one of the more serious issues in sales force management. In order to gain the affection and support of the sales reps, the manager may feel great pressure to give the reps more flexibility and discretion than permitted by a strict interpretation of policy. The tendency to grant such requests may reflect a stronger identification with the sales reps than with management, part of the "supersalesman" problem to be discussed at the end of this section.

Up to this point we have been dealing with supervision, the field sales manager's principal responsibility. We looked at five different dimensions of the supervisory task: creating the work environment, establishing standards of performance, developing manpower, acting as a communication link, and interpreting and enforcing policy. While the field sales manager's activities, in practical terms, do not divide themselves into these neat categories, these five components highlight in a conceptual way the major elements of the manager's supervisory tasks. We now turn to a consideration of four other duties of the field sales manager: developing the sales organization, personal selling and managing key accounts, office administration, and representing the company to the local community.

Developing the Sales Organization

As the local manager, the field sales manager may have the major responsibility for developing the sales organization through programs for recruiting, selecting, and training sales representatives and for organizing them into effective operating units. This whole area of responsibility will be the subject of Chapter 4. Here we will consider only the broad dimensions of that responsibility and the major reasons that it often falls on the shoulders of the local field sales manager.

Over the long run, the quality of the personnel brought into the organization and the training and direction they receive are the major determinants of organizational performance. Turning that statement around, the level of current performance will be a direct reflection of the quality of organizational development that has occurred in the past. Managerial time and effort spent on recruiting, selecting, and training sales representatives are an investment in the future. A failure to make that investment may reflect an excessively short-term, current performance orientation on the part of the field sales manager.

The local labor market is an important source of potential sales personnel, and the local manager is the person in the best position to develop specific programs to exploit that labor market. It is clearly more efficient for a local management representative to keep informed about local needs and to do the necessary advertising, following up of leads, and interviewing, and to implement programs developed at regional and national levels of the organization, than it is to attempt to manage such details of implementation from a national headquarters. While programs and budgets can be developed and coordinated at the highest levels of the sales organization, the local manager is often responsible for implementing the programs and producing the results. Furthermore, that local manager will be more comfortable with selection decisions, and more willing to do the necessary coaching and training, if he or she feels a personal responsibility for having brought the new rep into the organization.

The quality of personnel attracted will reflect the care with which the local manager has developed and nurtured relationships with colleges and universities, local business and community organizations, distributors, customers, and other potential sources of sales talent. While the appearance of an attractive candidate may seem to be simply a matter of good luck, in fact it probably is the result of effort exerted over a long period of time and a careful plan by the local manager to be in the right place at the right time.

Personnel turnover of 10–20% per year in a sales organization is not uncommon. The highest rates of turnover are likely to occur among the younger people, especially those just hired into their first sales job. As a result, the local manager probably will have a continuing need for new sales reps, and a need for continuing recruitment, selection, and training as a result. Because it may take several months to produce a new sales rep ready to assume account responsibilities, and because turnover often cannot be easily predicted and controlled, having new people "coming along" in the training program is desirable. While some cost is involved, such persons can be called upon to perform valuable tasks in the assistance of sales reps and the field sales manager as part of their training. Having fully prepared, new sales reps ready to go when the need arises can avoid the significant opportunity costs associated with leaving accounts uncontacted. Without such preparation, the departure of a sales representative can lead not only to a scrambling to get major accounts covered by other reps, but to the neglect of smaller accounts and new business development, inefficient routing patterns, more selling and less managing by the field sales manager, and similar problems. To repeat, a failure to develop the sales organization will inevitably lead to shortcomings in sales performance. While some companies centralize all recruiting, selection, and training at a national level, assigning sales reps to local territories based on demonstrated need, it is also common for the local manager to have a major role in developing the sales organization.

Selling and Managing Key Accounts

It is a rare sales organization in which the local field sales manager does not have some personally assigned accounts. Smaller organizations may simply not be able to afford the overhead costs of a full-time, non-selling local manager. More characteristically, there may be important customers who demand, and may require, the attention of a sales official with a management title. Especially if the regular sales representatives are relatively young and inexperienced, management selling may be a necessity. In many cases, however, management selling reflects an unwillingness and inability on the part of the manager to take the time and effort required to develop a relationship between a sales rep and the account. This is another aspect of the "supersalesman" problem.

The local manager with selling responsibility may have a sales quota for a significant portion of the district's total performance and may be assigned the larger and more prestigious accounts. To a significant degree, then, total district performance can depend on the personal selling performance of the local manager. Under these conditions, the manager's first priority is going to be selling, not managing, and there is large risk that the functions of supervision and developing the organization will be short-changed, with serious long-term consequences.

The manager's performance in the selling role can be a major influence in establishing standards of performance for the sales reps, setting the pace as we said. This positive effect may be counterbalanced, however, by the perception that the local manager is ignoring the reps and has the best accounts for himself/herself, which means reduced opportunities, and perhaps reduced income, for the reps. In this important sense, the selling manager may be perceived as a competitor by the sales reps.

All in all, the practice of holding the local sales manager responsible for personal selling, while common, is not without its problems.

Office Administration

The local sales operation must be housed in an office and within that office there are likely to be several staff members, such as a secretary, service representatives and technicians, order processing and other clerical personnel, sales trainees and sales supervisors, and so on. The sales reps may use the local office as a base of operations, perhaps maintaining a desk there. In addition to personnel, the local office will also have a variety of systems and equipment that need to be managed and maintained. Accounting, record-keeping, order processing, and other management information systems will be involved as well as office equipment of all kinds, automobiles, and perhaps tools and instruments used for product installation and service. In some situations, the local manager may be responsible for accounts receivable, payroll, cash management, and related treasury and accounting functions. Finally, the local manager may also be responsible for inventories of products, spare parts, and supplies of all kinds.

Office administration can therefore be a significant dimension of the field sales manager's total responsibility. In many respects, the local manager's responsibility for the office, personnel, systems, equipment, merchandise, and so on, can be as great as those of a general manager running a multimillion-dollar manufacturing operation. The field sales manager must protect these assets entrusted to his or her charge.

Equally important, the manager must use those assets wisely in day-to-day decision making in the pursuit of the ultimate objective of generating profitable sales volume. Among those areas of decision-making activity are customer service, inventory management, credit and collection, assigning delivery dates to orders, granting promotional and advertising allowances, adjusting prices and terms, and the whole variety of activities relating to managing non-sales personnel. If the company sells capital equipment, the fields sales manager may have a critical responsibility in appraising used equipment and offering trade-in allowances or in preparing lease terms and contracts. The scope of these local manager responsibilities varies significantly from one company to another.

Representing the Company to the Local Community

In the community where the company field sales office is located, and in the surrounding area, the field sales manager is "The Company." To customers, present and potential employees, community organizations of all kinds, and so on, the local field sales manager represents the company in a management role and as a spokesman. This responsibility can involve speaking to local groups, responding to requests for charitable contributions, accepting applications for employment, answering questions from representatives of the press, and so on. Especially if the company is a large multinational corporation whose activities are often brought to public attention, this responsibility for representing the company to the local community can be a major demand on the time and talent of the field sales manager.

We have identified five somewhat distinctive sets of duties of the field sales manager: supervision, developing the sales organization, selling and managing key accounts, office administration, and representing the company to the local community. Clearly, these responsibilities require the full range of management capabilities, and make field sales management a challenging and rewarding position. At several points it has been noted, however, that the managerial dimensions of the field sales manager's responsibility often are eclipsed in practice by attention to the selling dimensions of the responsibility. Before turning to a consideration of the abilities required of the field sales manager, we shall examine the nature of the selling *vs* managing dilemma in greater detail.

SELLING VS MANAGING—THE SUPERSALESMAN PROBLEM

There really is a conflict between selling and managing, and it is built into the field sales manager's position in four ways: by a desire to control overhead and administrative expense, by the nature of the selection process, by the characteristics of sales reps who become managers, and by customer expectations.

Especially in a small firm, non-selling field sales managers may be viewed as an expensive luxury, an unnecessary element of overhead expense. While such a view is often short-sighted and understates the valuable contribution of supervisory and other field sales management activities to sales force performance, it may also be realistic given the size of the market to be covered and the number of sales reps to be managed. If the market potential is limited, the area to be covered quite large, and the number of people to be supervised small, say three to four persons, then the manager may have to assume some selling responsibility simply as a matter of economic necessity. The situation can be exacerbated by having a significant portion of the manager's income depend on successful sales accomplishment.

Secondly, and perhaps most importantly, a promotion to a field sales management responsibility is usually viewed as a reward for successful performance as a field sales representative. Often, the major motivation for the promotion relates to issues of compensation. In some companies, it is common for the move to sales manager to involve a cut in salary. But in many other firms, as the best sales reps reach the top salaries permitted by the company's sales compensation plan, promotion to field sales manager is often seen as the only way to pay the person enough to make it attractive to stay with the firm. (If that is true, it may indicate an important weakness in the sales compensation area.) More generally, promotion to a manager's position may be regarded as the ultimate reward for superior sales performance.

Whether motivated by the desire to provide increased income or recognition, promoting a sales rep to a manager's position can be unwise if the person does not have the interests and abilities required to perform competently as a manager. The firm may lose a good sales representative and gain a weak manager. Sales organizations provide some of the best empirical support for *The Peter Principle,* a tongue-in-cheek but nonetheless valid analysis of a tendency in organizations to promote persons based on success in the previous position until they reach their "level of incompetence" in the hierarchy, where performance will be inadequate and they will therefore not be promoted further.[4] Thus, the nature of the manager selection process can contribute directly to the *"supersalesman"* problem and the emphasis on selling *vs* managing.

This leads directly to the third set of factors influencing the problem, the characteristics of sales reps who become managers. If the manager was promoted because of his or her skills as a sales rep, those skills are very likely to be the skills depended upon to bring success in the new job. It may seem entirely appropriate and expected for the manager to play "supersalesman," as a role model for the other reps and as the leading contributor to the district's accomplishment of its sales goals. The manager in this situation is simply doing what he or she does best, a perfectly understandable course of action but one that reflects a lack of understanding of the nature of a field sales manager's responsibilities and a lack of preparation to assume those responsibilities. If the selection process has not focused on the abilities required to be a manager, chances are these will also be overlooked in the training and supervision of the new manager.

Finally, there is pressure from customers to keep the manager in a selling role. Old customers may want to keep the rep's attention even after the rep becomes a manager. New customers may need to be wooed by a person with the manager's title before they will agree to change suppliers, hoping for greater assurance of product availability and service as a result of the management-level contact. Problem cus-

[4]Laurence J. Peter and Raymond Hull, *The Peter Principle* (New York: William Morrow & Co., Inc., 1969), esp. p. 26.

tomers, those with complaints, service problems, or complex product requirements, for example, may also need the manager's attention, especially if the manager has neglected the development of sales reps who might have been able, with proper training and supervision, to deal with these problems themselves. Large customers may be able to insist on managerial responsibility for their accounts simply as a matter of their importance to the selling firm.

In addition to these four sets of factors—cost considerations, the selection process, manager's selling skills, and customer insistence—there is a general tendency to focus on short-term, operating decisions that contributes to the emphasis on selling rather than managing. Every manager faces this problem to a degree, in the day-to-day pressures to attend to problems that arise in the normal course of events rather than to delegate them to subordinates so that the manager can keep his or her attention focused on longer-term administrative and strategic issues. In a sales organization this tendency is heightened by the ever-present and overriding demand to achieve forecasted levels of sales volume, contribution margin, new accounts, and so on. The basic issue here is that excessive focus on short-term activities and results (selling) by the field sales manager can significantly hamper the ability of the sales organization to perform effectively over the long run. Neglecting supervision, organizational development, and administration (managing) can lead to serious future problems, especially in the form of ineffective sales reps.

ABILITIES REQUIRED OF THE FIELD SALES MANAGER

For purposes of discussion we can define six reasonably distinct sets of abilities required of the effective field sales manager:

1. *Administrative* ability—to set priorities, organize resources, organize one's own time, develop systems and programs for accomplishing desired results, and give direction.
2. *Human relations* skills—to be sensitive to other people, their needs and perceptions, and to sense how other people respond to oneself; to understand how people work individually, in groups, and in the context of a formal organization.

Both of the above sets of abilities are particularly relevant in the performance of supervisory functions, as well as in office administration and developing the sales organization.

3. *Analytical and decision-making* abilities—to define a problem and break it into its component parts, to identify cause-and-effect relationships, to assess risks, to define and evaluate alternative courses of action and choose among them, and to implement a course of action once decided upon.

4. *Planning* ability—to set objectives, to analyze trends and forces likely to influence the environment in the future, to organize resources, and to develop programs to accomplish stated objectives.

Analytical, decision-making, and planning abilities will be more important at higher levels of the field sales management hierarchy, although not unimportant even for the first-line supervisor. Both types of abilities (and they obviously are closely related) involve a basic ability to reason logically, to think critically, and to use concepts. These abilities can be developed through formal education as well as through job experience.

5. *Selling skills*—to develop and deliver effective sales presentations, to listen carefully, to understand customers' needs and buying behavior, to identify and stress product benefits relevant to the customer, to build rapport with the customer, and to create a sense of trust and confidence. Selling skills are in essence communication skills and interpersonal interaction skills. At their root they have a lot in common with human relations skills.

6. *Technical* knowledge—about products and their uses, about customers and their industries, and about the market, including competitors and forces shaping supply and demand.

Selling skills and technical knowledge are the essential abilities of the successful sales representative and they are the abilities most completely developed through experience in the selling role. Human relations skills may also be developed in the performance of the sales representative's duties. All three sets of abilities are necessary in the field sales manager. Even if the manager does not have personal selling responsibility, selling skills and technical knowledge can be invaluable assets in the performance of supervisory functions, especially direct coaching. But the other abilities—administrative, analytical and decision-making, and planning—may not be well developed in the normal course of events as a person gains experience as a sales representative.

SELECTION AND DEVELOPMENT OF FIELD SALES MANAGERS

One conclusion from the foregoing analysis is that effective field sales managers are not going to arise fully developed from the ranks of the field sales representatives. Companies need well-designed programs for identifying and developing potential field sales managers from both within and outside the organization.

The most likely source of new field sales managers is the company's own sales organization, although it may be necessary to go outside if the company faces a need for a new manager and has not been nurturing such talent internally. In the larger and better-managed sales organizations, young men and women will have been recruited into the sales organization from colleges and universities with the expectation that they would move from sales rep positions into management, not that they would make selling a life's work.

Persons with the potential to become field sales managers can be identified through normal, routine performance evaluation. In addition to successful achievement of quotas, demonstrated sound work habits, and the necessary degree of personal ambition, the candidate should have a true interest in managing as opposed to a career in selling. Often, social pressure and cultural norms can make a person avow an interest in management when in truth he or she would prefer to remain in selling. As part of ongoing organizational development activities, a sales manager may give the rep several opportunities to test his or her own interests and to assess his or her abilities by assigning non-routine tasks and projects that resemble field sales management duties. Among the tasks that might be assigned are working with junior sales reps as a trainer or supervisor; analyzing a particular market segment, major customer, or competitor and writing a report to management: developing a formal key account selling plan; reviewing and recommending improvements in office systems or reporting procedures; and interviewing applicants for a sales representative's position.

In some companies where the need to develop field sales management talent has been recognized, a position like Senior Sales Representative has been created to provide an experienced sales rep with the opportunity to test his or her interests in, and to develop the abilities required for, management. A position description for such a senior responsibility is presented in Figure 2.4. These positions can recognize the experience and expertise of the sales rep, provide a higher level of selling responsibility, give important accounts more professional attention, and help the first-line manager with some supervisory assistance while developing the sales rep as a manager. The job description in Figure 2.4 should be compared with those for a sales engineer (Figure 1.2) and a branch manager (Figure 2.2) in the same company—Gould, Inc. Instruments Division.

When he or she has demonstrated the necessary interest and potential, the prospective field sales manager needs to be prepared through formal training and supervision to assume those responsibilities. Learning by doing or "on the job" is often not the most effective method. Rather, formal seminars and courses to develop the abilities required of a field sales manager are usually a preferred method. Equally important is the careful supervision and training of the neophyte field sales manager by his or her manager. Without such preparation, direction, and support, the supersalesman syndrome is likely to appear. This was one of the central conclusions of a classic study by Robert T. Davis involving field sales managers in 54 companies:

> They excel at personal selling, at trouble shooting (which is usually customer-oriented), and at the mechanics of running the field office; they are weakest at developing and supervising salesmen and at analyzing and planning their operations.[5]

Davis found a pattern of lack of management training and preparation underlying this mode of performance:

[5]Davis, *op. cit.*, from the abstract accompanying the book, p. 2.

TITLE: Senior Sales Engineer
RESPONSIBLE TO: Branch Manager

Major Responsibilities

I. Call on service customers to promote sale of company products.

    A. Establish and maintain a uniform level of customer contact in accordance with defined standards.

    B. Establish and maintain a level of product sales at approved prices within his assigned territory to meet and/or exceed his sales quota. This level of product sales should be approximately 25% above those of other sales engineers for comparable circumstances.

    C. Develop a negotiation backlog sufficient to provide a stable, uniform flow of orders entered.

    D. Assume responsibility for the installation and service of all company products delivered in his territory. Demonstrate to and instruct users in equipment operation and first-line maintenance.

    E. Inform other sales personnel of problems encountered and solutions thereto in the sale and use of company products. Maintain at all levels a free flow of information on a company-wide basis.

    F. Maintain and upgrade present customers, and establish new accounts at a minimum rate of 10% per annum.

II. Establish favorable customer relationships.

    A. Manage his territory professionally, ethically, efficiently, and in such a manner as to establish the company as a favored supplier.

    B. Investigate problems and complaints and work out settlements equitable to the customer and the company.

III. Acquire and maintain competence in the operation and application of company products.

    A. Acquire a high level of technical product knowledge. Participate in educational and training activities designed to improve technical competence.

    B. Properly care for all demonstration equipment and sales aids at his disposal. Be sufficiently skilled in equipment operation to permit optimum demonstrations without detraction from the sales effort.

    C. Continue to broaden knowledge and increase proficiency in the application of company products.

    D. Acquire knowledge of equipment modifications available as non-standard products and develop skill in applying modifications to satisfy customer requirements.

Figure 2.4. A job description for a senior sales representative in Gould, Inc. Instruments Division.

IV. Acquire and maintain adequate administrative skills.

    A. Assume all responsibility for proposals, price quotations, and correspondence connected with his sales activities. Acquire sufficient skill to function independently. Remain current on all sales information.

    B. Acquire sufficient knowledge of company organization to establish liaison with anyone whose assistance is required in the sale or service of company products.

    C. Prepare and submit reports as directed by supervisor. Compliance should be complete, timely, and in accordance with established schedules.

    D. Obtain, use, and disseminate information relating to potential and current customers, market trends, new markets, competitive products, product performance, and customer testimonials and complaints.

V. Acquire skill in accomplishing special assignments.

    A. Competently assist at trade shows.

    B. Become proficient in team sales efforts, conducting seminars, and formal product presentations.

    C. Participate in group and individual sales and product training activities as organized periodically in the branch, region, and factory.

    D. Assist in the orderly transfer of territories and accounts.

    E. At the direction of his manager, execute other assignments for which he has special skills and which are intended to accomplish primary sales objectives.

VI. Develop maturity and self-discipline.

    A. Respond cooperatively to management direction. Benefit from performance critiques. Discuss problems factually and objectively.

    B. Develop a well-organized approach to daily activities.

    C. Develop well-balanced and mature relationships with co-workers and customers. Develop leadership skills.

    D. Formulate career objectives and strive for their achievement.

VII. Acquire training and supervisory skills.

    A. Develop skills in training personnel assigned to him for that purpose. This training to encompass development of skills in sales, operation, and application of company products; administrative capabilities; and in the responsibilities of the job of sales engineer.

    B. Develop supervisory and leadership capabilities in preparation for next logical assignment.

Figure 2.4. *(Continued)*

Managers had received little or no management training and consequently . . . continued to do what they knew best—to sell . . . the basic pattern seemed to be determined by the path of progression the typical manager followed: from star salesman to local manager.[6]

That conclusion is probably just as valid today, in most companies, as it was when the research was conducted.

SUMMARY

This chapter has sketched the principal duties of the field sales manager and the abilities required to perform those duties well. The first-line manager's major responsibility was said to be supervision, defined to include creating the work environment, establishing standards of performance, providing for manpower development, acting as a communication link, and interpreting and enforcing policy. The other duties examined were developing the sales organization, selling and managing key accounts, office administration, and representing the company to the local community. A tendency to let attention to selling drive out attention to managing, labeled the "Supersalesman" problem, was seen to reflect cost considerations, the nature of the process by which field sales managers are selected, the characteristics of the individuals who get promoted to field sales management, and demands of customers. Effective field sales management was said to require not only the selling skills and technical knowledge of the successful sales representative but also administrative, human relations, analytical and decision-making, and planning abilities as well. Finally it was argued that future field sales managers must be selected, prepared, and managed with this full range of abilities in mind.

While sales managers' responsibilities do not come in such neat packages in actual practice, and while the abilities required are not easily separated from one another, these are reasonable descriptions of the requirements for an effective field sales manager. As the three different job descriptions illustrated, there is a wide variety of field sales management responsibilities in actual practice, and we should be cautious in calling any one manager or position typical.

[6]*Ibid.*

THREE

The Buying Process and Buyer–Seller Interaction

Selling has been defined as "helping customers buy." While that definition contains a large degree of oversimplification, it usefully focuses our attention on the basic fact that the customer, not the sales rep, makes the buying decision. The buyer holds ultimate authority in the buyer–seller relationship. As noted in Chapter 1, the basic dictum of selling and sales force management is "Know your customer."

We can return to a figure originally presented in Chapter 1 depicting the forces determining the sales representative's effectiveness. Now, in Figure 3.1, we must direct our analysis to the right side of the model, which is really a model of buying behavior in formal organizations. Formal organizations are goal-directed organizations consisting of many persons with formally assigned tasks, technology, and structure and are usually budget-constrained. This broad definition includes both business firms and non-profit organizations, the types of customers that are usually called upon by field sales representatives. We are excluding from specific consideration in the analysis of the buying process households and individual consumers, which are the prospects for door-to-door sales reps, insurance agents, investment brokers, and so on. However, our analysis of buyer–seller interaction will apply in general terms to these kinds of selling situations as well. A brief additional commentary on this distinction between industrial and consumer selling is in order.

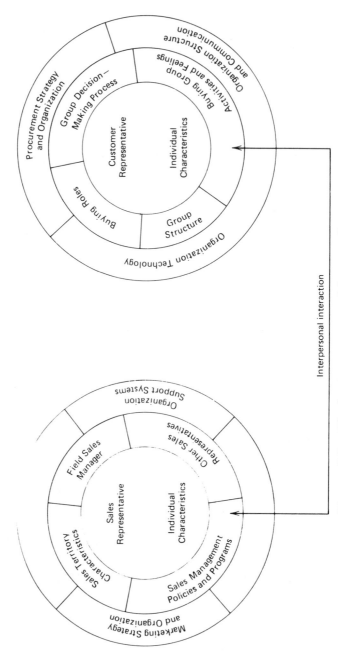

Environmental Factors
(Competition; General Economic Conditions; Laws and Regulations)

Interpersonal interaction

Figure 3.1. The buying process and buyer–seller interaction.

THE NATURE OF INDUSTRIAL CUSTOMERS

The distinction between industrial and consumer *marketing* is often hard to make in practice, although distinguishing consumer and industrial *products* may be easier. For example, consumer packaged goods such as alcoholic beverages and consumer durables such as automobiles are easily distinguished from industrial raw materials such as polyethylene film and industrial machinery such as a drill press. But what happens when the alcohol beverages are sold in large quantities to an airline for resale to passengers? when fleets of autos are bought by car rental firms and by companies for use by their sales forces? when the polyethylene film is converted and sold as plastic sandwich bags? when the home hobbyist buys the drill press? Other products such as typewriters, diesel fuel, fasteners and adhesives, and kitchen appliances are clear illustrations of products with both large consumer and large industrial/institutional markets.

Is the General Foods sales representative whose position was described in Chapter 1 an industrial or a consumer sales rep? While selling what is obviously a *consumer* product—grocery items such as coffee, frozen foods, and powdered soft drinks that move from the store shelf into the hands of the consumer—the General Foods sales rep is probably best thought of as an *industrial* sales representative. The sales rep's customer is not the consumer; it is the retailer, and the retailer is a profit-motivated and budget-constrained business firm. The persons who work for that retailer—buyers, merchandise managers, inventory controllers, and the like—and who are involved in the buying decision process for General Foods products are functioning in their roles as employees of the retail firm. To understand whether a sales rep is functioning in a consumer or an industrial sales organization, the central question is "Who is the customer?" not "What is being sold?"

Referring back to the discussion of push and pull strategies in Chapter 1, the consumer product sales force selling to business customers has a much different strategic role, that was characterized as one of *facilitating distribution* in support of the firm's basic consumer-oriented marketing strategy. For the industrial product sales force, the role is much more typically one of direct responsibility for demand stimulation because the buyer will actually use the product rather than resell it.

In the discussion that follows, we are considering the activities of all sales forces, for both consumer and industrial products, whose customers are organizations. We will emphasize the fact that the customer's buying process is an *organizational* decision-making process, which means that there is more than one person involved in the decision. Therefore, the sales representative must manage a complex set of relationships with the customer, involving interaction with several individuals.

THE ORGANIZATIONAL BUYING PROCESS

Organizational buying is a decision-making process involving persons who are functioning in their roles as members of an organization. These persons have formally assigned roles within the organization but they are motivated by their own personal needs, wants, and perceptions. Each person is likely to use a unique set of criteria in evaluating potential vendors' offerings and to have unique perceptions of the merits of those offerings. These persons interact with and influence one another. The sales representative will be interacting with them as individuals and as a group.

The Buying Decision Process

The organizational buying process takes time, often several months or even years, and the amount of time is correlated with the number of people involved in the process as well as the amount of risk involved for the buying organization. The buying process can be described, for analytical purposes, as consisting of a series of stages although the stages may not be discrete and sequential in practice. There are several models of the stages of the buying process. One that has achieved some popularity is the BUYPHASE model developed by Robinson, Faris, and Wind.[1] The BUYPHASE model describes the buying process as consisting of eight stages, or phases:

1. Anticipation or recognition of a problem (need) and a general solution.

[1]Patrick J. Robinson, Charles W. Faris, and Yoram Wind, *Industrial Buying and Creative Marketing* (Boston: Allyn & Bacon, 1967), pp. 11–21.

2. Determination of characteristics and quantity of needed item.
3. Description of characteristics and quantity of needed item.
4. Search for and qualification of potential sources.
5. Acquisition and analysis of proposals.
6. Evaluation of proposals and selection of supplier(s).
7. Selection of an order routine.
8. Performance feedback and evaluation.

The explicitness of each stage in the buying process, that is, the ease with which it can be identified as a distinct stage in decision making, will vary from one buying situation to another. The simplest buying situations, where something purchased before is purchased again from the same vendor, would perhaps involve only steps 1 and 8. The role of the sales representative and the nature of the selling process will vary, obviously, as a function of the complexity of the buying process—the number of persons involved, the extent to which each stage of the buying process receives explicit attention, and the amount of time required to pass through the decision stages.

A somewhat different model of the industrial buying process has been proposed by Bonoma, Zaltman, and Johnston. The intent of their model is to focus on the basic nature of industrial buying as an interaction between the buying center and representatives of the selling organizations. Thus, they define industrial buying behavior as:

an explicit or implicit transactional decision-making interaction through which formal or informal profit centers represented by authorized delegates:

1. establish the need for products or services,
2. search among and identify potential suppliers,
3. evaluate the marketing mix, product, price, promotion, and distribution of potential suppliers,
4. negotiate for, and enter into agreement about, purchase terms,
5. complete a purchase, and
6. evaluate the purchase's utility in facilitating organizational goals.[2]

[2]Thomas V. Bonoma, Gerald Zaltman, and Wesley J. Johnston, *Industrial Buying Behavior* (Cambridge, MA.: Marketing Science Institute, Report No. 77–117, December 1977), p. 4.

The essential feature of this definition is its assertion that industrial buying is not an act performed by the buying organization, but rather an interaction process between buyer and seller. Outcomes are not either/or possibilities defined before the process begins; they are negotiated as part of the process. The product offering is seen as the total marketing mix of the supplier—product, price, promotion, and distribution—because all of these influence the vendor's ability to satisfy the customer's needs. While the seller may have defined the product offering as part of the planning of the sales call, and the buyer may have developed the specifications for the purchase before interacting with the potential vendors, the actual buying outcome will be the result of the interactions that take place between the members of the two organizations. The Bonoma, Zaltman, and Johnston model is therefore a much more dynamic model than the BUYPHASE model of the buying process and it provides a realistic and necessary linkage between buying and selling. Neither process can take place without the other, and neither should be analyzed except in the context of the other. To understand the selling process we need to understand the buying process and vice versa.

Types of Buying Situations

To consider how the role of the sales rep varies as a function of the complexity of the buying process, it is helpful to characterize three rather distinct types of buying situations, called (1) straight rebuy, (2) modified rebuy, and (3) new task by Robinson, Faris, and Wind,[3] or (1) routinized response behavior, (2) limited problem solving, and (3) extensive problem solving in a more general theory of buyer behavior developed by Howard and Sheth.[4] Using the first set of categories, each type of buying decision can be characterized briefly as follows:

Straight Rebuy. Routine handling of a repetitive buying requirement with no search for alternatives. Characterized by loyalty to brands, vendors, sales reps, and other sources of information. For

---

[3]*Op. cit.*, p. 28.

[4]John A. Howard and Jagdish N. Sheth, *The Theory of Buyer Behavior* (New York: John Wiley & Sons, 1969), p. 27.

the "in" supplier, the selling problem is to maintain necessary levels of service. For the "out" supplier, the challenge is to create dissatisfaction with the presently purchased product offering, to alter perceptions, to move the buying situation to a higher level of complexity (the next type of buying situation).

Modified Rebuy.   Consideration of possible new sources or different product options for products or services purchased previously. May be used to keep present vendors "honest," with respect to prices, terms of sale, and so on. Sales rep's role emphasizes demonstration of product/service superiority *vs* competitors.

New Task.   Buying organization faces need to buy something unique and not purchased before, and needs assistance in defining buying goals and evaluation criteria as well as in developing and evaluating alternative purchase options. The sales rep's role emphasizes a high level of creative marketing activity, an educational–consultative–problem-solving mode of interaction with the buying organization.

In reality, buying situations do not come in three neat categories but range along a continuum of complexity. The most complex situations, the new tasks, take the longest time, account for the largest expenditures of money per transaction and perhaps in total money spent, and involve the most people, but they are only a small percentage of the total number of purchase and sales transactions. The simplest situations, the straight rebuys, typically account for more than 80% of the purchase transactions, that is orders in the narrow sense of actual purchase orders, but perhaps as little as 20% of the total dollar value of purchase.

There is a tendency for both new tasks and straight rebuys to evolve toward modified rebuys over time. The new task problem, once solved, may settle into a pattern of repeat purchasing of similar products according to familiar and well-defined specifications from a small list of qualified vendors. The straight rebuy may move up the ladder of complexity as the result of creative effort by sales reps or due to a perception by a member of the buying organization that there are attractive alternatives to present arrangements. Thus, even in a straight rebuy situation, the sales rep is well advised not to take current success for granted. To maintain competitive advantage and to deliver increased value to the customer, the sales rep for an "in" supplier may from time to time create a modified rebuy situation by presenting new product and service alternatives for the consideration of the customer.

Participants in the Buying Process

A buying situation is created when someone in the buying organization defines a problem in such a way that it potentially can be solved by buying something. The buying situation reflects, therefore, a perception by someone of an organizational need that can be satisfied by purchasing goods or services. The refinement of that perception into an operational problem definition is described by the first two steps of the BUYPHASE model, leading to the development of explicit, written purchase specifications in phase 3.

The definition of the buying situation and the careful determination of the characteristics of the item to be purchased, along with the desired terms and conditions of purchase, typically involve many persons who will influence the buying process in unique and varied ways. It is obviously a prime responsibility of the sales representative to identify those persons and to analyze their roles in the buying process. These persons interact with, inform, and influence one another. This group of interacting decision makers and influencers has been called a *buying center* in a general model of organizational buying behavior developed by Webster and Wind.[5] This general model defines five buying roles within the buying center:

1. *Buyers*.   Buyers are given specific authority for issuing purchase orders on behalf of the organization, which means they can enter into contractual relationships with vendors. Buyers are usually members of a purchasing department or are administrative officers.

2. *Users*.   Users are those who actually use the product or service in their work.

3. *Influencers*.   Influencers are persons who add either information or constraints to the buying process.

[5]Frederick E. Webster, Jr. and Yoram Wind, *Organizational Buying Behavior* (Englewood Cliffs, NJ: Prentice-Hall, 1972), pp. 77–81.

4. *Deciders*. Deciders are persons with the true authority, formal or informal, to choose among the various purchase alternatives available. Technical personnel or general management often have such authority, in contrast with purchasing personnel who may only execute the decisions made by others.

5. *Gatekeepers*. Gatekeepers exercise influence by controlling the flow of information and materials into the buying center. They might include secretaries who arrange appointments and schedule meetings, or purchasing personnel who maintain files of product information and approve visitor privileges for sales reps.

A buying center may have several persons in each buying role—several influencers, for example—and one person may occupy more than one buying role, as when one person is user, influencer, and decider. The buying center is the target for all marketing effort, and the sales representative must know the individuals involved in terms of their roles in the organization, their motivations and perceptions, how they interact with one another, and how they feel toward one another. The general model of organizational buying behavior developed by Webster and Wind can be used as an analytical framework for that analysis, as can an alternative model proposed by Sheth as an extension of the Howard and Sheth model mentioned earlier.[6]

The basic structure of the Webster and Wind model is diagramed in Figure 3.2. Organizational buying is seen as being influenced by four sets of variables—environmental, organizational, interpersonal, and individual. (These same four classes of variables are depicted in Figure 3.1 as well, where the right-hand side of the model is really a simplified representation of the Webster and Wind model.) Selling effort must be directed at specific individuals, not at the abstract organization. Defining the individuals in the buying center is the first task for the sales rep. The individual members of the buying center are characterized in the model by their motivations, cognitive struc-

[6]Frederick E. Webster, Jr. and Yoram Wind, "A General Model for Understanding Organizational Buying Behavior," *Journal of Marketing*, Vol. 36 (April 1972), pp. 12–19. Jagdish N. Sheth, "A Model of Industrial Buyer Behavior," *Journal of Marketing*, Vol. 37 (October 1973), pp. 50–56.

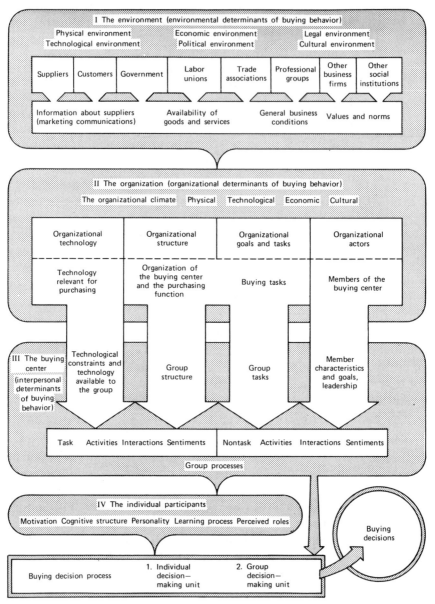

Figure 3.2. A model of the industrial buying process. Source: Frederick E. Webster, Jr. and Yoram Wind, "A General Model for Understanding Organizational Buying Behavior," *Journals of Marketing*, Vol. 36, No. 2 (April 1972), pp. 12–19. Reproduced with permission of the American Marketing Association.

ture, personality, learning process, and their own perceptions of their buying roles. The buying decision process includes both individual and group decision-making processes leading to buying actions. Members of the buying center interact with one another and have feelings toward one another that influence the buying process. These activities, interactions, and sentiments have both task and non-task dimensions, that is, directly or indirectly related to the specific buying task and buying situation. For example, the purchasing manager may accept the recommendations of a production engineer concerning specifications for a new machine tool because the manager respects the engineer's technical expertise (a task-related activity), even though he doesn't like the engineer personally (a non-task-related sentiment) and tries to avoid interaction with him. A sales rep working with these individuals must be aware of both the task and non-task dimensions.

The Influence of Organization

Members of the buying center are functioning in their buying roles as members of the formal organization. To understand their buying behavior it is necessary to understand how the organization influences them. In the Webster and Wind model, the organization is defined by four sets of variables—people ("actors"), tasks, structure, and technology. That model places special emphasis on the need to examine the influence of organization structure, because it is the most subtle and least obvious of the organizational variables. In particular, effective selling strategy must be based on an understanding of how the individual members of the buying center perceive, and are influenced by, the organization's systems of communication, authority, status, rewards, and work flow. Each of these systems is highly intangible and has several subsystems, which makes its influence both subtle and complex. For example, the communication system influences behavior in at least four functionally distinct ways: by informing members of the buying center; by issuing commands and instructions in the form of policies, operating procedures, and other types of directives; by messages from individuals intended to influence and persuade other individuals; and by messages designed to coordinate and integrate the activities of individual actors. In a complex buying situation, the sales rep clearly can benefit from understanding the organization's communication system.

Furthermore, the various organization structure systems interact with one another in their influence on the individual actors. In one of the more significant interactions, the *authority* system (which defines who can command and evaluate whom) interacts with the *rewards* system (which defines the rewards and punishments given to organizational actors). Because most selling efforts require individual members of the buying center to behave in some manner (respond, don't respond, grant an interview, evaluate a proposal, decide to buy or not buy, and so on), because that behavior is likely to be evaluated by someone, and because that evaluation will likely lead to some reward to the actor, positive or negative, all buying behavior (even the simple act of listening) may involve some personal risk to the individual. The sales representative must be aware of the organization's systems of communication, authority, status, rewards, and work flow in order to comprehend and cope with the risk perceived by the members of the buying center as a result of their interactions with the sales rep.

In these few paragraphs we have only begun to sketch the outlines of the influence of organizational variables on the buying process. The purpose has been to suggest the importance to the sales rep of understanding the formal organization *per se*, as well as the composition and functioning of the buying center and the motivations and perceptions of its members as individuals.

One of the specific organizational variables of obvious significance in the buying process, and for the sales rep, is the organization's purchasing strategy, an important subset of the organizational goals and tasks defined in the Webster and Wind model. A few simple definitions will be helpful. A strategy is a planned course of action is pursuit of clearly stated objectives and, usually, in the context of some environmental uncertainty. Purchasing strategies are plans of action for dealing with suppliers, actual and potential, in order to obtain goods and services. As in all strategic planning, some organizations have very well-developed purchasing strategies, whereas others have none at all. Because strategies provide the links between organizations and their environments, we now shift our attention to the environmental variables in the buying process model.

Environmental Variables and the Buying Process

Purchasing strategies can also be thought of as plans for satisfying the organization's evolving needs for goods and services in the context of a changing environment. That changing environment includes suppliers of goods and services, competitors for those goods and services, and economic and political conditions, especially the rate of economic growth and the regulatory environment, evolving technology, and changing social values and norms. Changes in any of these environmental variables can require significant modifications in purchasing strategy. It is the fact of a changing environment that creates the need for a purchasing strategy, the need for a plan to improve purchasing performance as the organization's goals, problems, and opportunities are redefined in that changing environment.

Among the most significant events in the procurement environment are changes in the number, characteristics, and performance of supplier firms. A key selling objective may be to keep all potential customers informed of the supplier's evolving capabilities in comparison with competitors. That is true for both "in" and "out" suppliers. A creative marketer may be able to play a significant role in the development of the customer's purchasing strategy.

The purchasing strategy, if it is well thought out, will set specific objectives and goals for the buying center. It will define the problem that the buyer is trying to solve, and the opportunity available to the sales representative.

THE SELLING PROCESS

For the past several pages we have been focusing our attention on the buyer side of the buyer–seller relationship. We have looked at models of the buying process that consider only half of the interactive process that links buying and selling organizations. We can begin to correct that imbalance by shifting our attention back to the seller side of the relationship and to the sales representative.

The selling process consists of one or more sales calls upon one or more members of the buying center. The *sales call* can be defined as one continuous interaction with one or more persons at a single buying location. A typical sales call might take 20 minutes or so, but the range can involve extremes—from a few minutes for a pharmaceutical detailer calling on a physician, for example, to a full day's presentation by a computer sales rep to the buying committee for a large potential customer. (McGraw-Hill Publishing Company conducts an annual survey of the costs of field sales activities and estimated the cost of an average industrial sales call to be $137 in 1981.)

There are many different types of sales calls and they can be classified according to the purpose of the sales call. In the kinds of buying-selling situations we have been considering, it is probably true that the majority of sales calls do not have the objective of making a sale—actually writing an order—on that particular call. Some possible, and typical, sales call objectives might be: to submit a formal proposal; to check on the progress of product evaluations in the customer's laboratories; to pick up a set of specifications; to correct a product performance problem; to discuss evaluation criteria with a key decision influencer; to attempt to convince a buyer of the potential supplier's reliability for product quality and delivery; or to obtain information from the customer about future purchasing plans. All sales calls, however, have the ultimate objective of generating profitable sales volume from this customer.

SIMPLE MODELS

The selling process can be thought of as an analog of the buying process, what the sales rep does to move the buying center through the stages of the buying process. This is a rather crude analogy, however, one that thinks of the sales rep as doing something to the buyer. It is a simple stimulus–response view of the selling process, one that overlooks the essential nature of the selling process as interpersonal (dyadic) interaction in which each party influences the other and both influence the outcome. Here we can continue our discussion of views of the sales rep's role that we began in Chapter 1, with more emphasis on the selling process *per se* rather than on the sales rep.

Among the most common of the traditional models of the selling process are the AIDA model: (1) get Attention, (2) arouse Interest, (3) stimulate Desire, and (4) get Action; the steps-in-the-sale model: (1) prospecting, (2) preapproach, (3) approach, (4) demonstration, (5) handling objections, and (6) closing; and the stimulus–response model, in which the sales representative learns a repertoire of specific things to say (as in the use of memorized or "canned" sales presentations) that are believed to have a high probability of producing a predictable and desired response from the prospect. A somewhat more complex view of the selling process was the need–satisfaction model, which emphasized the value to the sales rep of stressing product benefits and thereby customer need satisfaction in the selling process. Other models such as the mood selling and barrier theory of selling approaches (stressing, respectively, the need to establish a positive, professional climate in the sales call and the need to define and then deal with specific barriers to the successful sale) continued to emphasize the sales representative's action.[7]

Such simple views of the selling process have been characteristic of traditional approaches to the study of salesmanship and, in fact, may be reasonably effective paradigms for helping people to learn how to sell. These simple models are easy to understand and to remember, and can assist the neophyte sales representative in planning and executing sales calls. But they are inadequate as guidelines for sophisticated analysis of the selling process and are of very limited usefulness to both academic researchers and industrial sales planners. The selling process is more interesting, more complex, and more unpredictable than it is described to be by these simple models.

Behavioral-Communications Models

It has been characteristic of models developed in the last couple of decades to adopt a "communications" view of the selling process, stressing an active role for the buyer in the sales interview and the two-person dyadic interaction nature of the selling process. These approaches typically place emphasis on the sales rep's ability to listen to the prospect and to tailor selling messages to the specific customer and buying situation. Even these behaviorally based approaches, however, presented a viewpoint that was focused on the sales rep and heavily manipulative in tone, as in these five guidelines developed in an article on the application of social science findings to selling:

1. An atmosphere of mutual compatibility must be achieved;
2. The customer's attention must be focused on the salesman and his message;

---

[7]These models, and others like them, are described in Joseph W. Thompson, *Selling: A Behavioral Science Approach* (New York: McGraw-Hill Book Co., 1966), pp. 136–155.

3. An atmosphere of permissiveness must be established by evoking a felt need on the part of the customer;

4. The natural aggressiveness of the salesman must be changed to enhance the customer's ego; it should not be allowed to express itself in self-assertion, dominance, or hostility;

5. An atmosphere conducive to decision and action toward the resolution of the customer's felt need must be established through the development of feelings of satisfaction and profit.[8]

The author went on to observe that although the good sales rep was implicitly aware of these things, an explicit understanding would allow the rep to "manipulate the sales environment with more sureness and awareness."[9]

Another widely used salesmanship text of the late 1960s, based on a communications framework, was equally forthright in its preface to the reader:

> We believe a personal salesman must develop an insight into the process of perception if he is to successfully manipulate the attitudes, thinking, emotional responses, and, ultimately, the behavior of others . . . . a salesman must develop a persuasive communication based on his insight into client perceptions and make use of factors of attention, reasoned proof, personality, and emotional proofs. He must learn to overcome obstacles and to master closing techniques. He uses these techniques to alter client perceptions in order to win a favorable response.[10]

One suspects that this continued emphasis on selling as persuasion and what the sales rep could do to the prospect reflects a historical concern, implicit in the selling literature, more or less exclusively

---

[8]Samuel N. Stevens, "The Application of Social Findings to Selling and the Salesman," in *Aspects of Modern Marketing*, AMA Management Report No. 15 (New York: American Management Association Inc., 1958), pp. 85–94, reprinted in James H. Beardon (ed.), *Personal Selling: Behavioral Science Readings and Cases* (New York: John Wiley & Sons, 1967), pp. 85–91, at p. 88.

[9]*Ibid.*

[10]Richard M. Baker, Jr. and Gregg Phifer, *Salesmanship: Communication, Persuasion, Perception* (Boston: Allyn and Bacon, 1966), pp. v–vi.

with cold calls and with consumer selling—that is, one-on-one selling situations where the sales rep took the initiative and where the prospect had to be convinced that a product need existed. This set of assumptions is obviously inappropriate for a large portion of the kinds of buying situations faced by the industrial field sales representative.

Shapiro developed an eight-step format of the sales process intended to help sales managers in industrial firms plan their selling activities. This scheme is a more realistic view of the complexities of the typical industrial buying-selling situation, and emphasizes the need to think in terms of complex selling strategies, not the single sales call:

power cable

1. *Opening the Sale*.   Often done by telephone, with the objectives of introducing the sales rep and the selling company and learning whom to contact in the customer organization.

2. *Qualifying the Prospect*.   Assessing the buying organization's need for the product and the probabilities of making a sale.

3. *Developing the Sales Strategy*.   Planning on whom to contact and how to approach the buying center, systematically covering all members of the buying center, based on careful prior information gathering and analysis.

4. *Organizing the Justification*.   Developing the facts to be presented that will justify the cost of the purchase to the buying organization in terms of its effects on the customer's operations, budgets, cash flows, profits, and personal concerns of members of the buying center.

5. *Making the Presentation*.   Organizing and presenting the relevant information in the form of a proposal, either to assembled members of the buying center or to them as individuals. (Each of the members may have been contacted before the group presentation and may be contacted afterward as well.)

6. *Coordinating Resources and Personnel*.   Pulling together all persons and departments of the selling firm that may be involved in creating and delivering a solution to the customer's buying problem.

7. *Closing the Sale*.   Actually asking for the order in the form of a signed contract; may be tried first at the end of the formal presentation.

8. *Nurturing the Account Relationship*. Continued sales calls to build and maintain specific relationships between buying and selling organizations after the sale has been made; servicing the account in the broadest and most positive sense.[11]

While Shapiro's model is not a true behavioral-communications model in a specific sense, we have included it here because it has implicit within it a view of the selling process as buyer–seller interaction, and it is a realistically complex view of the process.

In Chapter 1 we presented briefly a view of the sales rep as a communicator in the buyer–seller dyad. We introduced some basic concepts from role theory to provide some structure to the analysis of dyadic interaction between buyer and seller. These concepts will not be repeated here,[12] but we should reiterate that this view of the selling process as interpersonal interaction is a much richer and more realistic framework for understanding the complexities of most industrial buying situations, and for relating the industrial selling process to industrial buying behavior. Now that we have considered both the buying process and the selling process separately, it is time to bring them back together in an integrated view of buyer–seller interaction.

BUYER–SELLER INTERACTION

The fundamental activity in selling is the interaction between the sales rep and a member of the buying center in the customer organization. The sales rep represents the selling company and presents its capability to the customer organization and the customer's buying problem to the potential vendor. The outcome of the interaction is determined in the interaction itself and not solely by the characteristics and actions of the individual actors. To repeat an earlier assertion, this is why we cannot realistically study buying and selling independently of each other. Bonoma, Zaltman, and Johnston make the point in this way:

---

[11]Benson P. Shapiro, "Making the Major Sale," *Harvard Business Review*, Vol. 54., No. 2 (March-April 1976), pp. 68–78.

[12]For a more complete presentation of a model of selling as dyadic interaction, see Frederick E. Webster, Jr., "Interpersonal Communication and Salesman Effectiveness," *Journal of Marketing*, Vol. 32, No. 3 (July 1968), pp. 7–13.

The defining characteristic of the dyadic interaction is the *social relationship* existing between actors. The interaction is not specified by the properties of the actors or even the actions of the parties. Further, it is not, as sometimes thought, equivalent to a stimulus–response sequence of communication, rewards, or punishments emanating from one actor, proceeding to a second actor, and back to the first actor. Rather, a dyadic interaction is characterized by the connections, shared experiences, interdependencies, or alliances between social actors.[13]

The central notion here is that the outcome of the sales interaction is a function of the *interdependencies* of the individual actors and of the buying and selling organizations. Potentially, each party's welfare can be enhanced by interacting with the other; each recognizes this mutuality of interests with the other; and each tries to influence the other to maximize his or her self-interest but not necessarily at the expense of the other's interests. The interaction is guided and constrained by a variety of forces, as specified in the model in Figure 3.1, including: norms and values; organization goals, policies, and procedures; the influence of other persons including supervisors, other sales reps, and other members of the buying center; and such environmental factors as intraindustry competition and government regulations.

Negotiation and bargaining are the principal influence processes at work in the buying–selling process, with some use made of compromise and persuasion. *Negotiation* as a social influence process recognizes specifically the strategic interdependency of the members of the dyad, and that cooperation can increase the value of the interaction to both parties. Negotiation attempts to maximize the total value of the interaction to both parties over the long run, not necessarily to maximize the short-term benefits which could block long-term maximization. The words bargaining and negotiation are more or less synonymous, but negotiation is sometimes defined as that special type of bargaining where both parties are committed to an objective of maximizing the total value of the relationship. *Bargaining* is a more general concept, which describes situations in which both parties recognize their strategic interdependence, and each bases his or her

---

[13]*Op. cit.*, p. 21.

choices on estimates of the likely actions of the other with the objective of enhancing his or her share of the outcomes as well as the total value of the interaction.

Compromise is a negative process, in which both parties give up something, thus reducing the total value of the relationship, in order to reach an agreement. For this reason, agreements based on compromise are likely to be unstable, since at least one of the parties will feel that something was lost in reaching the agreement and may seek to regain it by nurturing relationships with other sellers or buyers.

Persuasion is the influence process at the heart of most traditional views of selling. It is the process of convincing customers to buy, something the sales rep does to the prospect. The sale is seen as a conquest, and the customer can feel that he or she was "sold" rather than having particiated in a process that led to a buying decision. Persuasion can work in the short run. Its major strategic shortcoming is that it leaves the customer open to counterpersuasion by another sales rep with a better presentation. Persuasion may be most effective in those situations in which the buyer has few, if any, options, that is a seller's market. Even here, however, the outcome may be unstable and short-term in its orientation, especially if the buyer sets out after the sale to develop new options for future bargaining. The relative power of the buyer and seller, often a function of the number of competing suppliers and the size of the potential market, determines which of the methods of social influence will be most effective in the buyer–seller interaction.[14]

This view of selling as interaction has a set of fundamental implications for the sales management function that was summarized effectively in the title of an article by Shapiro: "Manage the Customer, Not just the Sales Force."[15] If the sales manager views the sales rep as a persuader, management attention focuses on sales policies in such areas as compensation, evaluation, and control in terms of how to get

[14]See Thomas V. Bonoma, "A General Theory of Interaction Applied to Sales Management," In Richard P. Bagozzi (ed.), *Sales Management: New Developments from Behavioral and Decision Model Research* (Cambridge, MA: Marketing Science Institute, 1979), pp. 145–173.

[15]Benson P. Shapiro, *Harvard Business Review*, Vol. 52, No. 5 (September-October 1974), pp. 127–136.

the rep to make more sales calls and more persuasive sales presentations. In the interaction and negotiation context, the sales rep is seen as a member of the team that represents and delivers the company's capability to solve the customer's problem. Instead of worrying primarily about motivating the sales people, management commits more resources to analyzing customer needs and buying behavior and to developing effective solutions to customer problems, and works hard at coordinating personal selling with all other elements of the marketing mix.

BOUNDARY ROLES AND BUYER–SELLER INTERACTION

This brings us back to the analysis in Chapter 1 of the sales rep as a boundary-role person, and now we can extend that concept to recognize the buying–selling process as a source of complex problems of negotiation and coordination for the sales representative and for the sales manager. The sales rep must represent the buying organization back to the marketing organization as well as representing his or her own organization to the customer. To some degree it is inevitable that this will involve conflicting expectations and demands for the sales rep. Certain sales policies intended to constrain the discretion of the sales rep and to proscribe the rep's behavior can conflict with the marketing objective of creating a satisfied customer.

Just as the sales rep must negotiate with members of the buying center, so must he or she also negotiate with members of the selling organization in developing solutions to customer problems. Some reseachers have argued that this often leads to a distrust of sales people by members of their own organization, partly because these other members cannot observe the sales reps in their interactions with customers.[16] Anxiety will be created in the sales rep who senses this cloud of suspicion and distrust. A supportive supervisor must be aware of this anxiety and must help the sales rep to reduce it, while at the same time assisting the rep in negotiations with other members of

[16]Robert E. Spekman, "Organizational Boundary Behavior: A Conceptual Framework for Investigating the Industrial Salesperson," in Bagozzi, *op. cit.*, pp. 133–144.

the organization. Role conflict and role ambiguity are perhaps greater for sales personnel than for any other members of the organization. Sales management policies, especially in training, supervision, and motivation must deal with these issues, as we shall attempt to show in later chapters on these subjects.

AN INTEGRATING CONTINGENCY FRAMEWORK

A view of the selling process as buyer–seller interaction leads to a much more complex view of the determinants of sales rep effectiveness and of the forces influencing the outcome of the sales interaction. This more complex view also explains why different studies of sales rep performance often have produced conflicting results on such questions as the effectiveness of different selling techniques, whether sales reps are more effective with prospects who are similar to themselves, and whether such characteristics of the sales rep as age, education, intelligence, product knowledge, sales experience, and empathy are correlated with effectiveness. The answer to such question is "It depends"—upon the nature of the customer and the type of buying situation. It is quite obvious, in retrospect, that there can be no one set of sales rep personal characteristics or selling behaviors that will be equally effective for all buyers and buying situations.

A *contingency framework* has been proposed by Barton A. Weitz as a guideline for future research on determinants of effectiveness in sales interactions.[17] This model (Figure 3.3) also has some important managerial implications for recruiting, selecting, and training sales reps, for assignment of reps to accounts and territories, and for the assessment of sales performance. The contingency framework says that the effectiveness of a sales rep's behavior is a function of three sets of variables—the rep's resources (skills, knowledge, and support); the customer's buying task; and the nature of the interpersonal relationship between buyer and seller—and of the interactions among these three sets of variables. The repertoire of selling behaviors avail-

[17]Barton A. Weitz, "Effectiveness in Sales Interactions: A Contingency Framework," *Journal of Marketing*, Vol. 45 (Winter 1981), pp. 85–103.

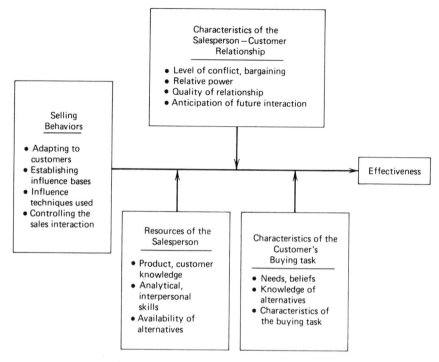

Figure 3.3.   An integrating contingency model of sales rep effectiveness. Source: Barton A. Weitz, "Effectiveness in Sales Interactions: A Contingency Framework," *Journal of Marketing,* Vol. 45 (Winter 1981), pp. 85–103, at p. 90. Reproduced with permission of the American Marketing Association.

able to the sales rep is characterized by four dimensions: (1) the degree of adaptation of selling style for an individual customer; (2) the presence of a basis of influence (e.g., company reputation—source credibility, and other sources of perceived legitimacy such as technical expertise); (3) the influence techniques used, including such choices as persuasion *vs* negotiation, and the type of selling messages to be delivered; and (4) the degree of sales rep control over the sales interaction.

The contingency framework integrates many of the notions of buyer–seller interaction developed in this chapter, and is consistent with our general model of the determinants of sales representative effectiveness (Figures 1.4 and 3.1). The contingency framework focuses on the behavior of the sales rep and leaves out the influence of supervision, management policies, organization, and strategy. Weitz's main purpose in developing the contingency model was to provide guidelines for future research, his own and others, on sales rep effectiveness. To that end, he outlined a number of propositions that could be tested empirically, propositions that focus on interactions among elements of the model. For example:

> Proposition 1: Engaging in adaptive sales behaviors across interactions is positively related to effectiveness in the following circumstances:
>
> > Salesperson resources—the salesperson has the resources, both personal abilities and product alternatives, to engage in adaptive sales behaviors.
> >
> > Customer buying tasks–the salesperson's customers typically are engaged in complex buying tasks that could result in large orders.
> >
> > Customer–salesperson relationship—the salesperson has a good relationship with the customer characterized by a low level of conflict, and the salesperson anticipates future relationships with the customer.[18]

In discussing this proposition, Weitz points out that adaptation of the selling approach to specific buying situations requires information, and information collection and adaptive selling are time-consuming processes. Thus, increasing effectiveness with an individual customer may cause a decrease in overall effectiveness across all customers, and it is important to be specific about the level and measure of effectiveness. The effectiveness of adaptive selling behavior is a function of the nature of the customer and the type of buying situation.

Once again, this complex model reminds us of several requirements for understanding issues of field sales management and of the need to avoid simple conclusions about complex problems. The field sales manager must be very specific in defining what is expected of the sales representatives, and these expectations must be clearly stated in a formal job description. This job description becomes a major tool for developing programs for recruiting, selecting, training, deploying, supervising, motivating, evaluating, controlling, and compensating sales personnel. Goals and objectives for performance

[18]*Ibid*, p. 94.

in the coming period must also be defined and communicated clearly. Performance evaluation and compensation systems should recognize the many factors mediating the relationship between the sales rep's efforts and customer response and the actual sales result. The bottom line on this discussion is a warning about the dangers inherent in a view of the sales rep strictly as an individual contributor and in seeing the solution to every sales problem as one of a kick in the pants or a pat on the back to make the rep work harder. In the industrial buying–selling situation, life isn't that simple.

SUMMARY

Buying and selling are two sides of the same process in which buyers and sellers are linked together through processes of dyadic interaction, especially negotiation. We looked at the buying decision process in complex formal organizations in order to develop an elementary understanding of the task faced by the sales rep. The buying center was defined as the key element in the buying process, including its membership and its functioning as a decision-making unit. Models of organizational buying behavior were reviewed, and seen to call for a more comprehensive view of selling than that represented by traditional models of the sales process, even those more recent models that take a behavioral–communications viewpoint. A view of selling as social interaction was seen to have significant implications for defining the role of the sales rep and for sales management policies and programs. An integrating contingency framework (model of the determinants of sales rep effectiveness) was presented, in which the major elements were the behavior and characteristics of the sales rep, the buying task faced by the customer, and the nature of the buyer–seller relationships. These are the principal elements of the buying–selling process, each of which has been examined in this chapter. Interaction among all three classes of variables is seen to determine the outcome, over time, of the buying–selling process.

FOUR

Developing the Field Sales Organization

From the first-line sales supervisor up to the national sales manager, the major responsibility and challenge for the field sales manager is to develop the field sales organization. The manager's principal opportunity for enhancing the long-range effectiveness of the sales organization is through recruiting and developing competent individuals for sales representative positions and as the future managers of the sales team. As noted in the previous chapter, pressures for the accomplishment of short-term performance objectives, especially current sales volume, often conflict with the need to develop an effective field sales organization.

The first level of field sales management has its impact on the development of human resources primarily through the supervisory process, and most especially in the coaching and "working-with" dimensions of the supervisory responsibility. As one moves up the organization ladder, recruitment, selection, and formal training become increasingly important dimensions of the organizational development process. At the top of the hierarchy, national and regional sales managers must determine the size and structure of the field sales organization in the context of marketing objectives and strategy. At these higher levels of the organization, more attention should be devoted to longer-term objectives and more time committed to organizational development rather than to short-term sales and profit goals. Even at the highest levels of management, however, the tendency for attention to short-term problems to dominate attention to long-term goals remains a persistent issue in many sales organizations.

In this chapter, our attention will focus on the issues of recruitment, selection, and training, and on determining the size and structure of the sales organization. The topic of supervision, and the related area of sales force motivation, will be covered in Chapter 6, after we have considered the deployment of the sales force in Chapter 5.

THE ROLE OF FIRST-LINE MANAGEMENT

There is wide variation in the extent to which companies assign formal responsibility for developing sales personnel to the lower levels of field sales management. At one extreme, the local manager (who might typically be called a district manager or branch manager) has little or no responsibility other than supervision, that is, the on-going development of sales personnel. Recruitment, selection, and training of sales personnel are all planned and conducted by line managers and supporting staff at the national level. This would more likely be the case in firms with relatively small sales organizations and where highly qualified, professional sales people are required and where each hiring decision has major significance for the firm. Final decision authority might still rest with the local manager.

At the other extreme, the local manager has the major responsibility for these activities, with only minimal direction or support from headquarters. In this case, headquarters support may consist of suggested copy for newspaper recruiting ads, application forms, standardized tests to be administered to applicants, or perhaps a manual or guide to assist the manager in the processes of recruitment, selection, and training. Such arrangements might be found in sales organizations where there is frequent turnover, where the selling job requires relatively low levels of knowledge and skill, and where large numbers of people are hired on a continuing basis.

Chapter 3 noted that the typical field manager grows out of the sales representative ranks. His or her sympathies and understanding are likely to lean more toward the sales rep than to management, especially if the management training of the field sales manager has been minimal or nonexistent. The manager needs direction and supervision to be sure that he or she is not simply "hiring in his or her own image," and trying to hire and train carbon copies of the people already in the sales force. The typical field sales manager tends to be more doer than planner, more implementer than strategist. This argues for careful guidance for the recruiting, selection, and training functions when responsibility for them has been delegated to first-line management.

AN OVERVIEW OF SALES ORGANIZATION EFFECTIVENESS

Selling is not an abstract process. It is a set of activities (observable and definable) carried out by people who are seeking to achieve a variety of personal goals while at the same time serving the goals of the selling organization. These people can be described by a set of personal characteristics including their knowledge, skills, and attitudes. Those characteristics reflect both innate and learned capabilities; the extent to which those responsibilities are obtained in the recruiting and selection process or developed through training and supervision is a function of sales management objectives and plans. The relationship between sales representative characteristics and sales force performance, as noted often in earlier chapters, is not a direct one but is influenced and mediated by many other factors including the field sales manager, company marketing strategy, and sales force management policies and programs.

How is sales organization effectiveness to be defined and measured? There are many options. Obviously, sales force performance is only one determinant of total organizational effectiveness, which can be defined by such measures as return on investment, return on equity, and so on. Sales organization performance is also to be differentiated from sales representative performance and from total marketing performance. We might visualize these relationships as follows, with the arrows meaning "contributes to" and "is one determinant of":

Sales representative performance
↓
Sales organization performance
↓
Marketing performance
↓
Organization performance

Performance is used here to mean accomplishment of objectives; effectiveness is a different concept, meaning the ability (of the sales rep, the sales organization, or the marketing strategy) to achieve those objectives. Effectiveness leads to performance.

Different measures are required for each type of performance. Some possible measures at each level are:

Sales representative performance:
    Dollar sales volume
    Unit sales
    Percentage of quotas achieved
    Product mix sold
    Qualitative measures
Sales organization performance:
    Total dollar revenues
    Percentage of sales forecast realized
    Expenses *vs* budget
    Return on assets managed
Marketing performance:
    Total dollar revenues
    Profit contribution margin
    Market share
    Rate of sales growth
Company/organization performance:
    Return on investment
    Return on equity
    Market share growth or decline
    Profit margin on sales

Performance is the ultimate objective of all sales management activities, policies and programs, including recruitment, selection, training, organization, planning, deployment, supervision, compensation, and control. However, to repeat an earlier point, these activities, policies, and programs do not lead to performance directly. Rather, their influence is mediated by the characteristics of the sales representatives themselves, including their aptitudes, skills, and motivation, and their perceptions of their roles. This overview of the determinants of sales organization effectiveness is summarized nicely in a model developed by Churchill, Ford, and Walker,[1] and depicted in Figure 4.1. The model shows the relationships between marketing strategy, sales organization and management, and sales force performance in a fashion very consistent with the viewpoint developed in this text.

A key concept in this model is that of role perceptions, described in terms of accuracy, ambiguity, and conflict. The role perceptions of the sales representative are an intervening set of variables between sales management activities and performance outcomes. Concepts relating to role performance were introduced in Chapters 1 and 3 in our considerations of the role of the sales rep, buyer–seller (dyadic) interaction, the sales rep as a boundary role person, and determinants of sales rep performance. Up to this point, the emphasis in examining the concept of role performance has been on buyer–seller interaction and the buying–selling process. Now, the focus shifts to the relationship between the sales representative and the field sales manager.

DEFINING THE ROLE OF THE FIELD SALES REPRESENTATIVE

From a strategic perspective, the role of the field sales representative is to implement the marketing strategy by making personal calls on present and potential customers, as defined by the marketing strategy, and to "make the numbers" for sales revenues and expenses contained in the marketing plan. The specific duties that are required by

---

[1]Gilbert C. Churchill, Jr., Neil M. Ford, and Orville C. Walker, Jr., *Sales Force Management* (Homewood, IL: Richard D. Irwin, 1981), pp. 18–27.

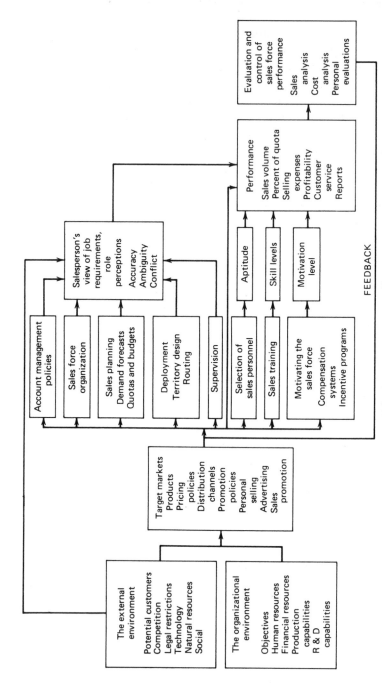

Figure 4.1. Determinants of sales organization effectiveness. Source: Gilbert C. Churchill, Jr., Neil M. Ford, and Orville C. Walker, Jr., *Sales Force Management* (Homewood, Ill.: Richard D. Irwin, 1981) P. 19. Reproduced with permission.

92

particular types of field sales assignments were suggested by the three position descriptions presented in Figures 1.1 to 1.3 in Chapter 1. While the job description is an essential management tool, which we will consider in more detail in the following section, the contents of the job description do not influence sales rep performance directly. Rather, the sales rep's performance is influenced by his or her perceptions of that role and of expectations held by other persons as to how he or she should play that role. The job description, while important, is only one of many determinants of the sales rep's role perceptions.

Role Perceptions

A social role is defined by the activities and behaviors expected of a person who occupies that position. Speaking of the sales rep's social role, Churchill, Ford, and Walker note that:

> The activities and behaviors associated with a particular job are defined largely by the expectations and demands of other people, both inside and outside the organization. Thus, a salesperson's job (or role) is defined by the expectations and desires of his or her customers, sales managers, other company executives, and family members. The salesperson's ability to do the job well, then, is partly determined by how clearly he or she understands those role expectations.[2]

In elaborating upon this part of their general model of sales management, the authors note that the sales rep's role is defined in a three-step process. First, expectations and demands, and pressures to conform to them, are communicated to the sales rep by members of that person's *role set*, those people with a vested interest in how the sales rep performs the role. Second, the sales rep develops his or her own perceptions of the expectations and demands of the role set. Third, the sales rep transforms these role perceptions into actual behavior. It is the second step in the process, the perceptual step, that is the source of difficulty. The perceptual problems can be classified into three sets of issues—perceived role accuracy, perceived role ambiguity, and perceived role conflict.

[2]*Ibid.*, p. 23.

Role inaccuracy results when the sales rep simply doesn't understand the expectations and demands of some portion of the role set, when the role perceptions are objectively wrong. The rep is not likely to realize that the perceptions are inaccurate, however.

Role ambiguity occurs when the sales rep is unclear as to what is expected and demanded by the role set. The sales rep will be aware of role ambiguity, by definition, in the form of feelings that role expectations and demands are unclear, that he or she lacks information about what is expected in a particular situation and how his or her performance will be evaluated.

Role conflict results from the perception that two or more members of the role set hold competing and conflicting expectations for the rep's performance and are making conflicting demands. For example, a spouse who objects to late hours may have expectations and demands different from a manager who insists on frequent customer entertainment. The sales rep is, once again by definition, aware of the existence of role conflict and is likely to feel it psychologically.[3] The sales rep's position as a boundary role person makes the position susceptible to higher degrees of role conflict than most other organizational positions. The ability to tolerate and manage such role conflict is clearly an asset for a person interested in a selling career.

It is essential that the field sales manager understand the concepts of perceived role accuracy, role ambiguity, and role conflict. The manager must work hard to reduce each to minimal levels, and must help the rep manage the residual conflict. A first step for the manager is to communicate his or her own expectations and demands for the sales rep's role performance as accurately and completely as possible. We will return to this set of issues in Chapter 6 when we more completely examine sales force motivation and supervision.

THE JOB DESCRIPTION

The field sales manager's attempts to communicate role expectations and requirements, including performance standards, to the sales representatives will obviously be easier if there is a clear and complete

---

[3]*Ibid.*, pp. 245–247.

organizational position description for the sales representative. The job description performs a number of other useful functions as well, and is a major tool for sales organization development, an essential guide in the many activities associated with recruitment, selection, training, supervision, evaluation, motivation, compensation, and control. It is therefore surprising that in many firms the sales rep's job description is incomplete, outdated, or missing altogether. Developing and maintaining an up-to-date job description is a time-consuming activity and should be done by, or in cooperation with, professionals. An argument that the selling process and the determinants of sales performance are too subtle and complex to capture in a written job description is an invalid excuse for not having one.

Job Analysis

Analysis of the sales representative's position is a necessary first step in developing an effective sales organization. The results of that analysis can be put in written form to produce a job or position description. The job analysis should examine those factors that determine the sales representative's functions and responsibilities and define the work environment. Among the most obvious things to be considered are the nature of the product, customers and their requirements, the buying process, competition, relationships between the sales rep and other departments, and the physical demands of the job. Basic data for the job analysis can be obtained by observing and interviewing sales reps and their managers and asking such simple questions as "What do you do?" "What do you need to be effective and successful?" "How do you spend your time?" "How are you evaluated?" The answers to these questions describe things as they really are, the actual nature of sales rep role performance.

A second set of inputs to the job analysis is provided by the company's marketing strategy and the role of the sales representative as defined by that strategy. If that strategy is not clearly spelled out in a written marketing plan, then the necessary information may be obtained through interviews with marketing executives, sales executives, product managers, and other marketing managers. These inputs are more normative, describing things as they should be. Among the areas to be examined with respect to strategy are the relative importance of selling versus service; the frequency and size of orders;

how the sales rep figures into the differentiation of the firm *vis-à-vis* competition; relationships with distributors and the sales rep's role in those relationships; and the importance of the sales rep as a continuing source of market information.

It is common for larger firms to have personnel specialists who can do the necessary job analysis and develop the position description, in consultation with national and regional sales managers. In the absence of such professional colleagues, the sales managers may be well advised to work with an outside expert, such as a management consultant, who will have both the knowledge and the time required to do the job competently and thoroughly. One of the more complex parts of the job analysis is to examine discrepancies between what sales reps say they do, what they are observed doing, and what management says they should be doing. Developing an understanding of the reasons for these discrepancies, and resolving them may be easier for an outside consultant or staff specialist who does not have a vested interest and has no need to defend existing practices and perceptions. Such analysis can also reveal the presence of perceived role inaccuracy, role ambiguity, and role conflict.

Contents of the Job Description

The task of putting role expectations and demands for the sales representative position into written form provides a very useful discipline for sales management. If the job description remains in the head of the manager, high degrees of perceived role inaccuracy, ambiguity, and conflict for the sales reps are virtually assured. Only through the exercise of committing thoughts to writing can inconsistencies, incompleteness, and conflicts be revealed and resolved. There is no better way to avoid fuzzy thinking than to put things in writing.

Job descriptions can take a wide variety of forms, depending on completeness desired. Brevity is always preferable to excessive length but has no particular virtue versus the need to be thorough in describing the sales rep's activities and responsibilities. At the minimum, a job description should contain these features:

1. A clear statement of the responsibilities and duties of the sales representative, stated wherever possible as specific activities

to be performed, with some indication of their priorities such as percentage of time to be allocated to each.

2. A description of reporting relationships—to whom the rep reports and any personnel who report to the rep.

3. A description of the work environment including products, types of accounts, and other relevant dimensions.

4. A clear indication of how performance will be evaluated, the specific standards to be used in evaluating performance, and who does the evaluation.

5. The knowledge and skills required by the position, including product, company, and market knowledge, and how those knowledge and skill requirements are to be updated.

6. A normal career path for people entering and being promoted from this position within the company job hierarchy.

Job Qualifications

Most job descriptions also contain a statement of job qualifications, the abilities and background required of persons who will occupy the position. These can also be contained in a second, supporting document to the job description. A separate and demanding analytical step is required to translate the job analysis and the job description into a statement of job qualifications. Obviously, the job qualifications should be consistent with the job description. It is as wasteful to recruit and hire overqualified persons as it is to attract unqualified personnel.

The statement of job qualifications specifies the attributes to be sought in applicants for the position of sales representative. These would include education, previous work experience, particular technical expertise, and so on. Desired aptitudes and interests may also be stated. (Equal employment opportunity regulations prohibit any specification of age or gender requirements except under very unusual circumstances.) Job qualifications should be a prominent part of any advertising and other recruiting literature so that the applicant pool has few if any persons who are clearly unqualified for the position.

DETERMINING SALES
PERSONNEL REQUIREMENTS

Two basic questions must be answered in initiating a program for develop-sales personnel: What kinds of people are required? and How many do we need? Job analysis and the development of a written job description and job qualifications statement provide answers to the first question. The second question requires a different type of analysis, including assessment of past and projected turnover patterns, market and sales potential, marketing plans, sales forecasts, financial conditions, competition, and the details of the marketing budget.

It is not uncommon for 10–20% of a sales organization to turn over every year as people leave the company or are promoted to management or other positions. In some sales forces, the rate is much higher, especially in organizations with large numbers of relatively unskilled sales people who sell primarily to friends and neighbors. Some amount of turnover is necessary and even desirable to eliminate ineffective personnel, to allow competent personnel to move into positions of greater responsibility and challenge, and to create opportunities to attract and develop new talent. The reasons for turnover, especially if the rate is increasing, should be examined continually, however. The analysis may reveal such problems as inadequate recruitment effort, careless selection procedures, incomplete training, poor supervision, low compensation, and a perception that there are no opportunities for advancement (which may reflect sales management ranks filled with managers who have reached their "level of incompetence").

Hiring must be done in anticipation of projected turnover and sales growth rates if the organization is to achieve planned sales levels. This means there must be a plan, to direct and coordinate the efforts of sales management at all levels involved in the hiring process. Specific hiring goals should be established and managers held accountable for their attainment. For reasons discussed earlier, these goals are as important as sales goals as determinants of long-range organizational effectiveness and performance. An understaffed sales organization, or one with people who are not properly qualified for their responsibilities, is less effective than required to achieve company objectives.

It does not necessarily follow, however, that a forecast of $x\%$ increase in sales requires an $x\%$ increase in the size of the sales force. In an inflationary period, some portion of the projected sales increase simply will reflect increases in prices. With rising costs of travel, lodging, entertainment, and related costs, and with product prices actually decreasing in many industries (e.g., computers), many sales management teams are under very strong pressure to increase sales force productivity, that is to increase the sales revenue to sales expense ratio. In summary, there are many reasons that the determination of number of new sales representatives (and supporting personnel) to be hired must go much deeper than simply looking at the sales forecast.

Rigorous mathematical approaches to determining the optimal size of the sales force are available in the management science literature and these are subject to the normal strengths and limitations of such approaches. Any model for determining the optimal level of selling effort (i.e., sales force size) must incorporate a *response function,* a stated relationship between effort and sales response. The response function can be based on management judgment, the model-builder's judgment, statistical analysis of historical data, or an experiment to measure changes in sales volume associated with changes in selling effort. Actual company practice has been reported using each of these approaches. The validity of the optimization model solution is directly related to the validity of the response function.

The optimum number of sales reps is theoretically defined by the point where marginal profit contribution and marginal cost are equal—where the incremental profit margin on sales due to adding the last sales rep is just equal to the incremental cost of maintaining the rep in the field. This assumes that marginal profit margin decreases as sales reps are added; that is, a sales response function which shows decreasing return to selling effort in the relevant range of effort. In actuality, incremental revenue, profit margin, and selling costs, and the response function itself, are very hard to estimate for many reasons, not the least of which, in most industrial selling situations, is the presence of significant time lags between the application of selling effort and the achievement of sales results. Nonetheless, the basic logic of marginal analysis, outlined here, provides a useful approach for a sales manager who is thinking through the question

"How many sales representatives do I need?" When combined with sophisticated estimation and modeling procedures, the approach can be quite powerful and useful. In a large sales organization the improved results may very well justify the effort.

Having defined the numbers and qualifications of needed sales personnel, management has the basis for developing a program for recruiting, selecting, and training sales representatives as required by the marketing strategy and sales plan.

RECRUITING

Recruiting is the process of attracting qualified applicants for the sales rep position. The success of the recruiting process will be seen almost immediately in the observed quality of the applicant pool. Over the longer term, the recruiting process will determine the ultimate success or failure of the total process of organizational development because it defines the raw material for that process. Unsuccessful and inadequate recruiting will force sales management to select sales representatives who are deficient in one or more desired characteristics. The costs of substandard recruiting and hiring are hard to quantify, but will be reflected in sales force and sales management dissatisfaction, high rates of turnover, and poor sales force performance. The ultimate costs, of course, are lost revenue and unprofitable sales activity.

Stated differently, the objective of recruiting is to maximize the number of qualified applicants within the constraints of time and expense available to the recruiters. The applicant pool is developed through a variety of techniques for making persons aware of the sales position, including advertising, personal contacts, campus recruiting visits, and so on. There are professional recruiting firms that specialize in the management of this process, bringing together those who are seeking positions with those who are seeking applicants. The quality of the information describing the position, and put forward in advertisements and other literature and through word of mouth, is a major determinant of the quality of the applicant pool.

The major sources of industrial sales applicants include other areas of the company (such as production, administration, and engineering); other sales organizations, especially those of competitors, distributors, and other firms in the industry; colleges and universities; newspaper and trade journal advertising; and professional recruiters, as mentioned. Relationships with potential sources of applicants must be developed and maintained over the long run, even if the hiring process is not a continuous one for the firm. The costs and difficulties of developing these contacts are significant and not likely to produce immediate results. There is a much lower probability of success associated with a recruiting process that is hit-or-miss and short-term in its orientation. An active file of names and resumes can be maintained for use when the recruiting program swings into the active phase.

The company's present sales representatives are likely to be a major source of leads for potential applicants, because they are the people most likely to be talking with others about the nature of the sales position and most able to stimulate interest in the position. Persons interested in the sales position, for whatever reasons, are likely to seek out someone who already holds a position in the sales organization in order to obtain more information. It makes good sense, therefore, to tell present sales reps how to respond to such inquiries and to be sure that they have all required information about existing sales career opportunities with the company, as well as instructions on next steps for the applicant to take.

How many applicants should be recruited for each sales position? One is tempted to answer that more is always better, since capable people are so hard to find and so valuable to the firm. But there are costs associated with developing the applicant pool and these should be taken into consideration. Most firms would probably be better off if they spent more on recruiting costs and reaped the associated benefits of a higher probability of securing applicants with the necessary qualifications. A rigorous sequential decision theory analysis of this problem has been developed and reported by Darmon, including the application of the analysis to the recruiting activities of a pharmaceutical firm.[4] This study confirmed that the incremental costs of identifying and interviewing an additional applicant for a sales position were minor in comparison with the expected net profit generated by an additional successful sales representative.

[4]René Y. Darmon, "Sales Force Management: Optimizing the Recruiting Process," *Sloan Management Review*, Vol. 20, No. 1 (Fall 1978), pp. 47–59.

SELECTION

Selection is the process of reviewing applicants and deciding which of them to hire. It can be thought of as a multistage process, beginning with the completion and review of the application blank and proceeding through interviews, checks of personal references, the administration and evaluation of psychological tests, a physical exam, and the final hiring decision. These steps could occur in a different order than this, and not all steps are used in every hiring situation. For example, not all firms make use of psychological tests.

The Application Blank

Even though the application blank is a relatively straightforward document, it is critically important in the selection process. It is the first step in the systematic collection and evaluation of data about the applicant. An illustration of an application blank is presented in Figure 4.2. The application blank should provide a record of the applicant's personal history including the followng data:

1. *Personal Data.* Federal and state legislation aimed at eliminating discriminatory hiring practices has significantly limited the type of personal data that can be requested, including questions about age, place of birth, sex, and marital status. The general rule is that all information requested should be directly job related. It would be appropriate to ask if the applicant has a valid driver's license, for example. Questions about hobbies and interests may also reveal something about the aptitude of the applicant for a sales position.

2. *Education.* It is common to ask for a listing of all high schools, colleges, and graduate schools attended, with dates of attendance and degrees received. Fields of study and grade-point averages may also be indicated, along with extracurricular activities and some indication of how much financial support the applicant was able to provide for himself or herself.

3. *Experience.* All previous employment should be indicated, including the employer's name and the dates of employment, as well as the nature of the work. Promotion and salary progress should also be given. These data are very useful indications of the interests and aptitudes of the applicant, as well as aids to judging whether or not

LAST NAME	FIRST NAME	MIDDLE NAME	SOCIAL SECURITY NO.	DATE

CURRENT ADDRESS - STREET	CITY	STATE	ZIP CODE	COUNTRY	PHONE
					AC Number

PERMANENT ADDRESS – STREET	CITY	STATE	ZIP CODE	COUNTRY	PHONE
					AC Number

FOR WHAT TYPE OF POSITION ARE YOU APPLYING?	APPROXIMATE SALARY REQUIREMENTS	DATE AVAILABLE

NORTON

Norton Company, an equal opportunity employer, is a diversified multi-national manufacturer of consumable supplies, advanced materials and related capital equipment with corporate offices located in Worcester, Massachusetts.

Check Division for which application is being completed –

☐ Akron, OH 44309 Chemical Process Products
        and Plastics & Synthetics
☐ Worcester, MA 01606, Corporate
☐ Abrasives Marketing Group
☐ Coated Abrasives
☐ Consumer Division
☐ Engineering & Construction Services

☐ Grinding Wheel Operations
☐ Industrial Ceramics Division
☐ Materials Division
☐ Safety Products Division
☐ Sealants, Northboro
☐ Other Locations _____

EDUCATIONAL RECORD

COLLEGE, UNIVERSITY AND GRADUATE SCHOOL (most recent first)

SCHOOL	LOCATION	FROM	TO	GRADUATED? Yes ☐ No ☐	DEGREE
MAJOR	MINOR	SCHOLASTIC AVERAGE/INDICATE RANGE OF GRADING SCALE			

SCHOOL	LOCATION	FROM	TO	GRADUATED? Yes ☐ No ☐	DEGREE
MAJOR	MINOR	SCHOLASTIC AVERAGE/INDICATE RANGE OF GRADING SCALE			

SCHOOL	LOCATION	FROM	TO	GRADUATED? Yes ☐ No ☐	DEGREE
MAJOR	MINOR	SCHOLASTIC AVERAGE/INDICATE RANGE OF GRADING SCALE			

LIST THESIS SUBJECT, INTERNSHIP PROJECTS, PUBLISHED ARTICLES AND PATENTS, IF ANY

COLLEGE HONORS AND LEADERSHIP ROLES HELD IN SCHOLASTIC OR PROFESSIONAL ORGANIZATIONS

CURRENT COURSES AND/OR FUTURE EDUCATIONAL GOALS

Figure 4.2. An application form for a sales position.

HIGH SCHOOL, PREPARATORY, TECHNICAL AND BUSINESS SCHOOLS (most recent first)						
SCHOOL	LOCATION	FROM	TO	DEGREE	MAJOR	
SCHOOL	LOCATION	FROM	TO	DEGREE	MAJOR	
SCHOOL	LOCATION	FROM	TO	DEGREE	MAJOR	

MILITARY EXPERIENCE

FROM	TO	BRANCH	RANK or RATING	DUTIES PERFORMED	SPECIAL SCHOOLS

EMPLOYMENT RECORD (most recent first)

EMPLOYER		COMPLETE ADDRESS		YOUR POSITION	
FROM Mo. Yr.	TO Mo. Yr.	NAME OF SUPERVISOR	TITLE OF SUPERVISOR		LAST SALARY

DESCRIBE DUTIES AND SCOPE OF RESPONSIBILITIES (These comments may be supplemented by attached resume.)

MAY WE CONTACT PRESENT EMPLOYER? ☐YES ☐NO

REASON FOR LEAVING OR CONSIDERING POSITION CHANGE

EMPLOYER		COMPLETE ADDRESS		YOUR POSITION	
FROM Mo. Yr.	TO Mo. Yr.	NAME OF SUPERVISOR	TITLE OF SUPERVISOR		LAST SALARY

DESCRIBE DUTIES AND SCOPE OF RESPONSIBILITIES (These comments may be supplemented by attached resume.)

REASON FOR LEAVING OR CONSIDERING POSITION CHANGE

EMPLOYER		COMPLETE ADDRESS		YOUR POSITION	
FROM Mo. Yr.	TO Mo. Yr.	NAME OF SUPERVISOR	TITLE OF SUPERVISOR		LAST SALARY

DESCRIBE DUTIES AND SCOPE OF RESPONSIBILITIES (These comments may be supplemented by attached resume.)

REASON FOR LEAVING OR CONSIDERING POSITION CHANGE

Figure 4.2 *(Continued)*

PERSONAL DATA

U.S. CITIZEN Yes ☐ No ☐	If not, what is your VISA classification?	Are you willing to relocate anywhere in the U.S.A.? Yes ☐ No ☐
IF NOT, GIVE RESTRICTIONS		WHAT IS YOUR GEOGRAPHIC PREFERENCE?
ARE YOU WILLING TO RELOCATE OVERSEAS? Yes ☐ No ☐	ARE YOU INTERESTED IN AN OVERSEAS ASSIGNMENT? Yes ☐ No ☐	IF SO, GIVE PREFERENCE

LANGUAGES – LIST LANGUAGES WITH WHICH YOU HAVE SOME DEGREE OF FLUENCY

ON SCALE OF 1 THRU 4 WITH 1 REPRESENTING NATIVE TONGUE FAMILIARITY OR EQUIVALENT, CIRCLE THE NUMBER CORRESPONDING TO YOUR LEVEL OF COMPREHENSION AND FLUENCY.

LANGUAGE																				
SPEAK	1	2	3	4	1	2	3	4	1	2	3	4	1	2	3	4	1	2	3	4
READ	1	2	3	4	1	2	3	4	1	2	3	4	1	2	3	4	1	2	3	4
WRITE	1	2	3	4	1	2	3	4	1	2	3	4	1	2	3	4	1	2	3	4

DESCRIBE SPECIAL INTERESTS AND VOLUNTEER AND COMMUNITY ACTIVITIES IN WHICH YOU ARE ACTIVE, EXCLUDING ORGANIZATIONS, THE NAME OR CHARACTER OF WHICH INDICATES THE RACE, CREED, COLOR, OR NATIONAL ORIGIN OF ITS MEMBERS.

NEW EMPLOYEES ARE REQUIRED TO PASS A PRE-PLACEMENT PHYSICAL EXAMINATION. DO YOU HAVE ANY KNOWN DISABILITIES WHICH MIGHT AFFECT YOUR ABILITY TO DO THE JOB FOR WHICH YOU'RE APPLYING?

YES ☐   NO ☐   IF SO, LIST

HAVE YOU EVER BEEN CONVICTED OF A FELONY?

YES ☐   NO ☐   IF SO, EXPLAIN (an answer of yes will not necessarily disqualify you from consideration).

HAVE YOU EVER PREVIOUSLY BEEN EMPLOYED BY ANY DIVISION OF NORTON COMPANY?

YES ☐   NO ☐   IF SO, GIVE WHERE, WHEN AND FOR WHOM.

HAVE YOU PREVIOUSLY FILED AN APPLICATION WITH NORTON COMPANY?

YES ☐   NO ☐   IF SO, WHERE AND WHEN

THROUGH WHAT MEANS DID YOU APPLY FOR A POSITION WITH US?

COLLEGE INTERVIEW ☐	ADVERTISEMENT ☐	EMPLOYMENT AGENCY ☐	PERSONAL REFERRAL ☐ BY NORTON EMPLOYEE	OTHER MEANS ☐
Name of School	Where Appearing?	Name of Agency		

Figure 4.2   *(Continued)*

REFERENCES			
REFERENCES WHOM WE MAY CONTACT OTHER THAN FRIENDS OR RELATIVES			
NAME	TITLE		HOW ACQUAINTED?
PRESENT ORGANIZATION	ADDRESS		PHONE
			Area Code Number Ext.
NAME	TITLE		HOW ACQUAINTED?
PRESENT ORGANIZATION	ADDRESS		PHONE
			Area Code Number Ext.
NAME	TITLE		HOW ACQUAINTED?
PRESENT ORGANIZATION	ADDRESS		PHONE
			Area Code Number Ext.

APPLICANT'S STATEMENT

If employed by Norton Company, I agree to abide by its rules and regulations. The above information is complete and true to the best of my knowledge. I understand that discovery of misrepresentation or omission of facts herein will be cause for immediate dismissal. I authorize the Company to contact any and/or all of my references, including confirmation of past employment.

_____   _____
DATE   APPLICANT'S SIGNATURE

Norton Company follows the usual practice of requiring new technically-trained, professional and other employees with access to confidential information to sign an agreement at the time of employment covering   a) non-disclosure and non-use of information,   b) restrictions on employment by others in the same fields for not more than three years after termination of the employment.

NOTE:

Consistent with Public Law 91-508, we advise you that a routine inquiry may be made in connection with the processing of your application for employment which will provide applicable information concerning character, general reputation, personal characteristics and mode of living. Upon written request, additional information as to the nature and scope of the inquiry, if one is made, will be provided.

Please return this application to:

Supervisor of Professional Staffing
Norton Company
1 New Bond Street
Worcester, MA 01606

Form 213 Rev. 3/80

Figure 4.2 *(Continued)*

the work and rewards of the sales position will be adequate to the needs of the individual.

4. *Personal References.* It is common practice to ask for the names of individuals who are willing to serve as personal references. These are best contacted by telephone and asked to respond to some specific questions about the applicant, as this avoids the vague generalities and uncritical praise that frequently appear in standard letters of reference. A major purpose of reference checks is to validate information contained in the application blank, such as dates of employment, school attendance, and degrees conferred. Previous employers are likely to be the most valuable personal references, and the questions "Why did he or she leave?" and "Would you rehire this person?" can produce very useful responses. Conversation is also likely to produce additional information about the application blank itself.

The application blank can be used to screen applicants according to predetermined selection criteria. For example, minimum required levels of education and work experience can be defined, and no applicant should be considered further if those minimums are not met. A second use of the application blank is to provide areas for discussion in personal interviews. Of special importance in this connection would be the nature of the applicant's performance and job satisfaction in earlier positions. Another area to focus on, as an indicator of potential trouble spots, is frequent job changes, or gaps in the dates given for education or previous work experience. If a period of time is not accounted for on the application or resume, it is important to ask what the applicant was doing during the period and to determine why it was not indicated on the application blank.

Firms that hire large numbers of sales representatives and therefore have a large data base on applicants and subsequent job performance may have the opportunity to develop rigorous, quantified rankings of factors on the job application. Variables such as amount of education, work experience, previous salary, and so on can be examined statistically for their relationship to subsequent job performance. Importance weightings thus developed can be applied to the application blank as predictive measures, and used to make the decision whether or not to allow the applicant to continue to the next stages of the selection process. Such a mechanical use of data on the application blank probably makes sense only where large numbers of applications must be processed, where more subtle managerial judgments about applicant quality are not called for, and when there are strong statistical relationships between application blank factors and actual sales performance. To repeat, all of this indicates the need for a large base of data on applicants.

Trade-offs Between Selection and Training

An underlying issue in the selection process, which presents itself first in a consideration of developing acceptance/rejection criteria based on application blank data, is the extent to which the firm expects to hire persons ready to assume selling responsibilities versus the extent to which it is prepared to train recruits who demonstrate the necessary aptitudes and interests. In simple terms, the firm must decide whether it wants to buy talent or to build it. If a firm is willing to pay the salaries and commissions necessary to attract people with significant educational accomplishments, solid work experience, and previous industry- and product-specific training, it can avoid the time and expense of elaborate training programs. On the other hand, if a solid training program is planned before the recruit is given actual field sales responsibility, then less-experienced people can be sought (perhaps at lower salaries) and selection criteria would focus on potential, interest, basic aptitudes, and trainability.

Personal Interviews

The core of the selection process is usually one or more personal interviews conducted by members of sales management and members of the firm's personnel or organizational development departments. The purpose of the interview, simply stated, is to assess the applicant's potential for successful performance in the sales representative's position and his or her potential for advancement into the sales management ranks. The interviewer must make complex judgments about the personality, interests, aptitudes, and motivation of the applicant.

Interviews can be either structured or unstructured. In the structured, or patterned, interview, the interviewers ask a set of predetermined questions, with the response typically recorded on a printed form. The major advantage of a structured interview is that it controls the quality of the interview and covers material that has proven to be important in making judgments about applicants. The use of structured interviewing techniques assumes that there is a large base of data on applicants—and large numbers of applicants—with which to develop the structured questions. It is more appropriate for use by relatively inexperienced and untrained interviewers and insures completeness, as well as making it easier to compare multiple applicants, perhaps interviewed by multiple interviewers in different geographic locations.

The unstructured interview is characterized by a freer flow of questioning, following directions established by the interests of both the interviewer and the interviewee. Rapport is established more easily in an unstructured interview. It has the potential to be both more interesting and more informative for both parties, but it runs the risk of incompleteness, irrelevance, and loss of comparability among applicants. Unstructured interviews provide a better opportunity to assess more subtle aspects of personality and to reveal unique characteristics of the applicant, as the applicant has the opportunity to take the initiative and to explore areas that might be prohibited in the structured format.

Some firms and managers use stress-producing techniques as part of the interview process, including such devices as asking aggressive or rude questions, maintaining silence to produce discomfort, or making outright challenges to the interests, abilities, and truthfulness of the applicant. The rationale for such approaches is that they simulate the sales situation, to a degree, and reveal how the person would respond under pressure. While sure approaches have a certain amount of validity and value, there is a real risk that the stress interview will offend the applicant and destroy his or her interest in the position. Frequently, such approaches go out of control when used by an insensitive manager. It is likely that the potential risks and costs of such gimmicky approaches to interviewing exceed the benefits.

Group interviewing is also used in some situations. While this may put some additional pressure on the interviewee, and this may be either a positive or negative feature, it can also provide a tempering influence on the interviewers. Not all sales managers are effective interviewers, even though they may have a legitimate need and interest in interviewing the applicants. Thus, group interviewing may be one way to insure a more positive result when such people are involved in the interviewing process. On the other hand, there is also the risk that managers will begin to compete with one another in the group interviewing process, seeing who can ask the most difficult questions or otherwise straying from the real purpose of the interview. More to the point, group interviewing permits managers to share perceptions based on the same data and experience and to develop a consensus about the strengths and weaknesses of a given applicant. Group interviews may also represent a more efficient use of time, especially if the applicant has only limited time for the visit and there are many managers who want to be involved in the interview process.

It should be remembered that the interview is not a one-way communication. It should be designed to do more than assess the qualifications of the applicant. Namely it should also be an opportunity to inform the candidate about the company, its products, customers, and opportunities, and to develop the candidate's interest in the position.

If multiple interviews are used, the initial interviews will have relatively limited objectives of screening applicants, checking information on the application blank, and obtaining factual data that cannot be obtained readily on the blank itself, such as information about personal appearance and other personal characteristics that cannot be requested for legal reasons. These earlier interviews may be conducted most economically by members of the personnel or administrative staff. Later interviews will have more complex objectives, such as assessing subtle personality characteristics and developing the candidate's interest in the position, and are conducted more appropriately by members of sales management, including those who will be working directly with the person hired. It is obviously important that managers who have interviewing responsibilities should be trained with the skills necessary to do such interviewing well. This is especially true when unstructured interviews are used.

Multiple interviews are preferred because this can avoid the problem of one or a few managers making judgments based on stereotypes, personal biases, and incomplete information. It can avoid the tendency to hire in one's own image, or to hire based on a narrow set of characteristics. A judgment based on a composite of managerial judgments is likely to be more accurate and more complete.

Should the spouse of the applicant be interviewed? That is a sensitive question, especially in the current environment of social attitudes toward dual careers, shared family responsibilities, and so on.

Opinions on this question vary widely. Common sense suggests that an informal meeting, perhaps by means of a dinner invitation at a nice restaurant for both the applicant and spouse, can be advantageous. This meeting should logically come late in the selection process, when there is a good chance that a job offer will be made to the recruit. The point is not to interview the spouse and use that information in the decision whether or not to hire the applicant; rather, the objective is to be sure that the spouse understands the nature of the position the applicant is considering, the implications in terms of demands on family life, the opportunities for advancement, and so on. It is part of the process of minimizing perceived role conflict when the person is hired, as well as serving to enlist the support of the spouse for the decision.

In earlier times, it was implicitly assumed in many situations that the firm was hiring the spouse as well as the applicant, and that the spouse had certain obligations, such as entertainment, with respect to the sales jobs. That set of assumptions is *passé* in today's social environment; typically, the spouse has a career of his or her own and cannot be assumed to be taking on any responsibilities with respect to the sales position. On the other hand, it is important to enlist the support of the spouse and his or her friendship toward the hiring organization. Personal acquaintance with the sales manager and good information about the company and the position can be developed to good advantage and with minimum expense.

Psychological Tests

Although not used in every hiring situation, psychological tests of various kinds are used frequently in selecting personnel for sales positions. The use of such tests is controversial, both with respect to the validity of testing procedures and to abuses in the use of the data. Nonetheless, tests can be a valuable aid in the selection process.

There are five different types of psychological tests—tests of knowledge, aptitude, interests, intelligence, and personality. If a company is going to use any psychological tests, it is likely to use more than one type of test in the total test battery given to an applicant. The nature and use of each type of test is described briefly.

Knowledge tests assess a person's knowledge of a particular subject area. They are only loosely related to true psychological tests, but are more akin to the type of tests every student has been exposed to. For the sales applicant, this might involve testing for knowledge about particular product technology or applications, or a test of basic mathematical and bookkeeping knowledge required in the job. Testing about marketing knowledge, especially as it relates to channels of distribution, for example, might be used by firms whose sales representatives call on the retail trade.

Aptitude tests are designed to measure the ability of the applicant to learn and perform certain types of tasks and activities. For a sales position involving servicing and repairing mechanical products, for example, it may be necessary to test for the applicant's mechanical aptitude.

Interest tests measure the applicant's interest in the type of work for which he or she is being considered. Most often these tests are not direct measures of interest in selling *per se,* but rather are indirect measures of a broad variety of interests. An assessment of the applicant compares the profile of interests revealed by the test with the profile of a large sample of persons who have been successful in similar positions. Probably the best known of such tests is the *Strong Vocational Interest Blank,* which has been scored, or keyed, for over 50 occupations, with separate scoring for men and women. The basic premise in the use of interest tests is that people in given occupations tend to have common interests. Whether that is a valid premise is open to some debate.

Intelligence tests measure a person's overall ability to cope with intellectual tasks, and are perhaps the most common type of psychological test. Virtually everyone takes intelligence tests at some point in the educational process, typically in the early years of grammar school. Most intelligence tests have been validated using scholastic achievement as a criterion. For this reason they have also been called scholastic aptitude tests, and may be used best in sales recruiting as an indicator of the applicant's ability to learn and benefit from a sales training program. There is a valid question whether or not more "intelligence" is necessarily better in many sales occupations; it can be argued that an extremely intelligent person is more likely to be bored by a routine selling position.

Personality tests are undoubtedly the most controversial of the psychological tests. They attempt to measure the motivational, emotional, and social aspects of behavior. The fundamental difficulty with such tests is that it is not obvious exactly what they attempt to measure, a difficulty inherent in the very concept of personality itself. A dictionary definition of personality is "the visible aspects of one's character as it impresses others," whereas the concept in psychology usually refers to the sum total of an individual's physical, mental, emotional, and social characteristics as they are organized into a recognizable pattern of behavioral characteristics. There is thus a virtually infinite array of traits that might be singled out for measurement on a personality test, and the labeling of those traits is largely at the discretion of the test developer; that is, there is no standard nomenclature for the concepts of personality. In fact, personality traits themselves are hypothetical constructs, defined by the tests that purport to measure them. It is clear that the central problem in personality testing is the definition of these traits, as illustrated by the following examples of traits measured by four different personality tests.

Guildford-Zimmerman Temperament Survey	Thurston Temperament Schedule	Bernreuter Inventory	Edwards Personal Preference Schedule
General activity	Active	Neuroticism	Achievement
Restraint	Vigorous	Self-sufficiency	Deference
Ascendance	Impulsive	Introversion	Ardor
Sociability	Dominant	Dominance	Exhibition
Emotional stability	Stable		Autonomy
Objectivity	Sociable		Affiliation
Friendliness	Reflective		Intraception
Thoughtfulness			Succorance
Personal relations			Dominance
Masculinity			Abasement
			Nurturance
			Change
			Endurance
			Heterosexuality

A fundamental issue related to the use of personality tests in the selection of sales personnel was discussed at some length earlier in this chapter, as well as in Chapters 1 and 3. The sales representative's personality characteristics are only one set of influences determining the outcome of the selling process. No single personality trait is likely to have a significant influence on selling success, and there is no basis for asserting strongly which set of characteristics is most important. The strongest arguments in favor of using a particular set of characteristics to predict sales success are made by those who sell the tests that measure such characteristics.

Another criticism of interest tests and personality tests is that these are easily faked. A reasonably intelligent applicant will have a good sense of those characteristics being sought by the firm, as well as what constitutes "good" and "bad" answers to test questions. Thus, test scores may not reveal the candidate's true interests and characteristics. There are procedures associated with most such tests, however, to identify and adjust for the extent of faking.

With any type of psychological test to be used in the sales selection process, the basic challenge is to validate the test in the specific use intended, which is to say as a vehicle for predicting success and failure in the sales job in that particular company. Most firms would find it difficult and expensive, if not impossible, to do the necessary validation. First, in order to provide an adequate data base for statistical analysis, there must be a large sample of persons who have taken the test. Second, the test must be administered to all applicants and the hiring decision must be made independent of the test results, until a large enough sample has been gathered. Third, the performance of all individuals hired must be tracked over time, for several periods. Fourth, statistical analysis must be done to examine the relationships, if any, between performance and test scores.

A substitute procedure, but not without problems, is to attempt to validate the test by administering it to all sales representatives already employed and to see if there are test measures that discriminate between strong and weak performers. Actual sales performance and test performance will both reflect the individuals' experience, training, management, and so on, as well as whatever psychological characteristics are being measured; that is, the measures will be biased, but not in predictable directions. It is not clear that recruits will answer the test in the same way and that the test will be able to predict which recruits have the best chance of successful performance in the selling situation.

Guidelines for Using Psychological Tests

Despite the difficulties inherent in the use of psychological tests, many companies find them a valuable tool in the selection process. Successful use of such tests requires that they be used with care. It is generally agreed that tests should be used as only one part of the total selection decision. That is, test performance should not be the only basis on which a candidate is accepted or rejected; final decisions should incorporate data from personal interviews and other sources as well. In no situation is the relationship between test scores and sales performance likely to be strong enough to permit the test score to be used as the sole decision variable.

There are also legal difficulties associated with testing. The firm must be able to provide evidence, if challenged by unsuccessful applicants, that its testing procedures do not systematically discriminate on the basis of the applicant's sex, race, national origin, age, and so on. In fact, some tests have been shown to discriminate in this fashion and they are obviously to be avoided. The firm using psychological tests must be able to show that there is a positive relationship between test scores and successful job performance; the burden of proof is on the using firm to show that the test is a valid measure and predictor of job success. That requirement, as noted, may be hard to satisfy. It is for this reason that some firms are moving away from the use of psychological testing in the selection process.

Tests should be administered and scored by trained specialists. Simple tests of aptitude may be administered and scored by the sales manager, but it is preferable that the more sophisticated testing instruments, those that measure intelligence, interests, and personality characteristics, be used only by qualified professional

THE PHYSICAL EXAM

The final data required in the selection process concern the physical health of the applicant. These data would not be gathered until all other steps had been completed and a positive judgment made. The purpose of the physical exam is obviously to make sure that the candidate is healthy and will be able to assume all of the responsibilities and duties of the sales position, which can be physically demanding. A complete physical examination is usually required by the various insurance companies that provide coverage for the firm and its employees, and to permit the new sales rep to quality for various benefit programs.

Physical handicaps can only be a cause for rejecting an applicant if they are directly related to performance of the sales task. A serious speech impediment, or hearing or vision impairment, for example, could significantly hinder the sales representative's ability to perform the job. Other handicaps that detract from a person's mobility, for example, that can be corrected using various devices, might not interfere with job performance. In general, management attitudes and company practice both seem increasingly prone toward hiring the handicapped whenever practicable.

AN INTEGRATED SELECTION PROCESS

The final selection decision should integrate data gathered from all sources—the application blank, references, personal interviews, psychological tests, and the physical examination. Each type of data has an important role to play. For a variety of reasons, the opinions of several managers should be considered in making the final decision, including all who have interviewed the applicant. In this manner, personal biases can be avoided and a better decision is likely to result. In addition, the person hired is likely to be an acceptable colleague to all managers concerned if they have participated in and agreed to the hiring decision.

TRAINING

The hiring of a new sales representative creates the need for a careful program to develop the attitudes, skills, and knowledge that the person will need to be effective in the rep's position. The job description provides basic guidelines for the requirements for effective job performance and, therefore, the broad requirements for a sales training program. Such training must be planned carefully, with specific programs and clearly defined managerial responsibility for executing those programs. The field sales manager typically carries a major portion of the responsibility for implementing the training program, especially in the later and ongoing stages.

The training experience includes providing the new recruit with information about the company, its products, its customers and markets, and the development of skills related to the selling process. A more subtle but equally important part of the total training process is to develop the attitudes toward the company, its products, its customers, and management, and toward the selling task itself, that will insure maximum effectiveness and growth for the sales rep. The ultimate objective of all training is to maximize the job performance and satisfaction of the sales representative and to develop the future management talent of the organization. After the new recruit is prepared to assume sales responsibility, there is a continuing need for training experiences that will keep him or her up to date on products, promotions, customers, and so on, and will further the development of the selling, planning, and managerial abilities of the rep.

The type and amount of training required will reflect two major sets of factors—the complexity of the selling task, which is a function of the products being sold and their applications, and the type of person recruited into the sales organization. A company that hires only people with 10 years or more of actual selling experience with similar products may need only a few weeks of training to stress company orientation. The firm that hires recent college graduates to sell complex products may require up to two years of training before the recruit is ready to assume full territorial responsibilities.

There is evidence that companies are placing increased importance on the training function in the form of better developed and more carefully integrated programs. They are also giving more attention to the development of sales training skills within the sales management structure, and thoughtful integration of training with the processes of management planning and evaluation of performance.[5] Companies today are more likely to make use of formal courses developed by outside consultants and professional firms, and to incorporate new train-

---

[5]David S. Hopkins, *Training the Sales Force: A Progress Report* (New York: The Conference Board, 1978).

ing and communications technology, such as videotape recording and playback, into the learning experiences offered to sales representatives. Such increased attention to training undoubtedly reflects an evolving view of the sales representative as not simply a salesman, but as a person responsible for managing the total relationship between the selling company and its customers. A manager for an office equipment firm observed that:

> The most significant improvements center around our realization that our industry requires the attention of a *total* representative who is not just a salesman, but a person equipped with full knowledge of the specific industry served, and knowledgeable in products, systems, *and* software. The person must be completely and professionally trained— even if at great cost, and without one eye on the clock.[6]

Another manager in this same study made the important observation that each year seems to bring a group of sales recruits that is more intelligent, sophisticated, and demanding than the last, with increasingly high expectations for what the company will provide as well as for their own performance and satisfaction. It is probably true that, as a result of both customer demands and sales rep qualifications and expectations, traditional forms of salesmanship are becoming increasingly irrelevant in industrial selling, and that more and better training is required.

Company Orientation

The necessary first step in the training process is to acquaint the recruit with the company itself. Literature, lectures, and informal conversations with management can be used to learn about the history of the company and the scope of its operations. Beyond that there is the need to develop a full understanding of company policies and procedures that relate to the sales representative, including such basics as how he or she will be paid, fringe benefits including such immediate concerns as moving expenses, and the nature of the training program itself. The career planning process within the firm should be outlined in detail at an early stage.

[6]*Ibid.*, p. 2.

Another immediate need is to introduce the recruit to colleagues and company management, most especially those persons who will be responsible for the recruit's development during the first several weeks with the company. Nothing should be left to chance during those early weeks.

Company knowledge relevant for the sales rep, and part of the sales training component of the training program, includes policies and procedures relating to order booking, credit, scheduling of orders, delivery scheduling, and the like. The sales rep needs to know how the company works in responding to customer needs and requests. The rep needs to understand in detail the internal operating system with which he or she will be interfacing in managing the customer relationship. This probably includes, at some early time, a thorough tour of a sample of the firm's manufacturing and distribution facilities, which should be interesting, informative, and a way of motivating the individual.

Included in company knowledge should be careful attention to the company's marketing and selling strategies. The sales recruit needs complete understanding of the company's overall marketing program, including market segmentation schemes, the strategy of product differentiation, pricing policy, channels of distribution, and promotional programs including advertising and sales promotion activities, as well as the details of the selling strategy. All of this marketing and sales strategy background should be presented in the context of the overall corporate strategy and objectives.

Product Knowledge

It is obviously important that the sales rep have an excellent understanding of the company's products and their applications (including their strengths and weaknesses) versus competitors' offerings. It is much less obvious how much product knowledge is enough and, specifically, how much technical knowledge the sales representative needs in order to sell complex industrial products. At one extreme, some firms require detailed understanding of the engineering and production of the product itself. This might make sense where the rep's responsibilities include installation and servicing. In many situations, however, such detailed technical knowledge is unnecessary for understanding the product's performance and applications. Time spent on technical knowledge may be better committed to an understanding of customer needs and product applications.

The amount of time required for training in product knowledge is clearly a direct function of the nature of the product. Complex products such as insurance, computers, or aircraft engines would require months of product-related training whereas industrial fasteners, promotional novelties, or transportation services might be understood much more quickly. Some amount of product knowledge can be most efficiently conveyed through a combination of classroom experiences and study of books and manuals. Another component may be better learned by observing the production and operation of the product, both in the factory and in the field.

Customer and Market Knowledge

Knowledge of the company's market segments, major customers, and competitors obviously is critically important for the sales rep. Some descriptive material can be given through reading assignments and lectures, but it may also be best learned in the field, under the direction of the field sales manager or a field sales trainer. One objective of any sales training program should be to provide for the best possible customer relationships. Complete understanding of customers, their needs, and the nature of the customer buying process is the necessary basis for effective customer relationships.

Customer knowledge includes detailed understanding of the nature of the customer buying process. In this part of the training program, simple models of buyer behavior may be used to describe, analyze, and organize knowledge about the buying decision process. An overview of such models was provided in Chapter 3, and this is the kind of material that might usefully be presented as part of the conceptual content of the section of a training program dealing with customer knowledge.

Weitz has found a positive relationship between a sales representative's performance and his or her ability to understand the customer's decision-making process. This research looked at "understanding of customer decision making" as a component of aptitude, as depicted in the model of sales organization effectiveness in Figure 4.1. Data were gathered from a sample of sales representatives of a large industrial firm, without any distinction as to whether this ability was the result

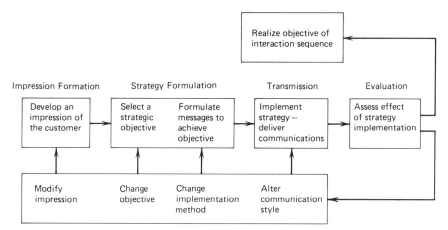

Figure 4.3. The ISTEA sales process model. Source: Barton A. Weitz, "Relationship Between Salesperson Performance and Understanding of Customer Decision Making," *Journal of Marketing Research*, Vol. XV (November 1978), pp. 501–516, at p. 502. Reproduced with permission.

of factors considered in the selection process or developed in the training process. Weitz proposed a communication process model of selling, which he called the ISTEA model (shown in Figure 4.3). The model posits four activities in which the sales rep must engage: (1) developing an impression of the customer, including the decision process and buying criteria used by the customer; (2) formulating a selling strategy, including the development of specific objectives and selling messages for this customer; (3) implementing the strategy by transmitting selling messages to the customer; and (4) assessing the effect of the strategy by evaluating feedback received from the customer. His empirical study focused on the first two steps in the process—impression formation and strategy formulation. The data showed strong positive statistical relationships between measures of the sales reps' abilities to accurately perceive the customers' beliefs about product performance, the ability to formulate strategy based on these perceptions, and the sales reps' performance.[7]

[7]Barton A. Weitz, "Relationship Between Salesperson Performance and Understanding of Customer Decision Making," *Journal of Marketing Research* Vol. XV (November 1978), pp. 501–516.

A strong argument can be made that such ability should be viewed as skills that can be developed through formal training experiences, rather than basic aptitudes that can be measured and screened for as part of the selection process. Viewed in that fashion, Weitz' research findings provide strong evidence of the importance of developing an understanding of the customer decision making process as part of the training program.

Selling Skills

The nature of the selling process was discussed at length in Chapter 3. The basic conclusion of that discussion was that buying and selling were two sides of the same coin, that we could not understand the industrial selling process without understanding the industrial buying process, and *vice versa*. It was also argued that selling skills are best viewed as the basic skills of interpersonal interaction, including the ability to listen and to develop carefully tailored messages in response to the feedback received from the other person in the interaction. Finally, the sales rep was positioned as a boundary role person, representing the customer to the selling organization as well as representing the seller and its products to the potential customer. All of these observations have direct relevance in the training of sales reps with the necessary selling skills.

Typical approaches to teaching selling skills include presenting the sales rep with simple models of the various steps in the selling process, such as the preapproach; the approach; the presentation; the trial close; handling objections; the close; and follow-up. Several such models were described and evaluated in the previous chapter. As frequently noted, such approaches essentially view selling as something the sales rep does to the customer, not as an interactive process. Nonetheless, for certain types of sales training, namely where simple products and relatively unsophisticated sales personnel are involved, such descriptions of selling may be useful as a model to which the sales rep can refer as a way of organizing the sales approach and keeping track of how the process is developing during an actual interaction. It isn't obvious, even in these circumstances, however, that such descriptive models contribute much to the development of actual selling skills. As pointed out in the previous section, part of the development of selling skills must be the development of an ability to analyze and understand the customer's decision-making process, and to develop selling strategy (objectives and messages) based on that understanding.

Current practice in developing selling skills emphasizes the use of role-playing techniques and videotape recording and playback to develop the full communication (i.e., interpersonal interaction) skills of the sales rep. Such techniques virtually require the use of trained professionals and are only rarely put in the hands of the field sales manager. Role-playing, with another trained person playing the role of the customer, can be a powerful and realistic simulation of the selling situation. Capturing the results on videotape provides the trainee with vivid and objective feedback on his or her performance. The impact of such data can be fully understood only by someone who actually has been exposed to it. Real learning occurs, although the initial reaction may be one of embarrassment and mild trauma.

The transition from the training laboratory to the actual field selling situation must be a careful one. The first step might be to go into the field with an experienced sales representative and observe a number of calls. This could then be followed by a role reversal in which the experienced rep, or manager, observes the trainee making a sales call and comments upon it afterwards. Needless to say, such critical evaluation must be done in a positive fashion designed to develop the skills of the trainee, build his or her confidence and self-respect, and maximize the learning potential of the joint calling experience.

To be avoided is a field training assignment that puts the trainee into the hands of an experienced person who has not been trained for the training responsibility. What some have called the "mother hen" approach, which involves assigning a senior sales representative to take the trainee around on his or her calls, typically results in little learning. The trainer must have teaching skills and sound conceptual knowledge of the buying–selling process. The senior sales rep who has been untrained must rely primarily on intuitive selling skills developed through the years, and may find it exceedingly difficult to articulate the reasons for success and failure. The so-called training sessions can the deteriorate into a "watch what I do and then try to do what I do" approach, where neither party can articulate what it is that is supposed to be watched and done.

While averages are not necessarily an indication of correct practices, it is interesting to note how a sample of firms allocates time among the various types of training. The mean percentage of time devoted to training for newly hired sales personnel reported by a Conference Board study of 152 sales organizations showed:

Company orientation	13%
Market/industry orientation	17%
Selling techniques	24%
Product knowledge	42%

This study also showed that on-the-job training was the most important training technique, followed by classroom coaching, observation, special outside courses, and home study, in that order.[8]

Continuing Training

The field sales manager has a major responsibility for the continuing training of all members of the sales team and for the development of that team as an effective entity. At the minimum, weekly or monthly sales meetings provide an ongoing opportunity for continued organization development. Annual meetings of the regional or national sales organization typically provide a period of several days that can be devoted to an update on such matters as the current marketing strategy, changes in policy, new products, and so on. Many firms use these meetings as an opportunity to bring in professional educators, trainers, and consultants to work with the organization in the development of particular knowledge. Management development, as well as the continued refreshment of selling skills, can be addressed in this fashion.

More generally, the field sales manager's first responsibility is that of supervision, and continuous development of the human resources assigned to his or her direction should be the focus of all supervisory activity. As argued in Chapter 2, the field sales manager should regard every interaction with a sales rep as a teaching/learning experience, an opportunity to develop the attitudes, knowledge, and skills of the sales rep and to make the rep independent of the need for the manager to solve specific problems for the rep. Equally important to the ongoing development of the sales rep is the continuous develop-

[8]Hopkins, *op. cit.*, p. 6.

ment of the manager as a supervisor and trainer, and preparation of the field sales manager to assume increased management responsibilities.

Continuing training of the sales rep should be directed not only to improving performance and satisfaction in the present assignment, but also to preparing the rep to assume larger responsibilities in account management, planning, first-line supervision of less experienced sales personnel, and other duties. Performance evaluation should be designed to assess the potential of the rep for advancement in either selling or management career paths, and to identify the need and readiness of the rep for specific additional training experiences designed to take him or her in that direction. Management talent must be consciously developed as part of the formal and informal training activities of the firm; it will not emerge of its own initiative except by accident. Without such careful attention to the development of management talent, that talent is likely to leave the organization in search of better opportunities; the best people will be the first to leave.

Team-Building

The sales reps assigned to a field sales manager's authority must be regarded not only as individuals, but also as a team. They are a true primary group in the social–psychological sense, interacting with one another face to face, influencing each other's behavior, and sharing a common set of norms and values. Those interactions, activities, and sentiments have a significant influence on the performance of the individuals and of the organization as a whole.

The social dimensions must be analyzed and managed by the field sales manager, just as the individual sales reps must be understood in terms of their needs, perceptions, goals, and aspirations. Through the goals that the manager sets for the group, and the feedback provided on performance, the manager has a significant influence on group attitudes, motivation, and performance. The manager can build supportive relationships among the team members, or he or she can tear them down. The manager can encourage positive attitudes toward the company's management, policies, programs, and strategies, or can instead encourage disrespect for company management and flouting of policies and objectives. In any situation, the field sales manager is a major influence through the example set by his or her own attitudes and behavior; the manager is a role model for the sales rep. Research has shown consistently that high-performing sales districts are characterized by managers who set high goals for their own performance and communicate these aspirations to their sales forces through their own performances and through the process of setting higher goals for the organization as a whole.[9]

Another dimension of the team-building responsibility of the field sales manager is to serve as an effective link between the sales reps and the rest of the organization. The manager must be sensitive to what it means for the sales rep to be a boundary role person, and the role conflict and psychological distance that characterize the boundary role occupant. The manager must manage a two-way flow of communication, interpreting and enforcing policy on the one hand and representing the needs, perceptions, and interests of the sales rep back to company management on the other hand. The pressures on the field manager accompanying the role of man in the middle are characteristic of any first-line supervisor, complicated in the sales management case by the physical separation of the manager from the people being managed.

Attitude development, as part of the total training requirement, cannot be assigned to formal training methods and sessions. Rather, it is part of the ongoing responsibility of the field sales manager, a function that can be performed by no other part of the organization.

SUMMARY

The development of an effective sales organization is the major long-term responsibility of field sales management at all levels of the organization hierarchy. Programs for recruiting, selecting, and training effective sales representatives must be based on a careful analysis of

[9]See, for example, Robert T. Davis, "A Sales Manager in Action," in Harper W. Boyd and Robert T. Davis (eds.), *Readings in Sales Management* (Homewood, IL: Richard D. Irwin, Inc., 1970), pp. 259–68, and Rensis Likert, "A Further Interpretation of the Study Results," in D. Bowers (ed.), *Applying Modern Management Principles to Sales Organization* (Ann Arbor, MI: Foundation for Research on Human Behavior, 1963), pp. 41–45.

the sales rep's position, the work performed, and the qualifications required of persons to perform that work. The basic aptitudes, education, and experience required are the focus of programs for recruitment and selection, whereas training is necessary to develop attitudes, skills, and knowledge. There are trade-offs of both time and money between recruitment and selection on the one hand, and training on the other, between buying talent and building it.

This chapter focused on issues involved in each of these areas—recruitment, selection, and training—against a general model of sales organization performance. It did not go into detail about company practice relating to each area and the assignment of responsibilities to various levels of the organization for meeting these requirements. Emphasis was placed on the role of the field sales manager as the person with primary responsibility for the ongoing development of human resources, and on higher levels of management's responsibility for developing the field sales manager. When training is ineffective, one must examine the programs that management has created and ask the fundamental question, "Who trained the trainer?"

FIVE

Deploying the Industrial Sales Force

The industrial sales force can be thought of, creatively and usefully, as the infantry of the firm. The infantry are the foot soldiers, those responsible for implementing a strategy, usually designed by people sitting around a table miles away from the field of battle. As noted in a popular encyclopedia: "Modern infantry forces may be transported to a battle area by airplanes, ships, trucks, armed vehicles, or helicopter; but once committed, they normally attack and defend on foot."[1] While the military analogy is not a perfect one, it is informative: "Modern infantry rarely fights alone for prolonged periods. In order to achieve decisive results quickly, it frequently is supported by armor, artillery, engineers, and signal and aviation units. To sustain itself on the battlefield, it requires a vast supply system encompassing the efforts of numerous support troops and complex logistical installation. . . . The infantry of all armies is part of a carefully organized and finely balanced team."[2]

The sales rep is the unit of attack through which a marketing strategy gets implemented. The sales rep is the foot soldier, out in the field trying to capture a territory against the efforts of an enemy—the competition. While truly hostile action is perhaps an exaggeration,

---

[1]A section on "The Infantry," prepared under the direction of Mark W. Clark, General, U.S. Army (Retired) in *The Encyclopedia Americana*, 1976 edition, Vol. 15, p. 143.

[2]*Ibid.*

the presence of competition in the field is certainly a major part of the reality faced by the industrial sales rep. The burden of "making the numbers" in the marketing plan falls squarely on the shoulders of the field sales organization.

The sales territory is the theater of action. While sales territories usually are defined by geographic boundaries, they are better thought of simply as collections of accounts, the responsibility for each account group being assigned to an individual sales rep. The issue of sales force deployment is essentially one of assigning sales reps to accounts, not just sales territory design but preparing, guiding, and supporting the sales reps as they seek to achieve company marketing objectives in the context of marketing and sales strategy.

OBJECTIVES OF SALES FORCE DEPLOYMENT

The ultimate objective of sales force deployment is to achieve the firm's profit goals. But that broad objective must be broken down into more manageable parts if it is to be made operational, and a number of issues must be resolved. Those issues can be seen as a number of potentially conflicting objectives. For example:

1. Sales revenue maximization *vs* sales cost minimization.
2. Short-term sales and profit goals *vs* longer-term goals.
3. Servicing existing accounts *vs* developing new accounts.
4. Maintaining sales volume on existing products *vs* developing markets for new products.
5. Taking business away from competitors *vs* developing new uses and applications and stimulating the total market for the product.

These are not false issues but real choices that must be resolved at the highest levels of the organization. If those issues are not resolved, the sales force will be subject to confusing and conflicting directions, incentives, measurements, and controls. It is the function of marketing strategy to make those choices and to focus and coordinate all of the efforts of the firm toward common objectives.

With a clear set of company objectives and marketing objectives in place, a set of objectives specific to the sales organization can be developed. Those sales objectives can also be divided into short-term and long-term components. Short-term objectives present choices about how resources are to be allocated among products, accounts, and territories. Long-term objectives represent similar choices over a longer-term planning horizon, but also include targets for developing additional resources—that is, growing and improving the sales organization itself. In the absence of a clear, long-term, strategic perspective, the sales rep is very likely to focus all effort on short-term objectives—maximum current sales volume from existing accounts and existing products, won in hand-to-hand combat with a well-defined enemy and with a heavy emphasis on price as a major weapon. A longer term view shifts some portion of sales effort toward expanding the customer base and creating new applications and uses for products sharply differentiated from those of entrenched competition, with less emphasis on price and enhanced profit margins as a result. The sales rep receives guidance from a marketing strategy in terms of customers to call on, products to be emphasized, and how those products are to be sold.

MARKET SEGMENTATION STRATEGY

At the core of every effective marketing strategy is a clearly defined market segmentation strategy that defines the market targets on which the firm will be focusing its marketing efforts. Segmentation strategies do several things:

Focus the company's resources on specific market opportunities that represent the best fit with the company's competitive strengths and weaknesses.

Tailor the elements of marketing strategy (product, price, promotion, and distribution) to the specific requirements of each segment.

Recognize differences in how customers respond to marketing effort, and organize customers with similar response patterns into distinct segments.

Establish a competitive advantage in a market niche, a part of the market where the firm can command high customer preference and loyalty *vis à vis* competiton.

Customer Selection

From a sales management perspective, the critical fact about the market segmentation strategy is that it selects customers. Whereas customer selection is a critical strategic issue for all firms, it is especially important for industrial firms. In much industrial marketing, products and services are tailored rather precisely to the unique needs of individual customers and market segments. The product, defined to include the total bundle of services offered along with the tangible, physical product, becomes a variable, not a given, in the marketing program, as the vendor seeks to provide the most effective and competitive solution to the customer's problem. But given limitations on its own resources and competencies, no firm can be all things to all customers. It will be much better at solving some problems, at meeting some customers' needs, than others. Market segmentation strategy is intended to maximize the differential competitive advantage of the firm by focusing on those customers whose needs are most consistent with the firm's resources and business objectives.

Good customers are those that place demands on the firm that are consistent with its capabilities. In the never-ending quest to find better solutions to customer problems, the typical industrial firm is continually evolving and developing its capabilities through product development, production process improvement, more efficient distribution, and so on. Much of this evolution occurs in response to specific customer requirements, as part of the ongoing buyer–seller relationship. In a very real sense, customers are a major force shaping the development of an industrial firm. It is for this reason that effective and efficient sales strategy, and especially the deployment of the sales organization in the field, must be based on a clear marketing strategy, with careful market segmentation at its core.

Costs of Inadequate Segmentation

Bad customers are those that ask the firm to do things that it cannot do well, that make demands that are very costly to respond to, or that take the company in directions that are inconsistent with its long-term strategy and objectives. There is a real danger in letting the field sales manager and the field sales representative opportunistically select customers to be called on. In the short-run, the principal danger is probably that the sales effort will be ineffective because the selling effort will be inconsistent with the firm's products, pricing, and distribution. Stated differently, the sales rep will not have the marketing support required to be effective with the customers selected. In the long run, however, a more serious strategic weakness may result from the failure to develop a strongly differentiated position with a well-defined set of customers. The sales organization will have failed in its implementation of marketing strategy. The infantry will have failed to capture its objective.

This set of issues can be recast in terms of the sales rep as a boundary role person, a concept developed in Chapters 1 and 3. If the sales rep is trying to develop customers that have requirements that are inconsistent with the selling firm's capabilities and strategies, role conflict will be high. He or she will be asking the firm to do things that it doesn't want to do or cannot do well, leading to charges that the sales rep is incompetent or uncooperative. The customer will perceive that the rep is making promises that cannot be kept or that the selling firm doesn't support its sales organization. Inadequate and ineffective programs may be submitted to the customer, failing to solve the customer's problem. Over time, the result will be lost sales, diminished profit margins, dissatisfied customers, and low levels of sales force performance and satisfaction. The sales force, by definition, will be doing a bad job of both representing the factory to the customer and representing the customer to the factory. Everybody loses.

In the absence of a strong, clearly defined marketing strategy, the opportunistic, current sales volume maximizing actions of the field organization will fill the gap. Marketing strategy will be dominated by sales strategy. Short-term goals will dominate attention to long-term objectives. The market segmentation strategy will be developed *de facto* by the sales reps. There is likely to be great inconsistency from territory to territory. Sales reps will be making conflicting and competing demands on the rest of the organization and the whole company will suffer from lack of strategic direction and sense of mission.

The major point being made is that carefully defined market segmentation strategy is the critically important starting point for sales force deployment. The absence of clear direction will have many adverse long-term consequences, including poor sales and profit results, a high degree of role conflict, sales force dissatisfaction, and dissatisfied customers. A good sales rep does not want to be left alone. A good rep values careful direction and organizational support. We will return to this issue of organizational morale in the following chapter.

THE SALES FORCE DEPLOYMENT PROBLEM

Deployment is the process of assigning sales effort to specified market targets or opportunities, in the form of market segments and actual and potential customers. These market targets can be defined at several levels of aggregation—individual persons, buying centers, buying locations, firms, groups of customers according to industry, geographic areas, and so on. The level of aggregation determines what is usually called a *control unit* in analysis of deployment problems. Control units are combined into a sales territory, a set of accounts (actual and prospective customers) assigned to a single sales rep.

There are many different types of management decisions required in the deployment of a sales force, and responsibility for those decisions may be found throughout the sales management organizational hierarchy. From a top-down perspective, some of the most important sales force deployment decisions include:

Types of customers to call on.
Balance between established accounts and prospects.
Number of calls, per period, by type of account.
Defining sales territory boundaries.
Degree of product specialization in the sales force.
Whether to add or drop customers.
Assignment of specific sales reps to territories.

Given a number of sales reps, with a given set of characteristics and abilities as the result of recruitment, selection, and training policies, the sales manager must decide how to assign them to the field in pursuit of such marketing objectives as sales volume, market share, contribution margin, return on investment, return on assets employed, and so on. Different levels of the sales management organization will have varying degrees of involvement at various stages of the deployment process. The following illustrates the hierarchy of deployment decisions and a reasonably characteristic definition of shared responsibility for those decisions within the sales management hierarchy.

Sales Management Hierarchy	Deployment Decisions
National Sales Manager or Sales Vice President	Market segmentation strategy
	How to organize the sales force—by product, customer type, geographic territories, etc.
	Define regional boundaries
	Estimate national market and sales potentials
	Define normal workload
Regional Sales Manager	Define call frequency by type of account
	Number of reps per region
	Estimate regional market potential
	Define district boundaries
	Estimate district market potential
	Number of reps per district
District Sales Manager	Define territory boundaries
	Assign sales reps to accounts
	Estimate territory and account potentials
Sales Representative	Develop routing plan in territory
	Develop key account selling plans
	Determine call frequency per account

There are obviously a number of interactions and trade-offs among these various decisions both in planning and in implementation. For example, as territory boundaries are expanded, call frequency would have to be reduced; as the definition of normal workload is reduced, more sales reps are needed; and so on. Sales force deployment and the allocation of sales effort is really a dynamic problem, requiring continuous adjustment and refinement from period to period as marketing strategy and market conditions change. Organizations differ tremendously in the manner in which such decisions are made, in the delegation of responsibility for these decisions downward through the field sales organization, and in the frequency with which adjustments in deployment occur.

Analytically, the sales managers can approach the deployment problem in either a top-down or bottom-up fashion. In the former, the process is essentially one of taking sales force size as given, judging how much potential and geographic area one sales rep can handle, locating customers within geographic areas, and drawing boundaries around areas or otherwise grouping accounts to define territories that represent some optimum combination of potential and workload. The remaining variable that must be decided by the sales rep and the district sales manager is the frequency with which to call upon various types of customers. In the bottom-up approach, the starting point is an estimate of the optimum call frequency for each account or type of account, based on account potential and other account characteristics. Accounts in a geographic area are aggregated until the total calls required for the group of accounts, combined with other territory characteristics, represent a reasonable workload for a single sales rep. These territories are aggregated into regions and the total number of territories determines the size of the sales force.

In actual management practice, some dimensions of both top-down and bottom-up are probably found, and the analysis is refined almost continually. While the opportunities for rigorous structuring and quantitative analysis of the deployment problem are obvious, the problem calls for a large number of qualitative managerial judgments about factors that are hard to estimate precisely in practice. At the core of every sales force deployment decision are estimates of two key variables: potential and workload.

Potential

Potential can be thought of as the capacity of a market to absorb the product under analysis. It is the amount of sales volume available from a given account, territory, district, or other grouping of accounts in a given time period, and can be defined in terms of either units or revenue. It combines measures of both ability and willingness to buy.

In some cases, especially where demand for the product is a function of the customer's rate of operation, potential may be estimated reasonably easily and precisely, as in the case of a trucking company's fuel requirements or a polyethylene plant's usage of ethylene. In other cases, requirements, and therefore buying potential (which must always be defined in a given time period if it is to be meaningful and useful), are much harder to estimate; say, an insurance company's potential for additional data processing equipment or a public utility's potential as a customer for steam turbines.

Needless to say, the quality of deployment decisions is significantly influenced by the quality of the data available for, and the manager's judgments about, market potential. Among the most commonly used measures of potential are number of employees, production volume, sales volume, plant capacity, and other measures of customer size. Number of customers (and prospects) by size category are aggregated to yield estimates of territory potential. Such data are generally available from government and trade association sources in most industries.

The analyst must make a difficult judgment about the difference between *market* potential—the total amount of business available from a customer, a geographic area, or market segment—and *sales* potential—the amount of business realistically available to a given selling firm in that period. Obviously, the two are very seldom the same.

The situation is complicated further by the realization that both market potential and sales potential are influenced by the marketing and sales efforts of prospective vendors. Pricing changes, new product developments, and advertising and sales promotion programs are three of the more obvious actions that can substantially influence market and sales potential. Limitations in the product line, for example, will make sales potential less than market potential. Thus, estimates of market and sales potential are based on some assumptions about marketing programs and their impact on individual customers, geographic markets, and market segments.

For products and services consumed by the thousands and millions of units on an annual basis, such as grinding wheels or small motors or air freight shipments, the analyst has the luxury of large numbers of customers and transactions to work with in estimating market and sales potentials. While small errors in judgment still can be costly, the estimates of demand will be fairly dependable and reliable, and it will be possible to determine at the end of the period whether or not the estimates were accurate. Very large capital equipment purchases represent the other extreme, where only a few units may be purchased during a given period. Examples might include oil drilling rigs, nuclear power generating plants, and wide-bodied passenger aircraft. Even after the period is over and sales results are in, the true market potential can only be estimated. The potential demand in such markets is a function of individual managers' judgments about a huge variety of subtle and complex economic, international, political, financial, legal, and technological factors. Quantification of those factors and judgments into estimates of market and sales potential obviously is difficult, yet sales and marketing managers in those industries must come up with such estimates as the basis for their strategic planning and deployment decisions.

Sales forecasts are estimates of what the firm actually will sell during a given period, with a specified marketing and sales program in force. The sales forecast will be less than the sales potential unless the firm has all of the resources necessary to realize the full potential available to it. The sales forecast is probably the single most important element of a firm's planning efforts, especially short-term, operational planning. Production, purchasing, personnel, financial, marketing, and sales plans all must be based on a sales forecast. Sales forecasting is one of the critical management functions performed by field sales managers at all levels of the sales management hierarchy.

If a firm's sales actually come close to the forecast, this may not indicate simply a high degree of accuracy and reliability in the sales forecasting procedure. Because all of the firm's operations become geared to the sales forecast, attainment of that level of sales is not an unexpected outcome; on the other hand, it is by no means a foregone conclusion. A number of competitive and economic conditions in the marketplace intervene between the application of marketing and sales effort to potential demand to produce a final sales result.

Workload

The concept of territory workload is less complex and subtle than the concept of potential, but not without difficulties of measurement. Workload, the amount of effort required by the sales rep assigned to a given territory, reflects the characteristics of the accounts in that territory (such as size, potential, whether contacted before, service needs, technical requirements, etc.) and the geographic characteristics of the territory (urban *vs* rural, concentration and dispersion of accounts, weather extremes, availability of public transportation, etc.).

A specific measure of workload is the number of sales calls required in the territory during a planning period. To derive such an estimate, the sales manager needs a list of all accounts in the territory, grouped according to desired call frequency. (Note that such groupings and assigned call frequencies cannot be said to be optimum in any sense; they do not take into account how sales response for any given account might change if call frequency was increased or decreased).[3] It may also be desirable to differentiate accounts according to desired length of call. These numbers together determine the workload in number of selling hours represented by a territory (group of accounts), as in the following illustration.

Type of Account	Number	Desired Call Frequency per Year	Average Length of Call (hrs)	Total Selling Time Required per Year (hrs)
A (large)	12	24	2	576
B (medium)	15	12	1	180
C (small)	18	6	0.5	54
				810

Actual selling time with customers is only part of the sales rep's total activity and therefore only one determinant of workload. Travel is another major activity that must be factored into the analysis of workload, and travel requirements will vary widely from one territory to another as a reflection of the location of accounts within the territory (concentration and dispersion) and the physical characteristics of the terrain to be covered. Staying with this simple illustration, the

[3] Lodish has called such a system for allocating effort to accounts based solely on size or potential "precisely wrong." See Leonard M. Lodish, " 'Vaguely Right' Approach to Sales Force Allocation," *Harvard Business Review*, Vol. 52 (January-February 1974), pp. 119–124.

manager might estimate that travel time required would be 75% of selling time:

$$0.75 \times 810 \text{ hours} = 607.5 \text{ hours travel time per year}$$

Using some ratio of travel time to selling time is probably an easier way to estimate it than to try to actually estimate travel time from each account location to the next in some kind of optimum routing plan. Another rule-of-thumb estimation procedure would be to estimate travel time available to a sales rep as a function of total time. Assuming a 250-day work year and an 8-hour day, each sales rep has 2000 hours per year to devote to all activities. If travel is estimated as requiring 30% of total hours, the estimate of travel time would be:

$$0.30 \times 2000 = 600 \text{ hours travel time per year}$$

Non-selling time requirements include not only travel but also a variety of administrative tasks, such as completing weekly call activity reports, writing customer orders, correspondence with customers and company personnel, responding to customer service requests and complaints, following up on orders and deliveries, gathering and reporting information on competition and market conditions, and so on. These activities also can be estimated either as a function of total time available or as a function of selling time. To keep the illustration simple, we can assume that administrative and service requirements are the same as travel time:

$$0.30 \times 2000 = 600 \text{ hours of service and administrative time}$$
$$\text{required per year}$$

To complete the illustration, we have defined a total workload for this group of accounts of approximately 2017.5 hours per year:

Selling time	810	hours
Travel time	607.5	hours
Service and administrative time	600	hours
	2017.5	hours

Thus, this particular grouping of accounts would represent a reasonable workload assignment for an individual sales representative, again assuming a 2000-hour work year.

Ideal Territory Design

An *ideal territory* is one that has just enough potential and workload to be managed by a single sales rep. In this ideal world, all sales reps are of equal ability and the sales manager is therefore indifferent as to which individuals are assigned to which territories. The sales reps are perfectly interchangeable and each territory is an exact replica of every other territory in terms of potential and workload. Stated differently, each territory represents the same earning opportunity for the sales rep and for the company. Therefore, differences in sales performance among territories will largely reflect differences in effort by the sales reps, and should be reflected in differences in compensation. Such a view of the relationship between effort, outcome, and rewards is based not only upon the assumption that sales reps are of equal ability (which may be a necessary assumption in analyzing and developing sales territories), but also on a view of the sales rep as strictly an individual contributor, not as a member of a total marketing and sales team, views that were compared in Chapter 3.

The ideal of sales territories of equal potential and workload may be useful as a target in designing sales territories, because it helps to define a reasonable assignment for a single individual as well as making it possible to compare territory performances, to move reps among territories, to allocate advertising and sales promotion effort in an equitable manner among territories, and the like. But the problem, of course, is that each territory will be idiosyncratic to a degree, because of the characteristics of actual and potential accounts in that territory, as well as other factors such as competitive activity, proximity to the firm's factories and distribution centers, the history of company effort in that area, and so on. Likewise, the characteristics of sales reps must be taken into consideration when people actually are assigned to territories. To the extent that the sales people are different, it may actually be desirable to have territories that differ. A new rep, newly recruited from college and freshly trained, needs a different territory assignment than does the old foot soldier with 20 years in the trenches.

As a practical matter, familiar geographic boundaries such as counties and states often become sales territory boundaries. Market data are often organized this way and it can be very difficult to analyze, plan, evaluate, and control sales activity on any other basis. It is obvious that it is virtually impossible to group such political and geographic subdivisions into units of equal potential and workload, except as a rough guideline.

OBJECTIVE OF TERRITORY DESIGN

Very few sales managers ever face the problem of developing a total national sales effort allocation scheme *de novo*. There is almost always a deployment scheme in place. Under extreme conditions, it may be necessary to restructure a whole national sales organization, realigning all sales territories, districts, and regions and reassigning a large proportion of all accounts. One can imagine a number of causes for such drastic action: the merger of two companies' product lines and sales forces; a major change in competitive effectiveness and market share; a major increase or decrease in the size of the sales organization; addition of a new product line with very large market potential; or a change from heavy reliance on distributors to direct sales coverage.

More commonly, a sales management team is faced with the need to make a more or less constant series of relatively minor changes in sales force deployment. This need results from many factors—the normal addition of new sales reps to accommodate sales growth; shifts in the location of customer buying centers; response to competitors' moves; resignations and retirements; changes in the rate of industrial activity and growth rates in different regions of the country; and the introduction of new products and the deletion of old ones, to give a few examples. Over time, existing territory boundaries and personnel assignments become obsolete. Some territories will have too much potential and/or workload for a single sales rep, others not enough. Some customers and distributors will receive inadequate sales coverage and service and may complain loudly. In other cases, sales expenses will be too high given the level of sales results.

The sales force deployment strategy must be approached as a total system. By definition, it is impossible to change the boundaries of one territory without changing at least one more, and usually several more, as well. One sales rep's assignment and workload cannot be altered, usually, without influencing the assignments and workloads of others. Such interactions obviously must be considered as the sales manager fine-tunes the allocation system and realigns sales territories.

A sales territory should represent a reasonable assignment of potential and workload for a single individual, enough to permit the rep to earn a reasonable income and to allow the company enough business volume to justify the expense of keeping the rep in the field. It should permit the accounts in the territory to be covered with the desired frequency.

As noted in our discussion of the ideal sales territory, a goal to strive for is to have sales territories that are as nearly equal as possible in terms of potential and workload. Such an ideal would permit the sales management team to achieve several objectives:

To permit equitable evaluation of sales representative performance across territories.

To assure that sales representatives will achieve equal pay for equal work, that is, to achieve equity in the compensation system.

To allocate sales effort in a way that maximizes the sales volume achieved from available potential and sales effort.

To avoid problems in sales force morale that will result from unequal potential and workload including turnover, poor performance, and supervisory problems.

An even more basic objective in territory design is to be sure that each actual and potential account is the responsibility of a single sales representative. This means that territory boundaries should not overlap. There should be only one answer to the question "Who's account is that?" This should be true even in those cases where a firm has two or more sales organizations, each specialized in certain products. Unfortunately, it is often not true in this kind of situation, because it often can be difficult to decide which of the product lines is best suited to a given customer's requirement—as in the case of a computer firm with two sales organizations, one handling small-to-medium and the other handling medium-to-large systems. In some instances customers are ignored; in others, the two reps find themselves fighting over the same piece of business.

DETERMINANTS OF SALES TERRITORY PERFORMANCE

One way to approach the problem of optimum sales territory design (the optimum allocation of sales effort) is to examine various answers to the question "What are the factors determining sales territory performance?" Several researchers have looked at this question. Some of the general models of sales force performance and sales representative effectiveness reviewed in earlier chapters could be cited here once again. Instead, we will examine only a few additional models and empirical studies that have focused specifically on the issue of sales territory design and the allocation of sales effort among territories. A common issue in all of these studies has to do with the relative importance of potential vs workload in determining territory sales response to selling effort.

Cravens, Woodruff, and Stamper used stepwise multiple regression analysis to examine the influence on territory sales performance of six variables: (1) market potential; (2) territory workload; (3) sales rep experience; (4) sales rep motivation and effort; (5) company experience in the territory; and (6) company marketing effort in the territory. To do the empirical analysis, these six factors were operationalized by a total of eight measures, which entered into the stepwise multiple regression solution in this order (from most to least important):

1. Number of accounts per sales rep—a measure of workload.
2. Industry sales in the territory—a measure of potential.
3. Market share change—year-to-year changes over a four-year period, a measure of company experience.
4. Workload per account—a weighted index based on the account's annual purchases and the geographical concentration of accounts.
5. Performance of sales rep—field sales managers' estimates on eight dimensions of performance.

The following variables had no significant impact on territory sales results:

6. Market share—a measure of company experience.
7. Length of employment—a measure of sales rep experience.
8. Advertising effort—a measure of company effort[4]

Both workload and potential had some significant influence on sales territory performance. Unfortunately the data base upon which these conclusions are based (25 territories) is really too small for the results to be meaningful statistically, given that eight variables were examined.

In a study of a national sales organization serving the retail apparel trade, Lucas, Weinburg, and Clowes also found that territorial potential and the sales representative's workload (number of accounts and their geographic dispersion) were associated with historical sales. As potential (measured by industry sales) increased, territory sales increased; as workload (number of accounts and number of counties) increased, sales went down. Both linear and curvilinear models were tested, and fitted the data more or less equally well. When the data were analyzed at a regional, rather than national level, potential was found to be more important than workload, but both were worth a look.[5]

In a later (1977) study, Beswick and Cravens used data for a later time period for the same variables on the same company as the earlier (1972) study of Cravens, Woodruff, and Stamper. Once again there were some problems with the data, and one can question the validity of the results. Among other problems, the predictor variables are highly intercorrelated and management judgments were used to change some of the input variables. The six variables examined were found to all have a significant influence on sales results and in the hypothesized direction.

[4]David W. Cravens, Robert B. Woodruff, and Joe C. Stamper, "An Analytical Approach for Evaluating Sales Territory Performance," *Journal of Marketing*, Vol. 36 (January 1972), pp. 31–37.
[5]Henry C. Lucas, Jr., Charles Weinberg, and Keith W. Clowes, "Sales Response as a Function of Territorial Potential and Sales Representative Workload," *Journal of Marketing Research*, Vol. XII (August 1975), pp. 298–305.

Sales in a geographic control unit increased as:

The sales rep's effort (percentage of time spent in the area) increased.

An index of buying power (potential) in the control unit increased.

Previous sales in the area relative to sales potential increased.

The amount of the sales rep's time allocated to the control unit increased.

The regional manager's time with the company increased.

Average account size (workload) increased.[6]

Bagozzi reported a study that showed that a model incorporating potential and workload was not as strong a predictor of territory sales results as was a model incorporating psychological variables, especially the sales rep's self-esteem and the amount of perceived role ambiguity for the sales rep. Another variable, verbal intelligence, had a significant negative influence on sales results, opposite to the hypothesized direction. Nonetheless, territory potential, measured by industry sales volume, did have a significant influence in the second model, in which there was no measure of workload.[7]

In the final study to be looked at here, Ryans and Weinberg reviewed each of the studies just reported and noted that a number of important variables, especially those relating to the characteristics of sales reps and their supervisors, had been left out. All of these earlier studies did support the importance of potential as a determinant of territory sales performance. Ryans and Weinberg studied three national sales organizations to determine the influence of six classes of variables contained in their model of territory sales response:

1. The company's marketing activities in the region.
2. Sales force supervision—span of control.
3. The field sales manager.

[6]Charles A. Beswick and David W. Cravens, "A Multistage Decision Model for Salesforce Management," *Journal of Marketing Research*, Vol. XIV (May 1977), pp. 135–144.

[7]Richard P. Bagozzi, *Toward a General Theory for the Explanation of the Performance of Salespeople*, unpublished doctoral dissertation, Northwestern University, 1976.

4. The sales rep's characteristics—time with the company in sales, time in the territory, and age.

5. Territory characteristics—potential (employment in customer industry in territory); concentration (employment per plant in customer industry); and dispersion (geographic area of the territory).

6. Competitor strength in the territory.

Data were available for Company A for two years and for Company B and Company C for only one year. Not all measures were available for all companies. In no case was there data on the field sales manager's characteristics. Results were not the same for all companies and there were some important differences between the two years of results for Company A. Their results can be summarized as follows:

Sales are lower for reps in territories that receive less marketing support.

Sales increase with increasing territory potential and with increasing concentration of potential in a territory's accounts.

Sales increase with increasing sales rep experience.

Sales decrease as the span of control the sales rep operates under increases (i.e., as closeness of supervision decreases), but this result was significant in only two of the four cases examined.

There was no consistent relationship between territory sales and geographic dispersion.

In the one case where data were available, territory sales were lower in areas where competition was stronger.

Comparing their own results, where possible, with the studies reviewed earlier, Ryans and Weinberg pointed to some interesting and useful conclusions. First, measures of potential were successful predictors of territory sales response in virtually every case. Second, measures of workload were never significant predictors in the hypothesized direction, which is that sales should decrease as workload increases. While Ryans and Weinberg do not discuss this result in any detail, it may be because of the measure of workload used. When the measure of workload relates to number of accounts, as it did in the studies of Cravens, Woodruff, and Stamper; Lucas, Weinberg, and

Clowes; and Bagozzi, it in fact may be a better measure of potential than workload. Clearly, better measures of workload are required. Third, there is no consistently observed relationship between territory sales response and either concentration (of potential in accounts) or geographic dispersion. Nonetheless, these are both important variables that warrant continued study.[8] The Ryans and Weinberg results, combined with those of Bagozzi, support the conclusion that models of territory sales response should incorporate not only measures of territory characteristics (potential, workload, concentration, dispersion, company experience, and competitors' strength), but also measures of the sales rep's characteristics (experience, ability, time in territory), the rep's psychological state (perceived role ambiguity, role conflict, and self-esteem), and the quality and closeness of supervision (manager's experience and ability and the span of control). Once again we come back to a complex view of the relationship between sales effort and sales results, rather than to a simple model of the sales rep as an individual contributor.

DEVELOPING SALES TERRITORIES

In this section, a simple procedure for developing sales territories will be outlined. Subtleties relating to the quality of the sales representative, the characteristics of the field sales manager, or the presence of major customers and distributors with unique requirements for sales coverage and service, of necessity must be left out of a generalized and simplified procedure such as this. The steps in this procedure are:

1. Establish clear objectives for territory design.
2. Select the control unit.
3. Estimate market and sales potential for each control unit.
4a. If possible, establish call frequency and average length of call for each type of account in the control unit.

---

[8]Adrian B. Ryans and Charles B. Weinberg, "Territory Sales Response," *Journal of Marketing Research*, Vol. XVI (November 1979), pp. 453–465.

4b. Judge the amount of potential that a single rep can handle reasonably.
5. Combine control units into initial territory clusters.
6. Evaluate workload requirements in each territory cluster and adjust territories as indicated.

Establish Objectives

The manager responsible for designing sales territories must have a clear notion of what would constitute an optimal territory. In addition to the frequently cited criterion of territories of equal potential and workload, there are some other obvious objectives, such as to provide complete coverage of the market and to be sure that all customers are contacted with the desired frequency. There are also a number of less obvious decisions required and choices to be made.

The objectives for territory design, as noted early in this chapter, must be closely linked to the company's marketing and sales objectives. An objective of building market share clearly calls for increasing the intensity of sales coverage. Specific objectives for increased penetration of particular market segments must be translated into higher call frequencies and more account coverage in territories where those accounts are concentrated. If reducing sales and marketing expense is a company priority, larger territories and reduced call frequencies are going to be a likely goal in territory redesign.

Select the Control Unit

The *control unit* is the basic unit of analysis in territory design, the unit for which data will be collected and analyzed. While it could be the individual account, it is more likely to be a geographic unit containing multiple accounts. Counties, states, U.S. Postal Service Zip Codes, and Standard Metropolitan Statistical Areas (SMSA), as defined by the U.S. Bureau of the Census, are all used frequently for this purpose. A basic rule in selecting the control unit is that it should be small enough so that no control unit falls in more than one sales territory.

The control unit chosen should also reflect the nature of the products and markets involved. Markets for products sold to the retail trade, for example, are analyzed most appropriately using control units that parallel available measures of retail activity, such as retail trading areas. Likewise, there is a significant tendency for a given type of industrial activity to be concentrated in particular regions of the United States and Canada. Ready examples are automobile assembly in Michigan, Ontario, New Jersey, California; high-fashion clothing in New York City; and electronics in "Silicon Valley" (California) and along Route 128 (Massachusetts). In these cases, relatively small control units must be used to provide the necessary detail in data on market potential.

Estimate Market and Sales Potential

Information about the number, size, location, and potential of actual and prospective customers is collected and organized by control unit. Among the most commonly used data for estimating market potential are industry sales, number of customer buying locations by size, or measures of industrial or economic activity such as electrical power consumption, manufacturing employment, or retail sales. Measures of customer size include number of employees, annual sales, and plant capacity.

In many instances, developing reasonable estimates of the amount of business available will require that measures of market potential be combined with estimates of market share, or share of specified customer business, to yield estimates of sales potential. As noted earlier, product line characteristics and other limitations in the firm's marketing mix usually mean that the total market potential is not available to a given seller. For very large customers, buying policies related to the development and maintenance of multiple sources may be a major factor in adjusting measures of market potential to useful measures of sales potential.

At this stage in the analysis, the manager has two options. If the number of potential accounts is small enough, as might be the case for an industrial market where the analysis is being performed at the district or regional level, it may be possible to analyze each control unit on an account-by-account basis with respect to call frequency and desired length of call. In this manner, the estimated call requirements can be estimated for each control unit. However, if the number of accounts is too large, as might be the case if the total national market were being analyzed, then the planner would have to make some judgments about the amount of potential that can reasonably be assigned to a single sales rep, without considering call requirements.

Group Control Units into Initial Territory Clusters

Contiguous control units can be combined until the amount of potential, or the estimated required number of calls, is approxiamately that which can be handled by an individual sales rep. This aggregation process continues until all control units have been combined into territories. Such a bottomup approach assumes that a sufficient number of reps is available, or can be recruited, to cover the resulting number of territories.

Alternatively, in a kind of top-down procedure, the estimated total national market potential could be divided by the number of reps to get a target potential per territory. This approach might be preferred if sales force size was fixed. In this case, initial territory boundaries would be determined by combining control units until the target potential for a sales territory had been approximately reached. In either case, the goal is to have sales territories of approximately equal potential.

Adjust for Workload

As the last step in this simplified procedure, the manager must look at tentative territories arrived at by clustering control units to arrive at territories of equal potential and factor in workload considerations. As noted above, some preliminary assessment of workload may have been made in the form of judgments about call frequency and duration as a function of the size distribution of accounts within the territory. If not, such judgments must be made now. The manager's attention is likely to focus on the major accounts in the territory.

There are other workload determinants to consider as well, such as territory geography and terrain, the clustering of accounts in certain parts of the territory, and other such factors that significantly influence travel time. Competition is another factor to be assessed; strongly entrenched competition may simply mean that the rep will have to work harder and cover a broader base of potential in order to achieve an adequate volume of sales. On the other hand, a commitment to increasing share of market in the territory, or an expected increase in competitors' marketing and sales activities, may call for a heavier allocation of selling effort relative to potential; that is, smaller territory and workload. Here is an area where clear objectives are necessary to guide decision making and where management judgment is crucial.

As a general rule, the territory planner must make adjustments that trade off potential with workload. As workload increases above averages or target levels (as measured by number of accounts, account size, miles to be traveled, distance between accounts, etc.), the amount of potential in a reasonable territory assignment should be lessened. Selling time is estimated by grouping accounts according to size and multiplying the number of accounts in each category by the number of calls and average call duration. Travel time, service time, administrative time, and so on also must be estimated by the manager, using his or her best judgment.

Several management scientists have developed sophisticated, computer-based models for assisting sales managers in the development and realignment of sales territories. These include the CALLPLAN model developed by Lodish,[9] the GEOLINE model of Hess and Samuels (originally developed for realigning legislative districts),[10] and the PAIRS model presented by Parasuraman and Day.[11] These more rigorous models can assist the sales manager's judgment, especially where a major territory realignment is undertaken.

When this analysis is complete, the manager will have not only a set of sales territories but also a data base containing estimates of market potential, sales potential, and workload for each territory. These can be totaled to produce estimates for districts and regions as well.

[9]Leonard M. Lodish, "CALLPLAN: An Interactive Salesman's Call Planning System," *Management Science*, Vol. 18, No. 4, Part II (December 1971), pp. 25–40, and "Sales Territory Alignment to Maximize Profit," *Journal of Marketing Research*, Vol. XII (February 1975), pp. 30–36.

[10]Sidney W. Hess and Stuart A. Samuels, "Experience with a Sales Districting Model: Criteria and Implementation," *Management Science*, Vol. 18, No. 4, Part II (December 1971), pp. 41–54.

[11]A. Parasuraman and Ralph L. Day, "A Management-Oriented Model for Allocating Sales Effort," *Journal of Marketing Research*, Vol. XIV (February 1977), pp. 22–33.

Such estimates provide the basis for sales and expense quotas, the standards against which subsequent results will be evaluated and rewarded.

ASSIGNING SALES REPS TO TERRITORIES

The next step in the sales force deployment process is to assign people to territories. At this stage, further refinements in territory boundaries can be made to reflect the ability and other characteristics of the sales rep. While territory design has assumed to this point that sales reps are of equal ability, actual differences in ability must now be taken into account.

In the typical situation where established territories are being realigned, relatively few people actually will be moved around in the sense that their office location will change or they will have to change residence. What is more likely to happen is that the individual will be assigned some new accounts to cover while others will be taken away and assigned to another rep.

If sales people differ markedly in the nature of their expertise, the manager may elect to give sales reps accounts that maximize the value of their expertise, even if this means overlapping territories and travel routes for the reps involved. While such arrangements can be justified at times, as a general rule they should be avoided because of the potential confusion and inefficiency that result.

The assignment of sales reps to accounts and territories calls for a high degree of sophisticated management judgment in matching the experience, interests, motivation, and abilities of sales reps with market and account requirements. One of the manager's objectives in making territory assignments may be to provide new challenges and learning opportunities for the sales representative. The trade-off between short-term effectiveness and long-term growth is always difficult to make in practice.

Lodish has also developed a mathematical programing model and a linear programing solution procedure for assigning sales representatives to accounts. The model solution also determines the appropriate allocation of selling time to those accounts. Managers' subjective judgments about the effectiveness of specific sales reps with specific accounts are a key input to the model. The model is said to be especially useful in situations where accounts are in close geographic proximity and the interaction of the sales rep with the account is relatively important in determining outcome. Several successful applications of the model have been reported.[12]

DEVELOPING THE ROUTING PLAN

A final step in the deployment of sales effort is to plan the route of travel for the sales rep through the territory. Some companies actually have management plan the routing for the rep but, more commonly in industrial sales organizations, the routing is done by the rep himself or herself.

The inputs to a routing plan are number and location of accounts, distance between accounts, desired call frequency, and length of call. The objectives are to minimize travel distance and expense while covering accounts with desired levels of activity. In the typical situation, the sales rep would return to the office or home location at least every second or third night. A common pattern of territory travel is three or four loops originating from the home city in a kind of clover leaf. There are also well-developed management science approaches to this problem, which has spawned a whole class of procedures, typically using linear programing, to solve what is called "the traveling salesman problem."

The need for careful attention to the routing plan is becoming increasingly serious as travel costs increase so persistently. When one considers the costs of car ownership, insurance, maintenance, and fuel, the average costs of restaurant meals and hotel rooms, as well as the sales rep's salary, commissions, and fringe benefits, it is easy to understand why studies now show that the cost of a single sales call in most industries exceeds $100, and averaged $137 for all industries, according to a 1980 study. At an estimated average of 4.3 calls required to close a sale, the average cost of a sale was calculated to be $589.00.[13]

---

[12]Leonard M. Lodish, "Assigning Salesmen to Accounts to Maximize Profit," *Journal of Marketing Research*, Vol. XIII (November 1976), pp. 440–444.
[13]Labratory of Advertising Performance/McGraw Hill Research, Studies No. 8051 and 8052.

In actual practice, it may be difficult for a rep to stick with the routing plan as problems and opportunities arise at particular customer locations. A major benefit of the routing plan, however, is the discipline it can provide, thus helping to maintain the coverage pattern and hold travel expenses to planned levels. Using the routing plan as the framework, the sales representative can let customer personnel know when to expect a visit, and can make the necessary appointments, rather than responding to problems and opportunities in a random, *ad hoc* manner. Such careful planning can reduce waiting time to a minimum, maximize selling time, and increase sales force productivity.

ACCOUNT PLANNING AND MANAGEMENT

The professional sales representative should have a carefully defined work plan for each of his or her major accounts. This plan should include specific selling objectives, both quantitative and qualitative, for the selling period. Planned call frequencies should be included. It should be a written plan, developed in consultation with the field sales manager and identify key personnel in the buying center. It should also describe customer programs and projects currently underway that will influence demand for the sales rep's products and services. In industrial selling, the focus must be on developing and maintaining long-term buyer–seller relationships, not just on current sales volume.[14]

SETTING SALES QUOTAS

A primary sales management tool for the planning, evaluation, and control of sales effort is the *quota*. A quota is a target, a goal, that becomes a standard against which to measure results. It defines an individual's share of the responsibility for achieving a total organization objective.

---

[14]Benson P. Shapiro, "Manage the Customer, Not Just the Sales Force," *Harvard Business Review*, Vol. 52 (September-October 1974), pp. 127–136.

Most commonly, we talk about *sales quotas*, which can be for a territory, a district, or a region. These usually are stated in revenue terms and the sum of all sales quotas is the firm's sales forecast. Sales quotas can be derived from the sales forecast by multiplying it by the percentage of market or sales potential within the sales area. Typically, sales quotas actually are derived through an iterative process of consultation between reps and their managers, up and down the line. The rep may be asked to estimate territory sales for the next period, and this is compared with measures derived from the combination of the national sales forecast and measures of local market potential. The rep and his or her manager can then factor in their knowledge of local market conditions and individual account situations. Participation of the sales representative in the sales forecasting and quota-setting process obviously can do much to assure that the quota will be acceptable to the rep as a fair standard against which to subsequently evaluate his or her performance. Sales quota achievement usually is tied to the compensation plan. Properly designed sales quotas can be a major incentive for the sales organization, both directly as targets for achievement and indirectly through their connection to the compensation plan.

Individual sales quotas may be divided into quotas for specific products, product lines, market segments, and so on, with some part of compensation tied to each. These product and market quotas can be instrumental in coordinating selling effort with the strategic details of the marketing plan, a critical consideration as discussed in the early pages of this chapter. Sales quotas can be modified to become quotas for profit contribution.

Sales quotas are concerned with sales results. Another type of quota is more concerned with selling effort. These are called *activity quotas* and include such things as number of calls to be made on specific types of accounts, new accounts to be obtained, and number of in-store displays to be set up.

In some organizations, expense control is facilitated by establishing specific quotas for selling expenses. *Expense quotas* can be established for advertising and sales promotion expenditures in the territory, district, and region, as well as for sales reps' travel and entertainment expenditures. In all cases, quotas can be thought of as that part of the company's budget that the individual sales representative or field sales manager is responsible for maintaining.

This discussion of quotas and their uses will be continued in Chapter 7, which is devoted to the evaluation and control of sales effort.

SUMMARY

In this chapter we have looked at the complex process of deploying a sales organization in pursuit of strategic marketing objectives. We began by stressing the importance of market segmentation strategy as the core around which sales deployment is planned, customers are selected, and the level of effort to be applied to customers is established.

Determinants of sales territory performance were examined by reviewing several empirical studies, and their underlying models, in some detail. The central issue here was the relative importance of potential versus workload in determining territory sales response. Potential was the winner, but the influence of workload needs further study, especially as to the best measures for it. Other variables found to be important include the motivation of the sales rep, the level of competitive activity, the closeness of supervision, and the experience of the field sales manager.

A simple procedure for developing sales territories was outlined. Assignment of sales reps to territories, development of the routing plan, account management, and setting sales quotas were considered briefly in concluding the chapter.

SIX

Sales Force Motivation and Supervision

Sales force effectiveness reflects the composite performance of the individual sales representatives and field sales managers. Performance is the result of the basic aptitudes, training, and experience of the sales reps, the assignment of that sales talent to territories, and the motivation of sales reps to accomplish the assigned work. The field sales manager is a central force in the development of that motivation, as well as in the development of the reps' basic abilities, through the day-to-day activities of supervision. The previous two chapters examined the development (Chapter 4) and deployment (Chapter 5) of sales force talent. In this chapter, the basic concept of motivation will be explained, the role of the field sales manager as a supervisor will be examined in depth, and some research relating to sales force motivation, performance, and satisfaction will be reviewed.

THE CONCEPT OF MOTIVATION

A motive is a force within an individual that impels and directs behavior. Motivated behavior is goal-directed behavior. (Not all behavior is motivated—examples of non-motivated behavior include all involuntary physiological responses.) A motive can be a need, a want, a goal, or a value. Motives both incite behavior and direct it toward particular objects, events, and tasks. Behavior thus reflects motivation, as well as many other individual characteristics including ability, knowledge and previous experience (learning), and perceptions. In a general sense, a motivated person is in a state of tension that reflects unsatisfied needs, and will seek to reduce that tension through goal-directed, need-satisfying behavior.

Theories of Motivation

The earliest theories of human motivation were rather simplistic, and focused on the individual's basic physiological needs. In the first theories, basic human instincts were emphasized in a kind of Darwinian orientation. Hedonism, the basic human urge to seek pleasure and avoid pain, was formally offered as an early theory of human motivation in the English Utilitarianism tradition that followed the philosophic tenets of Priestley, Bentham, Spencer, and their successors. Freud and his disciples looked to unconscious, sexually oriented drives to explain much of human behavior.

Whereas theories emphasizing instinctual and hidden motivations once enjoyed popularity as explanations of human behavior, modern motivation theory takes a more rational view. Today's views assume that most human behavior is motivated by conscious goal-seeking on the part of the individual. A person seeks outcomes (rewards) that will reduce perceived needs and achieve goals of which the individual is highly aware.

The psychologist C. L. Hull developed one of the first formal theories of motivation, published in 1943, called *drive theory*.[1] He defined *primary* needs or drives as the basic physiological and survival needs (hunger, thirst, rest, shelter, etc.), and *secondary* needs or drives as learned connections between behavioral outcomes and rewards that satisfy primary needs. The Hullian concept of drive replaced the more primitive concept of instinct in psychological conceptions of motivation and was a generally accepted view for the better part of two decades. The basic motivational mechanism in drive theory is an unsatisfied need that creates a felt tension that leads to behavior that satisfies the need and reduces the drive. A basic premise of drive theory is that a satisfied need does not motivate behavior.

A major shortcoming of Hull's drive theory is its rather simplistic emphasis on basic physiological needs, and its inattention to other

[1]C. L. Hull, *Principles of Behavior* (New York: Appleton-Century-Crofts, 1943).

factors that can impel and sustain behavior. As one commentator has put it:

> . . . it is difficult to see how Hull's explanation can help us understand why workers continue to work for more money even when their basic needs are satisfied.
>
> More damaging to Hull's view . . . is the great amount of evidence indicating that people . . . are attracted to many outcomes that do not seem to be directly related to primary needs.[2]

A more complex view of the drives motivating human behavior was offered by Maslow as early as 1943, although his theory, in its initial form, was more a typology of the outcomes that individuals would find attractive than it was a theory of motivation.[3] Later developments in Maslow's work rounded out its status as theory, however.[4] Maslow proposed a five-level need hierarchy as follows:

1. *Physiological needs.* For food, water, air, and so on.
2. *Safety needs.* For security, stability, and the absence of pain, threat, or illness.
3. *Belongingness and love needs.* For affection, belongingness, love, and so on.
4. *Esteem needs.* Both for personal feelings of achievement or self-esteem and for recognition or respect from others.
5. *The need for self-actualization.* A feeling of self-fulfillment or the realization of one's potential.[5]

Maslow argued that these needs existed in a "hierarchy of prepotency," that the needs at one level did not influence behavior significantly until the needs at the next lower level were satisfied. Thus, the physiological needs must be satisfied to some minimum degree before the safety needs become motivators, and so on. Needs at one

---

[2]Edward E. Lawler III, *Motivation in Work Organizations* (Monterey, CA: Brooks/ Cole Publishing Co., 1973), p. 16.

[3]A. H. Maslow, "A Theory of Human Motivation," *Psychological Review*, Vol. 50 (1943), 370–396.

[4]A. H. Maslow, *Motivation and Personality* (New York: Harper & Row, 1954) and *Toward a Psychology of Being* (Princeton, NJ: D. Van Nostrand, 1962).

[5]Taken from Lawler, *op. cit.*, p. 28.

level need not be completely satisfied before needs at the next level become important. Maslow originally argued that satisfaction of needs at any level reduced the force with which they drive behavior. In later revisions of his theory. Maslow asserted that for self-actualization needs, increased need satisfaction leads to increased, rather than decreased, need drive and motivation. "Gratification breeds increased rather than decreased motivation, heightened rather than lessened excitement."[6] He also added two other needs—cognitive (need to know and understand) and aesthetic (need to move toward beauty and away from ugliness), but these two needs were not related to the hierarchical arrangement, a further suggestion that Maslow may have been moving away from the concept of a hierarchy. Maslow's theory became very popular in the literature of management, including sales management, in the 1960s and 1970s.

In the late 1960's and early 1970's, Alderfer redefined the Maslow need categories somewhat and combined them into three new need categories—existence, relatedness, and growth, and proposed "the E.R.G. framework" as follows:[7]

Maslow Categories (modified)	E.R.G. Categories	Definition
Physiological Safety—material	Existence	Material and physiological desires, including desires for pay, fringe benefits, and working conditions.
Safety—interpersonal Love (belongingness)	Relatedness	Needs involving relationships with significant other persons, groups as well as individuals. Relatedness includes acceptance, confirmation, understanding, and influence.
Esteem—interpersonal Esteem—self-confirmed Self-actualization	Growth	Needs that impel a person to make creative or productive demands on self and the environment, to use existing capabilities, and to develop new ones.

Figure 6.1. The E.R.G. framework.

[6]A. H. Maslow, *Toward a Psychology of Being*, 2nd ed. (Princeton, NJ: Van Nostrand-Reinhold, 1968), p. 30.

[7]Clayton P. Alderfer, *Existence, Relatedness, and Growth* (New York: The Free Press, 1972), p. 25.

Alderfer dropped the strict prepotency assumption in the Maslow need hierarchy, and his theory does not require that lower-level needs be satisfied before higher-order needs become important. In Alderfer's model, a hungry man can still be concerned about and motivated by his self-esteem, for example. A highly creative person with high growth needs may need less satisfaction of his or her existence needs, and so on. Compared with Maslow's need hierarchy, Alderfer's theory proposes a much more complex interaction between the satisfaction of one set of needs and the drive force of another set. Alderfer proposed, for example, that the less relatedness needs are satisfied, the more existence needs will be desired. Likewise, he hypothesized that the less growth needs are satisfied, the more relatedness needs will be desired. While Alderfer's empirical work did not confirm these particular assertions, it did serve to confirm the basic E.R.G. categories as a way of viewing human motivation.

All of the theories reviewed so far are essentially theories of need types and their interactions as driving forces, and have relatively little to say about connections between drives and various outcomes or rewards. Whereas drive theories focus on past satisfactions and learned behavior, so-called cognitive theories look at individuals' beliefs, expectations, and perceptions about future events, and see behavior as rational, goal-directed, and consciously motivated. *Expectancy* theory, a term that replaced cognitive or valence theory, was developed in the 1950s and 1960s to explain the dynamic relationships between drives, behavior, outcomes, drive satisfaction, and the value of the reward as perceived by the individual. The principal theorist applying expectancy theory to people in formal organizations has been Victor Vroom, whose 1964 theory[8] has been called "perhaps the most widely accepted theory of work and motivation among today's industrial and organizational psychologists."[9] Recent studies of sales force motivation, supervision, performance, and job satisfaction have been based almost exclusively on expectancy theory models.

The following discussion will become a bit technical and complicated, but for good reasons. Worker motivation is a complex phenomenon. An astute manager will want to understand and appreciate that

[8]Victor H. Vroom, *Work and Motivation* (New York: John Wiley & Sons, 1964).

[9]M. A. Wahba and R. J. House, "Expectancy Theory in Work and Motivation: Some Logical and Methodological Issues," *Human Relations*, Vol. 27 (1974), pp. 121–147 at 121.

complexity. It is fair to state that the traditional literature of sales force management has been overly simplistic in its treatment of the subject of sales representative motivation. The question as to whether or not money, rather than other rewards such as personal recognition, is the major motivator, often has dominated the discussion. This emphasis traces back to another simplification as well—the tendency to view the sales rep as an individual contributor whose performance is largely the result of his or her personal characteristics and efforts, rather than in complex interactions with environmental and organizational variables and with significant other persons—customers, managers, other sales reps, and family members. In the following section we will consider a recent and rich model of sales representative motivation that is realistically complex and consistent with the general view of sales force effectiveness that we have been presenting through out this text.

EXPECTANCY THEORY APPLIED TO SALES FORCE MOTIVATION

The central proposition of expectancy theory is that the strength of a drive to behave in a specific way depends upon two factors: the actor's expectation that the act will lead to a particular outcome; and the perceived attractiveness or *valence* of that outcome to the actor. Drive strength equals expectancy times valence. Note that in its basic tenet, expectancy theory also traces back to hedonism. Vroom's theory, building on earlier expectancy models, was unique in its specific concern for motivation in a work environment.[10] Several other behavioral scientists have expanded and tested Vroom's model. Walker, Churchill, and Ford have further extended and adapted the expectancy model to an industrial selling context. [11] Their general model of the determinants of a sales representative's performance is presented in Figure 6.2.

---

[10]Lawler, *op. cit.*, p. 45.

[11]Orville C. Walker, Jr., Gilbert A. Churchill, Jr., and Neil M. Ford, "Motivation and Performance in Industrial Selling: Existing Knowledge and Needed Research," *Journal of Marketing Research,* Vol. XIV (May 1977), pp. 156–168.

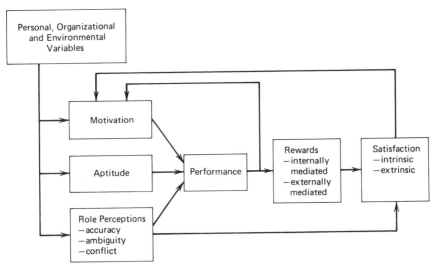

Figure 6.2. A model of the determinants of a sales representative's performance. Source: Orville C. Walker, Jr., Gilbert A. Churchill, Jr., and Neil M. Ford, "Motivation and Performance in Industrial Selling: Existing Knowledge and Needed Research," *Journal of Marketing Research*, Vol. XIV (May 1977), pp. 156–168, at p. 158. Reproduced with permission.

The basic proposition of the Walker, Churchill, and Ford model is that performance is determined by the interaction of aptitude, motivation, and role perceptions. (The role perceptions component of the model was described in Chapter 4.) The sales rep is seeking two kinds of rewards. *Internally mediated* rewards are those that the sales rep attains for himself or herself. They are tied to the higher-order needs—relatedness and growth in Alderfer's E.R.G. framework or esteem and self-actualization needs in Maslow's hierarchy. *Externally mediated* rewards are controlled by other persons in the rep's role set, such as customers and managers. These rewards generally relate to lower-order needs, that is, existence or physiological and safety needs, and take the form of financial rewards, promotions, job security, and recognition.

The relationship between performance and rewards in most industrial selling situations is far from straightforward. A central issue is how performance is measured, the basic problem being that there is typically a long time lag between the performance of job tasks (the exertion of sales effort) and the achievement of sales results. Sales management may use a variety of measures of both effort and results such as number of calls, number of accounts, percentage of quota attained, dollar revenues, unit sales, new accounts opened; and subjective measures of such areas of activity as customer service, coverage planning, reporting, and administration. The link between task performance (effort) and results accomplished may be complicated by many other variables, not all of them under the control of, or necessarily even perceived by, the sales rep or the manager. The sales rep may also not see a clear connection between performance and results or between results and rewards. This set of issues will be examined more carefully in the next chapter which deals with evaluation and compensation.

Expectancies and Performance Valences

The motivation component of the Walker, Churchill, and Ford model of sales rep performance is an expectancy model and is depicted in Figure 6.3. Motivation is defined as the sales rep's willingness or desire to expend effort on specific job tasks such as calling on established customers, calling on new accounts, providing customer service, completing call reports, and so on. *Expectancy* (E_{ij}) is defined as the sales rep's estimate (a subjective probability) of the likelihood that a given amount of effort expended on job task (i) will lead to an improved level of performance on performance dimension (j). *Valence* (V_j) for performance dimension (j) is defined as the rep's perception of the desirability of improving performance on dimension (j). The concept of valence as used here and in later discussion means attractiveness or desirability; if something has a positive valence, a person is attracted to it, whereas negative valence implies repulsion.

Expectancy is a prediction—a personal, subjective estimate of the probability that a given amount of effort expended on a task will produce a specific performance result. The sales rep's motivation (M) to expend effort on any sales task (i) equals expectancy times the perceived valence of that performance dimension:

$$M_i = E_{ij} \times V_j$$

Both expectancy and valence are themselves functions of other variables. Expectancies are perceptions based on previous experience,

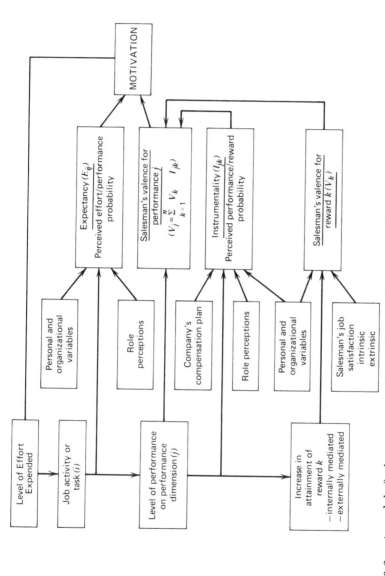

Figure 6.3. A model of sales representative motivation. Source: Orville C. Walker, Jr., Gilbert A. Churchill, Jr., and Neil M. Ford, "Motivation and Performance in Industrial Selling: Existing Knowledge and Needed Research," *Journal of Marketing Research*, Vol. XIV (May 1977), pp. 156–168, at p. 162. Reproduced with permission.

understanding of the job description, training in all its dimensions, and interactions with significant others in the role set—especially customers, supervisors, and other sales reps. An expectancy could be phrased in the form: "If I increase my calls on larger accounts by 20%, there is a 50% chance that sales volume from them will increase by 25% in the next year."[12] The strength or magnitude of such probability estimates reflects the sales rep's role expectations as well as personal characteristics, such as basic achievement motivation, general self-esteem, and job-specific self-confidence, which might in turn be a function of training and previous experience. The magnitude of the expectancies would also reflect the rep's assessment of general economic conditions, account and territory potentials, the strength of competition, and other market and environmental factors. The accuracy of the estimates will also reflect experience, training, and supervision, and the accuracy of the rep's role perceptions.

Instrumentalities and Reward Valences

The sales rep's valence for a given performance outcome is a function of the perceived link between that outcome and some reward, and the valence of that reward for the rep. *Instrumentality* (I_{jk}) is defined as the rep's subjective estimate of the probability that achieving an improved level of performance on performance dimension (j) will lead to increased attainment of a particular reward (k). Valence (V_k) for reward (k) is the rep's perception of the desirability of receiving more of a reward (k):

$$V_j = \sum_{k=1}^{n} (V_k \times I_{jk})$$

where V_j is the rep's valence for performance dimension (j) and there are (n) different rewards associated with that performance dimension. The earlier and simpler equation for motivation can therefore be rewritten as:

$$M_i = E_{ij} \times \left[\sum_{k=1}^{n} (V_k \times I_{jk}) \right]$$

[12]Expectancies are stated as simple probabilities; a more complex formulation would involve a probability distribution with specified mean and standard deviation.

To review and summarize these concepts, both expectancies and instrumentalities are subjective probability estimates made by the sales rep. Both performance dimensions and rewards have valences, which are the rep's perceptions of desirability. Performance valences are a product of reward valences and instrumentalities. Pulling these assertions together, the sales rep's motivation to perform a given sales task is a function of his or her (1) expectancy that more effort will lead to improved peformance, (2) perception of the link between performance and rewards, and (3) perception of the desirability of those rewards.

In a sense we are back where we started from—a simple hedonistic assertion that individuals are motivated to maximize rewards. But a number of important and subtle linkages and interactions have been added and the psychological realities of uncertainty and subjective perception have been introduced. The Walker, Churchill, and Ford formulation also implicitly recognizes that generalizations about what motivates most or all sales reps are highly suspect. An individual sales rep's motivation reflects individual needs and perceptions, all of which are a function of experience and interaction with the environment.

Like expectancies, instrumentalities (the perceived links between performance outcomes and rewards) can be described by their magnitude and their accuracy and are themselves a function of other variables—personal, interpersonal, organizational, and environmental. A major factor in determining a rep's instrumentalities is his or her understanding and perception of the firm's compensation plan. Another major factor has been called "locus of control," the tendency for some persons to have a general view that they can and do control their own destiny (internal control) vs a feeling that other persons and random events determine performance outcome (external control). Research confirms a logical supposition that internal-control people are generally better motivated to perform well since they see a more direct connection between behavior and rewards that satisfy their goals.[13] Job experience is likely to improve the accuracy of the sales rep's instrumentalities, as it should improve the accuracy of expectancies. The field sales supervisor is also a major factor determining both the magnitude and accuracy of instrumentalities.

[13]See Lawler, *op. cit.*, p. 57.

The missing ingredient here is the determinants of reward valences—how can a sales manager know which rewards will be most attractive to the sales rep? This is still the basic question to be answered: What motivates performance? The answer must first be phrased in terms of the individual's needs and goals, and here the Maslow need hierarchy, Alderfer's E.R.G. framework, and similar need typologies may provide a useful set of concepts. However, the critical point to be made in the context of the Walker, Churchill, and Ford model is that the linkages between needs and rewards are neither simple nor clear. Whether designing or administering a reward system, the field sales managers must work through, understand, and manage—for each sales rep—each of the linkages between needs, effort, outcomes, expectancies, instrumentalities, valences, and rewards. None of these, except the individual's needs (and then only to a degree), is a given. The field sales manager can influence each of these variables. The link between supervision and motivation is a direct one. Before turning to supervision, however, we must return to the question of reward valences. What determines the attractiveness of rewards for a given sales rep?

Influences on Reward Valences

Simply stated, sales reps will seek rewards that satisfy their needs. As we have just seen, however, that motivational process depends upon the rep's perception of the linkages between effort and performance and between performance and rewards. The Walker, Churchill, and Ford model of sales rep motivation distinguishes between internally and externally mediated rewards, and incorporates some of the basic assertions of the Maslow and Alderfer models, supported by some others' empirical findings. For the lower-level needs, those associated principally with externally mediated rewards, it is argued that the higher the level of need satisfaction, the lower the valence for increased amounts of those rewards. For the higher-order needs, however, it is asserted that increased levels of internally mediated rewards lead to still higher valence for increased amounts of those rewards.

In practice, financial compensation is the most important externally mediated reward. The motivational model we have been exploring would argue that the higher a sales rep's total compensation, the less important would be additional pay as a motivator for that individual. While that assertion has some intuitive appeal, it may oversimplify the situation, First, individual sales reps at the same compensation level may place very different valences on an additional amount of income, depending upon a variety of personal characteristics and the extent of financial obligations. The rep supporting a large family will view the extra income differently than will the single person without dependents. Some people simply place a higher value on financial well-being that do others. One could think of many individual characteristics that would influence the valence of additional amounts of externally mediated rewards, including factors related to family background, education, previous experience, and need for recognition.

Second, financial reward systems may appeal to many different needs. Money is valued not only for what it can buy but as a way of keeping score on one's development and progress. Comparison of one's pay *vis à vis* one's colleagues' pay may be a very important consideration in terms of self-esteem and the perceived respect of others. From this perspective, then, one could argue that more pay does not lose its value as a motivator as the sales rep's compensation increases. Compensation, and what it symbolizes, satisfies a variety of needs, not just physiological and safety needs, but needs for the esteem of others and for self-respect as well.

Externally mediated rewards also incorporate non-financial compensation including job security; management statements of thanks, praise, and support and other forms of recognition; more tangible rewards such as promotion and added job responsibility; and various non-monetary awards such as merchandise and travel for winning sales contests. As a general proposition it is probably true that a sales rep's valence for additional amounts of internally mediated awards increases as his or her satisfaction with all such externally mediated rewards increases. Internally mediated rewards include feelings of accomplishment, growth, personal challenge and self-fulfillment and by their very nature are harder to define and measure because of their personal, subjective, and intangible nature.

Ford, Walker, and Churchill conducted a field investigation of their expectancy model of sales representative motivation, focusing on the question of reward valences—which of the many alternative rewards for performance are most attractive to sales representatives?[14] As asserted in that model (Figure 6.3), the link between reward valences and motivation is seen as influenced by personal and organizational variables, including demographic/life style variables, stage in career cycle, and psychological characteristics. Six sales organizations from a total of three different industrial companies were surveyed in 1976 and again in 1981. A comparison of the findings of these two studies concerning performances for various rewards is presented in Figure 6.4. The rank orderings of preferences are interesting in themselves, but equally interesting are the findings relating these rankings to various personal characteristics.

Reward	1976 Study ($n = 227$)		1981 Study ($n = 108$)	
	Valence	Rank	Valence	Rank
Pay	87.5	1	83.7	1
Personal growth	79.2	2	68.5	4
Sense of accomplishment	78.1	3	69.8	3
Promotion	68.0	4	73.3	2
Job security	59.3	5	38.0	6
Recognition	51.5	6	41.9	5

Figure 6.4. Sales representatives' rankings of the attractiveness of alternative rewards. *Source:* Neil M. Ford, Orville C. Walker, Jr., and Gilbert A. Churchill, Jr., *Differences in Attractiveness of Alternative Rewards Among Industrial Salespeople: Additional Evidence*, Marketing Science Institute, Report No. 81-107, December 1981, p. 14.

The strength of the evidence supporting the contention that sales reps are motivated primarily by pay is surprisingly strong. Conversely, recognition and job security were ranked amazingly low in terms of average valence scores. Some of the stronger (statistically significant) relationships between valence for rewards and personal characteristics were the following:

A sales rep's valence for more pay was influenced only by whether the person owned a home. Marital status, family size, and job ten-

[14]Neil M. Ford, Orville C. Walker, Jr., and Gilbert A. Churchill, Jr., *Differences in Attractiveness of Alternative Rewards Among Industrial Salespeople: Additional Evidence,* Marketing Science Institute, Report No. 81–107, December 1982.

ure were also all positively related to valence for pay, but were not statistically significant.

People with six or more years of experience valued job security more highly than did those with less.

Promotion was valued more highly by those sales reps who were unmarried, were relatively young, and had less than six years of experience.

Feelings of accomplishment were valued more highly by reps with higher education levels (graduate work or graduate degree). There was some positive relationship with need for achievement and self-esteem, but not at levels of statistical significance.

High valence for personal growth was shown by females, younger reps, unmarried reps, those with high household incomes, and those who had relatively short tenure with their companies.

The researchers offered a summary conclusion that higher-order (internally mediated) rewards tend to become relatively more important when lower-order (externally mediated) needs are satisfied. Also, sales people appear to value internally mediated rewards more highly during the early stages of their careers. It is suggested that older sales reps, with more experience, come to concentrate on the monetary rewards as their chances for promotion decrease over time and they incur the added financial obligations of marriage, parenthood, and home ownership. Conversely, younger, better-educated sales reps are more highly motivated by chances for promotion, feelings of accomplishment, and personal growth in the early stages of their careers—when they have relatively less need for financial rewards. This suggests that sales management should spend at least as much time designing sales career paths as it spends on compensation plans. It must be repeated, however, that age is not significantly related to valence for pay; sales reps, across the demographic spectrum, appear to be primarily motivated by pay.

A final conclusion worth noting is the lack of any strong relationships of psychological variables with reward valences.

The theories of motivation we have been reviewing lead to the proposition that additional amounts of internally mediated awards have higher valence for sales reps with higher levels of satisfaction with those rewards. The more an individual sales rep feels that he or she is growing and achieving, the more he or she will want to achieve. Achievement can thus lead to a sales rep's setting increasingly higher personal goals and creating higher levels of expectation for rewards to be earned.

A key variable here is the individual's level of achievement motivation. Individuals show great differences in this characteristic and it is more likely to influence performance in jobs that are challenging and competitive (like selling) as opposed to those where the work is repetitive and boring.[15] Internally mediated rewards would logically seem to be more attractive to individuals with a high need for achievement. Not only do sales jobs tend to attract individuals with a high need for achievement (because selling involves taking responsibility for solving problems and some personal risk-taking), but they also tend to reward individuals for such activities. Doyle and Shapiro report a study showing that sales rep motivation and effort are directly related to need for achievement.[16] They noted that the sales rep selection process in the companies studied is likely to emphasize past accomplishment and other factors closely correlated with need for achievement. Looking ahead to our discussion of supervision, they also found that the number one determinant of a sales rep's motivation was the clarity of the sales task, defined as the relationship between the exertion of sales effort and the observation of a sales result. Sales rep motivation was also influenced by incentive compensation, when there was a strong link between reward and effort, and by what was called "good sales management," defined to include accurate and prompt feedback of sales results, rewards for reported results, and recognition for achieving those results and rewards.

To conclude, sales representative motivation is determined by perceived linkages between effort and performance outcomes and between outcomes and rewards. Those perceptions are a function of the rep's experience, training, and supervision. The desirability of particular rewards is a reflection of the individual's level of need satisfaction. In general the motivating power of internally mediated rewards

---

[15]D. C. McClelland, *The Achieving Society* (Princeton, NJ: Van Nostrand-Reinhold, 1961).

[16]Stephen X. Doyle and Benson P. Shapiro, "What Counts Most in Motivating Your Sales Force?," *Harvard Business Review*, Vol. 58, No. 3 (May-June 1980), pp. 133–140.

increases as the rep's satisfaction with the level of externally mediated rewards—such as pay and recognition—increases.

A key determinant of the rep's perceptions of the effort-performance-reward linkages is the closeness and quality of that rep's supervision. Motivation and supervision are intertwined very closely as determinants of sales rep performance.

SUPERVISION

Supervision is the management process of overseeing and guiding performance, and it is the principal responsibility of the first-line field sales manager. It is more or less synonymous with *direction,* but in its more complete and subtle meanings it also involves such managerial concepts as training, goal-setting, personal development, support, guidance, and counseling in the work situation. Peter Drucker has noted that IBM does not use the words "foreman" or "supervisor" in its production organization but instead speaks of an "assistant." He then goes on to observe:

> This is exactly the role the supervisor is supposed to discharge. He is to be the "assistant" to his workers. His job is to be sure that they know their work and have the tools. He is not their boss.[17]

Supervision is a relationship between the manager and the worker. In our introduction to the role of the field sales manager in Chapter 2, we defined supervision as overseeing, directing, and controlling the sales rep's activities and said that it included assigning tasks to be performed, monitoring performance on a continuous basis, and evaluating performance against standards. Supervisory functions were defined as (1) creating the work environment, (2) establishing standards of performance, (3) developing human resources, (4) acting as a communication link between sales reps and sales management, and (5) interpreting and enforcing policy. Each of these functions was examined in some detail.

---

[17]Peter F. Drucker, *Management: Tasks, Responsibilities, Practices* (New York: Harper & Row, Publishers, 1974), p. 261.

Organizational climate was defined as the sales rep's perceptions of the work environment, whereas job satisfaction was defined as the rep's attitudes toward and feelings about the perceived work environment. It was pointed out that the supervisor can and does influence not only the objective characteristics of the work environment, such as task assignments and job standards, but perceptions, attitudes, and feelings as well.

Traditional views saw job satisfaction as a result of job performance. More recently this causative relationship has been questioned, some arguing that improved job satisfaction leads to improved performance[18] and others asserting that both are simultaneous outcomes of selling effort, the result of common causative factors. Modern views in this area, once again, see that the nature of the relationship between satisfaction and performance depends upon several other factors including perceptions of the linkage between performance and rewards and the distinction between internally and externally mediated rewards.

DETERMINANTS OF JOB PERFORMANCE AND SATISFACTION

Bagozzi has examined the relationship between a sales rep's performance and job satisfaction in a study of two sales organizations, both selling steel and plastic strapping and related hand tools used in shipping.[19] Sales performance was found to be positively related to territory potential (a conclusion shared with the several studies reviewed in Chapter 5) and with job-specific self-esteem. The latter concept requires some brief explanation. Job-specific self-esteem is based on the person's previous experience with similar or related tasks and reflects the person's sense of competence to deal with the job. It is distinct from general or chronic self-esteem, which is a persistent personality trait and applies across a wide range of situations, and from socially

[18]J. P. Wanous, "A Causal-Correlational Analysis of the Job Satisfaction and Performance Relationship," *Journal of Applied Psychology*, Vol. 59 (1964), pp. 139–144.

[19]Richard P. Bagozzi, "Salesforce Performance and Satisfaction as a Function of Individual Difference, Interpersonal, and Situational Factors," *Journal of Marketing Research*, Vol. 15 (November 1978), pp. 517–531.

influenced self-esteem, which is a function of the person's perceptions of other people's expectations. All three forms of self-esteem could be assumed to influence a sales rep's job performance. Bagozzi tested for both generalized and specific self-esteem but found that only the latter had a significant influence on either job performance or satisfaction. In fact, job-specific self-esteem, the rep's own sense of competence as a sales representative, was far and away the most significant influence on sales performance.

Two other factors examined by Bagozzi were also found to influence sales performance, each in a negative direction—role conflict (job-related tension) and verbal intelligence. The fact role conflict (the perception of incompatible or opposing expectations or demands held by two or more role partners) has a negative influence on sales performance certainly comes as no surprise. But it is surprising that verbal intelligence—defined as a person's ability to perceive, attend to, and process information related to conversations, written instructions, and other forms of communication—has a negative impact on sales performance. The magnitude of this negative relationship was "relatively small and only borderline in significance," according to Bagozzi, who tentatively offered the explanation that "for those very high in verbal intelligence, the job was boring or in some other way unchallenging, thus leading these individuals to devote less time and energy to the job at hand."[20]

Job satisfaction was found to be influenced primarily by role conflict, which reduces satisfaction; and by job performance, which increases satisfaction. Thus, according to this research, performance leads to job satisfaction but job satisfaction does not influence performance, at least directly. Role ambiguity and self-esteem did not influence job satisfaction.

Bagozzi also examined his data for influences on self-esteem and found that general self-esteem was a function of "other-directedness" and sales performance. Sales performance had a positive impact on general self-esteem, but other-directedness, a measure of the rep's tendency to look to other people for direction and approval, had a negative relationship with general self-esteem. Specific self-esteem,

[20]Richard P. Bagozzi, "Performance and Satisfaction in an Industrial Sales Force: An Examination of their Antecedents and Simultaneity," *Journal of Marketing*, Vol. 44 (Spring 1980), pp. 65–77, at 71.

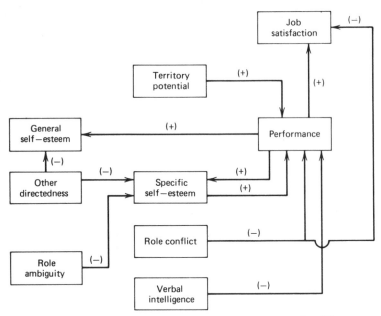

Figure 6.5.   Sales representative performance and self-esteem.

in contrast, was influenced by sales performance (positively), other-directedness (negatively), and role ambiguity (negatively). It will be recalled that role ambiguity is a measure of the degree of uncertainty perceived by the rep concerning the expectations of such role partners as customers and sales managers.

These interacting conclusions from Bagozzi's research might be summarized visually as in Figure 6.5; while other possible linkages were tested, only the statistically significant relationships are shown. It is important to note that Bagozzi's findings support a view of sales rep performance as influenced by the sales environment and by the process of interpersonal (buyer–seller) interaction, as well as the individual characteristics of the sales rep. This viewpoint, incorporating what Bagozzi terms "social learning and interactionist conceptualizations of human behavior," has been stressed repeatedly in earlier chapters, in contrast to traditional views of selling as something the sales rep does to the buyer, determined solely by the characteristics of the individual sales rep.

Performance is influenced not only by territory potential but also by specific self-esteem, role conflict, and verbal intelligence; performance in turn has a positive influence on both general and specific self-esteem. Sales performance has a positive impact on job satisfaction, but satisfaction does not, in this study, have any direct influence on performance. Role conflict has a negative impact on both performance and satisfaction and role ambiguity has a negative impact on specific self-esteem (and therefore indirectly on performance).

Implications for the Field Sales Manager

Bagozzi has suggested some specific implications of these findings for the field sales manager. If management wants to achieve heightened sales performance and job satisfaction, it might focus attention first on reducing role conflict by selecting reps who can cope well with job tension and by structuring the work situation to minimize interpersonal conflicts. The latter requires a strengthening of the supervisor–sales rep relationship, streamlining of procedures and policies, strengthening internal company support for the sales rep, and understanding customers and their needs well enough to ensure compatibility between the customers' expectations, managerial directives, and company policies and procedures.

Improving the sales rep's self-esteem has the potential to enhance performance. This can be done by reducing role ambiguity and by assigning reps to territories that are a good match with their capabilities, enhancing the probabilities of success. More generally, providing positive feedback on performance whenever possible can also enhance self-esteem.

These are duties directly assignable to the field sales manager as a first-line supervisor: to select and assign sales reps, to reduce role conflict and ambiguity, and to take a variety of positive steps to enhance the sales rep's self-esteem. As a boundary role person, physically separated from the supervisor, the sales rep is especially susceptible to conflicting expectations by role partners, inadequate positive feedback on performance due to infrequent direct contact with the supervisor, and distrust and misunderstanding on the part of the employees of the marketing organization. The sales supervisor's role in providing clear direction and positive feedback and in resolving role ambiguity and role conflict when they are present is a major determinant of sales force performance and job satisfaction.

Closeness of Supervision

The foregoing considerations point toward a close relationship between the sales representative and the field sales manager as a positive influence on job performance and satisfaction. The very essence of the supervisory process is a close, personal relationship between the sales rep and the manager, the latter providing direction and support, including training and organizing company resources as required by the rep to perform the selling task effectively. At the same time, the nature of the selling job is such that much of the work is carried on in the absence of direct supervision. How, then, can a field sales manager provide close supervision? The three answers to this question might be summarized as observation, communication, and participation.

An essential activity is working with the sales reps in the field, traveling with them, calling on customers, observing their work habits and their interactions with buyers, and discussing the reps' problems and progress. As noted in Chapter 3, these work-with sessions can lose their effectiveness if the sales manager essentially takes over the interaction with the customer and attempts to close the sale or solve the problem instead of coaching and helping the rep. The manager who acts like a supersalesman is making the rep more dependent on the manager rather than helping the rep to grow and to develop new capabilities. But used properly, the work-with session can be an extremely positive source of guidance, support, and feedback for the rep.

In the times between direct observation, other forms of communication, especially by telephone and in writing, are a vital supervisory tool. Maintaining contact with the rep can avoid misunderstanding about expectations, spot and deal with problems as they develop, and satisfy the rep's basic needs for support, security, and a sense of belongingness. The rep will be eager to have current information about company programs and progress that is being made in solving specific customer problems, for example. Simply acknowledging communications from the rep is one important function of managerial communication.

Participation in the goal-setting process, and in determining the standards against which he or she will be evaluated, is an essential ingredient in developing and maintaining the sales rep's motivation and morale. Such procedures often go by the label *management by objectives* or simply MBO. It is well known that workers are much more likely to accept and strive for goals if they feel they have participated actively in setting them. These goals then serve as a focus for periodic performance review and further goal-setting. In the sales force setting, these goals include not only performance targets—sales, expense, and call quotas, for example—but also the development of selling plans with specific key accounts and, equally importantly, the setting of specific goals for the sales rep's own personal development. The latter might include training sessions to be attended, analytical exercises to be completed, product or market knowledge to be acquired, and so on. Recall the research cited earlier on the importance of internally mediated rewards, especially for younger and more ambitious sales personnel. It is essential that active steps be taken by the sales supervisor to provide incentives and rewards that appeal to needs for personal accomplishment and growth and to enhance job-specific self-esteem as well as to enhance job performance and the necessary externally mediated rewards of pay and promotion.

These considerations argue for close supervision and are inconsistent with a view of the typical sales rep as a person who values independence and wants to be left alone. There is good empirical support for the argument that sales reps value close supervision, but one must distinguish between the quality and frequency of supervision. Churchill, Walker, and Ford found that industrial sales reps' job satisfaction was related positively and strongly both to the amount of influence they believe they have in determining the standards by which their performance is evaluated and to their feelings of closeness of supervision. Industrial sales reps appear to want clear direction and prefer that their performance be watched carefully. Job satisfaction was found to be directly related to the extent that the rep felt that he or she understood clearly what was expected and how to meet those expectations. Sales reps also were found to be more satisfied when they felt that they had an input to the determination of company policies and procedures that influence their jobs. Frequency of contact with the field sales supervisor was not an important determinant of job satisfaction; it was the perceived quality of the relationship that was important.[21]

[21]Gilbert A. Churchill, Jr., Neil M. Ford, and Orville M. Walker, Jr., "Organizational Climate and Job Satisfaction in the Salesforce," *Journal of Marketing Research,* Vol. 13 (November 1976), pp. 323–332.

None of this is surprising, but it is contradictory to a view of the sales rep as a kind of undisciplined "lone ranger" who regards every supervisory interaction as an imposition. These findings serve to underline the critically important role played by the first-line supervisor, the field sales manager, in determining sales force performance and job satisfaction.

SUMMARY

In this chapter we have reviewed the concepts of motivation and supervision, and have related them to the performance and job satisfaction of the sales representative. Familiar concepts of role ambiguity and role conflict, from earlier chapters, have been integrated with findings about the value of various forms of compensation and rewards to present a detailed and complex view of sales rep motivation, performance, and satisfaction. The central theme might be summarized as a view of the sales rep as an achievement-oriented person motivated by monetary rewards and by opportunities for personal growth and accomplishment. The major determinants of sales performance are territory potential and a strong sense of self-esteem specifically related to the selling task itself. The major contribution of the sales supervisor to sales rep performance comes in providing clear direction and positive support for the sales rep, reducing role ambiguity and conflict to tolerable levels, and helping the rep to manage the residual level of job-related tensions. Sales force recruitment and selection can contribute to performance and job satisfaction by selecting people with the ability to tolerate the role ambiguity and conflict that are inherent in the sales rep's boundary role, as well as people with a high need for achievement and a high general sense of self-esteem. (It was also suggested that high levels of verbal intelligence and other-directedness might best be avoided in sales applicants.) Sales career path planning may be at least as important as compensation planning in providing the best levels of sales force performance and job satisfaction. Close supervision is a key ingredient in sales force motivation, performance, satisfaction, and development.

SEVEN

Evaluation, Control, and Compensation

Getting things done in a business firm requires planning, organization, and control, and our treatment of field sales management has been organized around these three activities. In the first three chapters we looked at the nature of the field sales representative's duties, the responsibilities of the field sales manager, and the characteristics of buyer-seller interaction as the three basic elements that must be *planned* when managing a field sales organization. Chapter 5 also considered the problem of planning for market coverage and deploying sales effort against predetermined marketing objectives and market segments. Chapters 4 and 5 examined the activities involved in developing and deploying the field sales organization, including the recruitment, selection, and training of personnel, analyzing market potential and workload, designing sales territories, and assigning reps to those territories. Chapter 6 concerned sales force motivation and supervision, the process of bringing sales organization resources to perform at maximum levels of effectiveness.

In the current chapter we will be analyzing the interrelated questions of evaluating, controlling, and compensating field sales personnel, which, in turn, are intertwined closely with motivation and supervision. Evaluation is an integral part of the control process, gathering information to compare actual performance against predetermined objectives and standards. Compensation provides incentives and rewards for performance, directing effort toward those predetermined objectives and standards and distributing rewards

183

consistent with their attainment. Compensation systems should be viewed as a part of the organizational planning and control process, rather than as a separate administrative problem. In simplest terms, a compensation system is intended to secure sales effort and results that are consistent with company objectives, plans, and policies.

THE CONTROL PROCESS

Control is best thought of as an information handling process that monitors the performance of a system, compares performance against some predetermined standards or objectives, and sends information about any variance between actual and desired performance back to the system operator so that corrective steps can be taken. Implicit in the concept of control is the notion of directing, regulating, and constraining the operation of the system. A familiar example of a control process is the room thermostat in a building heating system—continuously sensing the room temperature, sending a signal to a heat source to begin operation when the temperature falls below a specified minimum level, and sending another signal to shut off the heat source when a specified maximum level is reached.

Any control process has four phases:

1. Setting standards and objectives for evaluating system performance.
2. Obtaining information on system performance.
3. Comparing performance against standards.
4. Taking action to bring the system operation into line with objectives.

We will be using these four steps to organize the following discussion of sales force evaluation and control, but we must first consider the unique problems of controlling a sales organization as opposed to the generalized concept of controlling an operating system.

The Human Element

A sales organization is a goal-seeking collection of individuals and, as elaborated in Chapter 6, those individuals are characterized by varying levels and types of motivation. Sales force performance reflects motivation as well as aptitude and role perceptions. Simply sending information about actual *vs* desired performance back to the system operators—the field sales reps and their managers—may do little to improve sales force performance. There are likely to be imperfect correlations between action instructions and action taken, and between action taken and results achieved. Feedback information on system performance also will be used by upper level sales management to alter areas of sales strategy and policy including recruiting, selection, training, deployment, supervision, organization, and compensation. The effects of these changes in strategy and policy will also be mediated by the sales reps' role perceptions, aptitude, and motivation.

Adding the human element to the concept of a control system complicates it considerably but does not alter its fundamental nature. At its core, control is a goal-setting and information-handling process. The sales manager must understand and manage the relationships between organizational goals and the personal goals of the sales reps and their field sales managers. The information to be gathered, analyzed, and sent back to the sales force must concern not only the more obvious aspects of system performance such as sales revenues, expenses, quota attainment, customer response, and competitive actions, but also must consider sales force motivation, aptitude, and role perceptions. System performance must be evaluated not only by quantitative measures relating to sales, expenses, and so on, but also by qualitative assessments relating to sales personnel, accounts, and the buyer-seller relationship. Sales force performance, and therefore sales organization evaluation and control, is a multidimensional problem.

One implication of this complexity in the control process introduced by the human variables is obvious: the control process itself is a major influence on sales organization performance. The critical dimension to consider in evaluating the impact of the control process on system performance is the quality of the information developed and communicated by the process—especially the accuracy, completeness, and timeliness of that information. Information quality is a major determinant of sales reps' role perceptions and motivation and of the quality of sales management decisions intended to correct and improve system performance.

The Field Sales Manager as a Communication Link

In Chapter 2, supervision was said to be the major responsibility of the field sales manager and was defined as the process of overseeing, directing, and controlling the work of the field sales representatives. To review, supervisory functions were said to include: 1) creating the work environment; 2) establishing standards of performance; 3) developing human resources; 4) acting as a communication link; and 5) interpreting and enforcing policy. From a control process perspective, the critical activities are establishing performance standards and acting as a communication link, and it is the latter that is to be highlighted at this point in the discussion. This emphasizes the centrality of the field sales manger in the control process. However, the five supervisory functions are intertwined closely; a single supervisory action—such as issuing a simple directive—easily can encompass all five functions.

As often noted in earlier chapters, sales management activities, policies, and programs do not influence sales force performance directly. Rather, their impact is mediated by the sales reps' role perceptions as well as their aptitudes, skills, and motivation levels. The field sales manager has a direct influence on role perceptions through planning, organizing, and directing the sales reps' efforts. It will be recalled that role perceptions can be characterized by inaccuracy, ambiguity, and conflict, and that a major responsibility of the field sales manager is to assure that reps' role perceptions are accurate and clear and that role conflict is minimized and managed effectively. The field sales manager is a critical link in the control process.

Individual vs Organizational Performance

It is useful to recall the important distinction between individual and organizational performance, developed in Chapter 4 in our consideration of the concept of sales organization effectiveness. First, we made a distinction between effectiveness and performance; performance refers specifically to actual results, the accomplishment of objectives, whereas effectiveness was defined as ability to achieve those objectives. Evaluation, control, and compensation depend primarily upon measures of performance, not effectiveness. Second, sales rep performance was said to lead to sales organization performance, which in turn contributes to marketing performance and, ultimately to the accomplishment of company/organization objectives.

Evaluating and controlling sales rep performance is a distinctly different problem from evaluating and controlling sales organization performance. Different measures and qualitative criteria are involved. An effective organization is likely to have some ineffective departments and individuals, and good organization performance does not mean that each member has performed satisfactorily. Obviously, however, a high-performing organization will not have many low-performing individuals. The point is simply that organizational and individual performance are distinct concepts.

Responsibility for evaluation, control, and compensation of individual sales rep performance is primarily the responsibility of the field sales manager—the first-line supervisor. The units of analysis are sales reps and their territories. Sales organization performance, on the other hand, is evaluated, controlled, and compensated by higher levels of the sales and marketing management hierarchy. The units of analysis in this latter case are *aggregates* of activity—districts, regions, product divisions, and the like—and their managers, policies, programs, and plans. Stated differently, evaluation and control of sales rep performance primarily involves assessment of people and their activities; evaluation and control of sales organization performance includes not only people but plans, policies, and programs.

SETTING PERFORMANCE STANDARDS

Setting performance standards is the first step in the control process. Sales reps are motivated, as elaborated in Chapter 6, by their perceptions of the linkages between their efforts and results, between results and rewards, and by the valences attached to those rewards. The central element here is the results that reps perceive they are expected to achieve. Role expectations, by now a familiar concept to the reader, are central to the problem of sales force control. There can be no control if sales reps and their field sales managers do not know what is expected of them and if they do not accept these goals and standards as reasonable and legitimate.

Role Expectations

Two basic sources of sales reps' role expectations, and therefore of their interpretations of the standards by which they are to be judged, are the job description and the sales supervisor. There are many other sources of role expectations for sales reps—their families, customers, friends, colleagues, and so on—but these are not sources of standards by which management will evaluate and reward their performance. As noted often, these non-managerial role expectations may conflict with company performance standards, creating tension for the sales rep. Not only must the sales manager be sure that the sales rep has a clear understanding about performance standards; the manager must also help the rep to cope with whatever role conflict inevitably remains.

Nothing is more fundamental to a sales rep's motivation and performance than his or her understanding of how performance is to be evaluated and rewarded. Problems often arise from discrepancies in the communication process, however. The sales manager, consciously or unconsciously, may set priorities different from those inferred from the job description; the field sales manager may misinterpret or intentionally countermand directives from the executive levels of the sales and marketing organization; the sales compensation system may reward performance different than is called for by the sales plan and sales management directives; and so on. Such conflicting signals in the communication process concerning role expectations can be a major source of role conflict and role ambiguity and reduced sales rep effectiveness, leading to poor performance. Research was cited in the previous chapter confirming that a major determinant of a sales rep's motivation is the clarity of the sales task—a clear relationship between the exertion of sales effort and the observation of a sales result, as well as a perceived link between results and rewards.

It is a basic tenet of management theory, as well as common sense, that people are more likely to accept performance standards as legitimate and reasonable if they have participated in setting those standards. This is one dimension of what has been called *participative management*, which involves people in the process of setting goals and standards for their own performance, against which they are subsequently evaluated and rewarded. Not only does this involvement increase the probability that such standards will be accepted as fair and reasonable; it also significantly reduces the chances for misunderstanding (role inaccuracy, role ambiguity, and role conflict). Participation by the sales rep in the goal-setting process can help management to understand customer plans and expectations, market conditions, and competition, and thereby can enhance the quality of sales and marketing management policies, plans, and programs.

Quotas

Quotas are quantitative standards or goals for sales performance in a given time period. Individual sales reps and field sales managers at several levels of the hierarchy may be held responsible for achieving one or more quotas. Most commonly, quotas relate to dollar or unit sales volume. Other types of frequently used quotas involve contribution margin, number of sales calls, number of new accounts, sales expense and promotional expenditures, and new dealer contracts. An aggregate quota for revenues or units may be broken into subquotas for individual products or market segments. Compensation usually is tied directly to quota achievement, although the formula relating compensation and results achieved may be quite complex.

A sales volume quota for a sales territory should reflect the sales potential and workload in that territory, as well as the ability and experience of the sales rep. That is, any quota should reflect both the characteristics of the territory and the person responsible for that territory. In practice, there are mechanical approaches to quota setting that yield targets that are relatively meaningless either as motivators or as standards for evaluating and controlling performance. Suppose, for example, that there is a national sales forecast for the company of $50 million for the coming year, and that a commonly used commercial or government publication reveals that the Virginia territory represents 2.0% of the total U.S. market potential for the firm's products. (That estimate might be based on a count of potential customers, by size, for example.) It would be easy to derive a sales quota of $1 million for the sales rep covering the Virginia territory.

This could be a useful starting point for quota-setting, but consider what has been left out of this analysis. First, consider territory characteristics. How strong is the firm's position in this area compared with competition? How does the geographic dispersion and size concentration of accounts compare with averages on a national basis? Is there more or less travel time involved? Are there strong account relationships, well-established programs with key customers in this area? How does advertising and sales promotion activity impact in this geographic area? How good are the distributors here?

Next consider rep characteristics: How long has the rep been in this territory? How long with the company? How well trained? Is the district manager strong or weak? What are the plans for continued development of the rep during the coming year? Has he or she been given any special assignments such as conducting a market analysis, developing new accounts or market segments, or enlisting new distributors? What sales volume does the rep think the territory is capable of producing in this coming year?

These are just a few of the more basic questions it is reasonable to ask in setting quotas, and they are questions that should be asked and answered in conversations between the sales rep and the field sales manager. Simple procedures such as multiplying the national sales forecast by percentage of total market potential, or incrementing last year's territory quota (or sales result) by a percentage equal to the increase in this year's forecast over the last, can be nothing more than a crude beginning in the quota-setting process.

The field sales manager needs the same basic data for quota setting that are needed for deployment decisions—market potential, sales potential, workload, account characteristics, and so on. While the analytically minded sales manager may be more comfortable focusing on territory/market characteristics in setting quotas, and using the quantitative measures that result as the basis for evaluating and controlling sales performance, it is important to factor the rep/manager/customer relationship into the calculation. Recall from Chapter 6 the research of Bagozzi, which concluded that psychological variables, especially the sales rep's self-esteem and perceived role ambiguity, were even stronger predictors of sales rep performance than were measures of potential and workload.[1] Throughout this text we have been presenting a model of sales force motivation and performance that emphasizes the complexity of the selling process. Our viewpoint highlights

[1]Richard P. Bagozzi, *Toward a General Theory for the Explanation of the Performance of Salespeople,* unpublished doctoral dissertation, Northwestern University, 1976.

the quality of the manager-sales rep relationship, the process of buyer-seller interaction, and the sales rep's role perceptions as determinants of effectiveness and performance, as well as customer, territory, and sales rep characteristics. (See Figures 1.4, 3.3, 4.1, 6.2, and 6.3 for summary depictions of these central themes.) That complexity has to be considered in setting quotas and other standards by which performance is to be evaluated and rewarded.

Relationships Between Quotas and the Sales Forecast

What is the proper relationship between quotas and the sales forecast? The primary function of a quota is to direct individual effort and measure results. A quota defines an individual's share of the responsibility for achieving a total organizational objective. At the level of the total firm, the sales forecast becomes the revenue goal for the period under consideration, and company expenditures are keyed to that level of activity. To return to the thermostat analogy, the forecast really sets the "temperature" in the control process. Forecasts sometimes get revised during the operating period when information indicates that the original estimate was clearly in error. More often, however, the forecast, once set, is modified only slightly or not at all, reflecting two considerations: first, a firm commitment to the goal once established and, second, the basic fact that the forecast determines the level of effort to be expended to achieve the forecast. That is, every forecast has an element of self-fulfilling prophecy in it—the forecast determines the level of effort that is expended to achieve the forecast.

As a general rule, the sum of individual territory quotas should equal the district quota; the sum of district quotas should equal the regional quota; regional quotas should sum to the national forecast. In actual practice, however, that is often not the case. If forecasts and quotas are developed at company headquarters and "imposed" on the sales organization without discussion, then quotas almost certainly will sum to the national forecast. It is when sales reps and their managers participate in quota-setting, a practice we have argued is highly desirable, that things become less straightforward.

In a typical sales organization, the quota-setting process might begin with an announcement from the national sales manager that the company's economic, financial, and marketing planning for next year calls for a 12% increase in sales revenue. Assumptions about the economy would be spelled out; new products and other significant marketing programs would be described. Field sales managers would pass this information on to their subordinates (lower-level managers and reps), asking them to review their markets and activities and to forecast sales in their territories and districts for the coming year. Information communicated from the national and regional offices at this stage would probably include year-to-date summaries of performance, by territory, district, region, and so on, to be compared with forecasts and quotas.

Each rep and field sales manager would likely begin his or her own analysis by comparing current-year performance-to-date with targets. The next step is to look ahead to the end of the current year and estimate how final results will look, and to draw some preliminary conclusions as to whether this year's goals were reasonable and accurate. The logical next step is to assess trends in the local market, such as customer activities and plans, changes in competition, and their impact on business. Finally, each person must come up with a "best-guess" forecast of the volume of business to be generated in his or her area of responsibility during the coming year. This process is highly interactive, with each person discussing the analysis and estimates with subordinates and superiors.

There are optimists and pessimists in any organization. In a sales organization, it is fair to assume that most people will tend to be optimistic—enthusiastic about prospects for the future and confident of their ability, and of their subordinates' abilities, to achieve ever-increasing levels of sales. The culture of selling and of sales organizations encourages this viewpoint; people assume that their managers expect them to be enthusiastic and optimistic. It shows they are interested in continued improvement and in the success of the firm. Therefore, one might assume that bottom-up forecasts of sales results, those that originate with the reps and their managers, will tend to be somewhat optimistic.

Unless, however, a significant share of compensation is tied directly to quota attainment. This significantly increases the degree of conservatism in those estimates. People want to increase their chances of earning the rewards associated with quota attainment. One argument, albeit not the major one, in favor of having some portion of sales compensation vary as a function of quota attainment is that it encourages better, more accurate forecasting on the part of normally optimistic sales reps and field sales managers.

An experienced sales manager develops a good sense of the relative optimism-pessimism of the people who report to him or her. That judgment, of course, gets communicated back to them in the iterative quota-setting process, and differences between the manager's and subordinate's assessments can become the basis for very productive discussions. The differences are likely to be narrowed as each party introduces and interprets information not readily available to the other. But a residual difference in estimates is likely to remain, especially about areas in which neither management nor the sales rep has much relevant experience. New products are a good example of this difficulty; no one can know with great certainty how customers will respond to new products. Management may forecast sales of new products based largely on what is needed to meet financial and production goals for the new product. The rep may estimate sales in the context of the risk of trading off sales of established products and the difficulties inherent in asking customers to try something new.

Such differences may not be resolved entirely. The national sales manager, for example, may put one estimate of sales in the financial plan and use a somewhat different basis for evaluating and rewarding the performance of regional sales managers, because the latter insisted on a set of regional quotas that were different. The field sales manager may decide that it is not worthwhile to impose his or her judgment on the reps. While there are practical reasons for leaving things this way, it also creates the potential for role ambiguity and conflict and future disagreement, and should be done, if at all, with caution and a clear awareness that there are discrepancies in the quota-forecasting system. With an eye to developing the sales rep or the field sales manager's forecasting abilities over time, the manager may opt to let the person "live with the forecast" for several months, expecting that it will get revised to a more realistic number as the year develops.

To conclude, the issue of whether or not quotas should equal the forecast is a complex one because of the inherent uncertainty in forecasting and because of the motivational considerations when reps and field managers participate in the forecasting process. At all levels of the organization, large quantities of judgment are required in quota-setting. How the issue is resolved will depend ultimately on the sales executive's management philosophy about the role of quotas and how to set them.

Types of Quotas

We have observed that there are many types of quotas. Dollar volume and unit sales quotas are undoubtedly the most common types. Other types of quotas concern profit margins, new accounts, sales calls, sales expenses, dealer enlistment, contract cancellations, promotional displays installed, and so on. In the multiple-product sales organization, separate quotas by product line are common.

What type of quota is best? The answer to the question depends primarily on management objectives for sales and marketing activity during the period, and on management's assessment of the role of the sales representative in the selling-buying process. How does the sales rep contribute to the actual sale? What is the relationship between sales effort and observable sales results? What priorities does management place on the various tasks performed by the sales rep? A few fundamental guidelines for resolving the question about type of quotas can be set forth.

First, sales reps should be evaluated and rewarded primarily on the basis of things they can control by their own actions and judgment. There should be a reasonably clear and direct relationship between the rep's activities and the performance measure used for evaluation. Depending on the product and the nature of the buying process, the rep may or may not be able to influence the mix of products sold and the profit margin derived on sales. It is worth remembering that product contribution margins often reflect rather arbitrary allocations, by accounting personnel, of costs shared among several products. In contrast, where sales reps have an active role in setting prices on orders, holding them responsible for profit margins would seem very sensible.

Second, quotas ought to be understandable to the reps. Not only does this relate to all the familiar arguments about role expectations, but also to the basic point that quotas should be seen as being reasonable. Quotas that are exceedingly complex (involving margin *vs* volume tradeoffs, for example), or that seem arbitrary instead of being based on careful analysis of sound information, will not be a strong driving force on sales rep motivation and performance.

Third, there should be, as already noted, a reasonably direct relationship between the exertion of effort by the sales rep and the achievement of the result referred to in the quota. The longer the lag time between the application of sales effort and the attainment of observable sales results, the less desirable are simple sales volume quotas as measures of sales rep performance. In these instances, activity quotas (e.g., number of calls, number of accounts, etc.) make more sense than do results quotas. Recall from the discussion of the expectancy model of sales rep motivation that the strength of a rep's motivation to expend effort on a sales task is determined by the strength of the perceived link between effort and the performance dimension being considered, as well as the perception of the relationship between performance and rewards and the attractiveness of those rewards. Viewed in this expectancy context, if the objective of a quota is to maximize sales force motivation, the type of quota selected should be that with the clearest, strongest perceived linkage to sales rep effort. Once the type of quota is chosen, it is the field sales manager's responsibility to help the rep develop a solid understanding of the linkages between sales tasks and performance outcomes.

Fourth, and this observation relates to the question of both *level* and *type* of quota, quotas should be attainable with reasonable amounts of effort. A simple as this sounds, it is not universally understood. There is a line of reasoning among a minority of sales managers that quotas should be set so high that each sales rep is stretched to the absolute limit of ability and effort, with only an outside chance at making the quota. The error in this line of reasoning is made clear by the expectancy model. To review the model, motivation is a function of expectancy, which is the rep's personal, subjective estimate of the probability that specified effort will produce a specific performance result, and of the valence of that performance dimension. Valence, in turn, is a function of instrumentality, the rep's personal, subjective estimate of the probability that achieving improved performance will lead to achieving a particular reward, and of the attractiveness of that reward to the individual rep. The key concepts here are the subjective probabilities, the rep's personal estimate of the strength and likelihood of the effort-performance-reward linkages. Excessively high quotas, or types of quotas that have very weak perceived linkages with effort, mean low probability estimates and therefore low motivation. To illustrate, imagine an industrial sales representative is given a quota to enroll four new distributors in the coming year, but is aware of at most two distributors that might consider switching lines from a competitor. The rep may conclude that, since the probability of this effort producing results is so low, the quota is meaningless. There will be little motivation to work to sign up new distributors. The quota will not be a motivator.

Against these general guidelines—quotas should be related to things reps can control, be understandable, be attainable, and should link effort and result—we can consider briefly the major strengths and weaknesses of the most common types of quotas.

Dollar Sales Quotas.   Dollar sales quotas have the great virtue of using a common metric across products and markets and of being consistent with the firm's normal accounting and management information systems. They are most desirable in those situations where the sales rep's overriding responsibility is to generate sales volume, and where there is a clear connection between sales effort and sales results, with other tasks being secondary. These are relatively easy to understand and can be justified by careful analysis of data such as measures of market potential or historical sales results. One reason for using dollar sales quotas is simply that they avoid the complexitites and ambiguities of other types of quotas. Dollar sales quotas permit the most straightforward comparison of sales performance across territories and the most direct analysis of selling expenses in relation to volume. Sales quotas also serve to coordinate sales and marketing activities with the firm's financial and operations (manufacturing, procurement, distribution, etc.) planning. It is probably a fair conclusion that dollar sales quotas are overwhelmingly the "quota of preference" and that a firm needs a very good reason *not* to have them.

Unit or Volume Sales Quotas.   Quotas are sometimes stated in terms of number of units or physical volume of the product to be sold; for example, number of computer systems, tank car loads of sulphuric acid, tons of low-density polyethylene resin, number of jet engines, and so on. Unit or volume quotas may be preferred to dollar sales quotas in instances where prices fluctuate considerably, as a function of market conditions or product specifications, and where the sales rep has little or no control over prices. Unit quotas become more common as the dollar value of the product and average transaction value increase. Unit or volume quotas have the advantage of neither penalizing nor rewarding the sales rep for major fluctuations in price, but they may also have the disadvantage of making the rep relatively indifferent to price. This shifts the burden for negotiating realistic prices on major contracts to other members of the sales and marketing team.

Margin Quotas. The sales reps and field sales managers may be held accountable for the profit contribution margin on their sales by means of margin quotas. Margin quotas may signify a firm that has moved from a production and sales orientation with its emphasis on sales volumes, toward a true marketing orientation with its emphasis on bottom-line profitability. The objective may be either to hold sales personnel responsible for prices, or for the mix of product sold, or both. Thus, if a sales rep is evaluated against a total-dollars-of-margin quota for the period, he or she will have to make judgments about whether or not to trim prices in order to make a sale, thereby facing the need to get additional sales in order to recapture the lost margin. Likewise, the rep may be willing to exert more effort on more expensive and harder-to-sell items in the product line if they have better margins and therefore will contribute more to the achievement of margin quotas. Margin quotas (or other types of quotas tying sales performance to financial criteria) are designed specifically to relate sales activity to financial objectives, especially where the sales rep does, in fact, have substantial influence—especially in terms of pricing and product mix.

There are a number of issues to consider whenever such quotas are used, and these issues raise a number of questions about this type of quota. The fundamental issue, really, is whether or not the sales rep should have to worry about financial performance, especially if product profit margins vary widely for reasons completely beyond the control of the rep. A related issue is whether or not the sales rep, indeed, has any significant influence on the mix of product sold, that is, on the mix of product demanded by customers. Should the sales rep try to influence the product mix that the customer buys? One can imagine margin quotas driving sales reps to emphasize a product mix less than optimally in tune with the customer's needs and preferences.

An implicit assumption in the use of margin quotas, usually, is that higher margin products are harder to sell. The validity of that assumption should always be checked.

In some cases, margin quotas are intended to force sales reps to worry more about sales expenses, that is, about the difference between revenue and sales costs. It is almost always easier, more straightforward, and more understandable, to control sales expense by relying on sales expense quotas *per se*, rather than tying them to margins. This would be especially true where prices also vary significantly—either under the sales rep's control or not. As a general rule, margin quotas of any kind tend to be complex, and therefore hard to understand and difficult to administer. There should be strong reasons for using them, given these difficulties. It may be more sensible to simply hold sales reps and field sales managers responsible for selling expenses *per se* rather than attempt to implement a system of margin quotas.

Activity Quotas. Activity quotas encompass two quite different types of quotas—those that govern effort and those that concern results. Effort quotas detail such measures of sales force activities as number of calls made, number of prospects identified and contacted, number of contract proposals written, and so on. This type of activity is a reasonable criterion for judging sales force performance when there is little direct relationship between effort expended and results achieved.

A second type of activity quota concerns results achieved, but that do not have a strong correlation with immediate sales results. Quotas for new accounts, new distributors signed up, promotional displays installed, and so on, tie sales force activity to specific results to be achieved, but stop short of sales revenue or unit volume measures. Activity quotas are preferred where specific goals for sales force performance are detailed by the marketing plan—for instance, to expand distribution, to broaden the customer base, or to increase customer awareness of the company and its products—but do not call for immediate increases in sales revenue or unit volume. Such intermediate sales goals can serve a very useful purpose in focusing sales effort when the buying and market development processes are complex and tend to be spread over several months or years. In these types of situations, it can be a mistake for the sales rep to make a premature attempt to close sales, generate major orders, and go for sales volume at the expense of developing customer and distributor relationships. Activity quotas can enhance sales force productivity by focusing sales effort on immediate, attainable results.

Two shortcomings of activity quotas are that they tend to focus on means, rather than ends, and that they impose significant reporting burdens on the sales organization. In the pursuit of activity quota attainment, the sales rep may spend too much time in "wheel spinning"—making calls for the sake of getting to the required numbers—without adequate concern for ultimate sales results. Likewise, to be sure that activity is accounted for and rewarded, sales reps and field sales managers may invest excessive amounts of energy to complete the necessary reports of sales calls and other activities. Activity quotas require frequent, careful checking of the validity of reports submitted, and are more difficult to administer than systems of sales quotas.

Whether or not to use activity quotas is a question best answered by reference to the firm's marketing and sales plans and by analysis of the nature of the buying process for its products or services. When a focus on immediate sales results is unreasonable because the buying process takes months or years, or because the firm is attempting to develop customers and markets where the immediate goals cannot be expressed in actual sales terms, then activity quotas are essential to direct and control sales force performance.

Weighting Systems. Weighting schemes are often introduced into quota systems to stimulate particular types of selling activity, usually for a brief period of time. The common element in such systems is that they weight specific types of results or activities unevenly in order to emphasize and reward particular kinds of effort. Usually, but not always, weighting systems are introduced as temporary modifications of existing quota systems. Probably the most common use of weighting schemes is to obtain additional selling effort on particular items within a product line by offering additional credit, in the form of multiples like 1.5 or 2.0 times normal dollar values for awarding credit toward quota attainment. New product introductions are often facilitated in this manner. Sometimes these systems take the form of points awards, with the featured products earning more point credits toward the sales quota, also expressed in terms of total points. Virtually any type of quota—dollar sales, unit or volume, margin, activity, or expense—can be modified by means of a weighting scheme designed to achieve particular emphasis from the sales organization. The major weaknesses of such weighting schemes are probably obvious—they can become complex and hard to understand and administer, and frequent adjustments to the basic plan can lead to confusion, role ambiguity, and loss of motivation. Weighting systems are not always temporary in nature, however. Different point values may be assigned to products with different profit margins, for example, in a type of margin quota.

In even more complex variations, weighting schemes may assign additional points or multiplier factors to sales results once sales on each of several products reaches a specified level. For example, assume three product lines—A, B, and C. Sales credit for the rep might be earned according to the formula 1.25 x (A + B + C) if the rep achieves quota on each of the three product lines. Such weighting schemes are intended to achieve balanced selling across product lines.

Combination Plans. More than one type of quota may be used in a sales organization—dollar sales, activity, and expense quotas, for example. The purpose in most instances is simply to try to avoid overemphasis on a single aspect of sales performance.[2] If only dollar sales quotas are used, for instance, the concern may be that sales reps (and their managers) may overlook such other areas of their responsibilities as profit margin, servicing, gathering market information, and developing new accounts.

When more than one type of quota is used, there is a higher risk of role conflict and ambiguity. The sales rep may feel that the different quotas make competing demands on their time and are unreasonable. If only one type of quota in a combination plan is tied directly to compensation whereas the others are not, the latter may be ignored. One common attempt to solve this aspect of the problem is to combine all quotas into a summary measure, using weights to assign management priorities to each element of the sales task, and to tie compensation to this summary measure.

[2]Allan Easton, "A Forward Step in Performance Evaluation," *Journal of Marketing,* Vol. 30 (July 1966), pp. 26–32.

An alternative method of controlling sales effort and performance that may be administered more easily than a combination of quotas is simply a management-by-objectives system in which the rep consults with the field sales manager, sets qualitative and quantitative goals relating to several performance dimensions, and subsequently has performance evaluated in a review session using multiple criteria. Such specific management direction, evaluation, and control may be more effective than reliance on the mechanics of a quota system.

Qualitative Evaluation

Many of the most important responsibilities of field sales representatives and sales managers cannot be quantified easily. These call for subjective assessments, but that does not mean that they should be casual, unplanned, or arbitrary. The field sales manager and the job description are the major sources of role expectations for the sales rep. Annual, semiannual, or quarterly planning and review sessions with each rep should be scheduled by the field sales manager, with the purpose being to set priorities and evaluation guidelines for the coming period. Such activities as working on technical product specifications on major customer procurements, developing new relationships with potential customers, doing a detailed analysis of a major market segment, training junior sales personnel, or creating a data base on the sales territory are not only terribly important to the effectiveness of sales operations but also in the development of the sales rep as a rep and as a potential field sales manager. If such qualitative activities are not planned carefully and evaluated, they are likely to be given inadequate attention under the day-to-day pressure to "make the numbers" in the sales quotas.

Likewise, the field sales manager must be held accountable for the accomplishment of these less easily measured objectives and tasks. An assessment of the care with which the manager plans and conducts these planning and evaluation sessions with the field sales representatives should be part of the periodic evaluation of the manager. In all instances, it is important that the understandings reached in these sessions be put into writing, for future reference and follow-up and to be sure that both parties have a common perception of the performance guidelines that will be used in evaluation at a later date.

OBTAINING INFORMATION ON PERFORMANCE

The second phase of the control process, after setting performance standards, is to gather information with which to assess performance against those standards. Professional sales management requires that performance appraisal be based primarily upon objective, factual, accurate, and thorough information, not upon subjective assessments, personal opinion, and hearsay evidence. Any company large enough to have its own field sales organization is likely to have a management information system that is adequate to provide, routinely, summary data on sales force activity, sales results, and the development of individuals within the sales organization. The sales manager also can obtain information for evaluating performance by direct observation and from the sales reps themselves, as well as from customers, distributors, and other members of the selling organization, such as applications engineers or field service personnel, who work with the sales reps and field sales managers on an ongoing basis.

Measuring sales performance is a relatively easy task compared with the more fundamental problem of trying to understand the causes of sales performance, both good and bad. Once again we can refer to the complex model of sales force effectiveness that has guided the development of our view of sales management. Performance results reflect not only the sales rep's ability, motivation, and role perceptions, but also the characteristics of the territory, the quality of the field sales manager, the nature of individual customers and buyer–seller relationships, and the specific impact of marketing programs on that customer set. Performance results may be assessed by means of activity reports prepared by the sales reps, by examining summary data from the firm's order processing and accounting systems, by direct observation of the rep's work in the field, and in the formal performance appraisal process.

Activity Reporting

Most companies require their sales reps to make regular reports on their activities. In some cases, each call on a customer or dealer is reported as a separate event. This would make sense where each customer or dealer accounts for a significant volume of sales activity and where relatively few calls are made each day. In these instances, rather detailed information about the customer or dealer may be requested, including business pending, any major shifts in personnel, the status of promotional programs, rates of product usage, service problems, and so on.

Summaries of call activities may be requested on a daily or weekly basis, requiring less specific and detailed information about individual customers or dealers than in the case of individual call reports. (See Figure 7.1.) Summary reports have the advantage of reducing the amount of "unproductive," non-selling time required of the rep for completing reports, and may be more than adequate for management's information needs. In many instances, in fact, management may have little use for detailed call reports, simply filing them away in an ever-expanding collection of expensive-to-gather-and-maintain, but relatively useless, data. Very little effective management control is obtained by the reporting process *per se*, that is by simply forcing reps to report regularly. The argument that requiring sales reps to report each call exercises discipline over them and "keeps them honest" isn't terribly convincing. Sales reps will soon catch on to the fact that reports are not being given careful consideration by management and will stop reporting in anything more than perfunctory fashion. Requiring reports on a less frequent basis may be a better way of obtaining information and avoiding the problems of information overload.

In some instances, activity reports are combined with expense reports, which the rep must submit regularly in order to obtain reimbursement for out-of-pocket expenditures. Expense reports serve, obviously, as a means to control selling expenses. Beyond that, however, they also indicate selling activity in terms of such measures as number of customers entertained, number of miles driven, number of nights away from home, and so on. While such measures can be useful, they really do not reveal anything about the substance or quality of the selling activity—problems defined and resolved, programs pending with customers, attendance at sales presentations, buying intentions, and so on. In the opinion of most, expense reports are best viewed as a supplement to, not a substitute for, sales activity reports.

KING—WAY WEEKLY CALL REPORTS

The Kingston—Warren Corp., Newfields, NH 03856

Region _____

Sales Manager _____

Week Ending _____

Page ____ of ____

Date	Dealer and Location	Contacts	Customer and Location	Contacts	Comments

Figure 7.1. A sales representative's call report for the **Kingston-Warren Company.**

Order Processing and Accounting System Data—Sales Analysis

Sales results are recorded in the firm's order processing and management/financial accounting systems. Sales records usually are maintained by customer, territory (sales representative), and product. For any period, it is usually possible for the accounting system to answer the question "How much (in dollars) of product X did sales rep A sell to customer N?" Summary statistics can be provided for every customer, territory, and product. The term *sales analysis* typically is used to describe the analysis and use of such data by sales management for sales force evaluation and control.

The most basic analysis that uses sales data considers performance in comparison with quotas, changes in activity, and results compared with the prior reporting period. Ratios such as percentage of quota to date, expenses-to-sales, sales as a percentage of market potential, average order size, current-year-to-previous-year sales results, and so on, can be generated rather easily and used by management to assess individual performance as well as to identify problems and trends that may require management attention.

The most productive use of such analysis is probably not in coming to final conclusions about what is good or bad, right or wrong, about a sales area's performance, but rather as a basis for a discussion with the sales rep or the district manager about business conditions in the territory or district. The manager needs to understand the reasons for the performance results revealed by the sales analysis, reasons that often do not reveal themselves directly in the data on performance. On the other hand, there is no substitute for hard, factual data as the basis for having a productive conversation about performance, selling problems, conditions in the territory, and the sales rep's personal development.

Personal Observation

A good field sales manager spends a major portion of his or her time in the territories, working with the sales reps. These work-with sessions have a number of purposes relating to the development of the rep and to evaluation and control, as well as supporting the customer relationship with a management presence. Only rarely is it legitimate to see the work-with session as an opportunity for the sales manager to take over the relationship with a customer and to solve a problem that the rep couldn't solve alone. As stated in Chapter 2, the underlying purpose of every supervisory contact should be to develop, educate, and train the sales rep, to make the rep independent and more able to solve problems alone. Solving problems for the rep in the work-with session will, in contrast, make the rep more dependent on the manager, increasing the likelihood that the manager will again be called on to solve similar problems when they occur.

Important information about the sales rep's performance can be obtained in the work-with session, information having to do with matters of planning, organization, and style, that will not be revealed in activity reports and sales accounting data. The experienced field sales manager will be able to spot subtle but important aspects of the rep's selling activity that have an impact on performance, positive and negative, highlighting and encouraging the positive while pointing out and correcting the negative.

A single work-with session may not provide adequate time for complete information gathering, analysis, and corrective action. The sales manager may want several such sessions before coming to strong conclusions, and may find it advisable to postpone serious discussion of observed strengths and weaknesses until a formal performance review session is planned.

To assist field sales managers in their use of personal observation as part of the performance appraisal process, some firms provide them with rating forms. While formal and somewhat mechanical approaches to performance appraisal can always be criticized, a small amount of training for the manager in how to use such systems intelligently and flexibly can help the manager develop a professional approach to the appraisal process. The use of a rating form has two principal advantages—it insures thoroughness and it permits the comparison of sales personnel on a common set of performance criteria judged to be important, countering potential personal biases of the evaluator. These common evaluation criteria can deal with aspects of performance not only related to immediate sales results but also to the long-term development of the individual as a sales representative and as a potential field sales manager. Another advantage of a formal rating system is that it results in a more permanent, written record relating to the individual's development, especially important when experienced field sales managers are reassigned or leave the company, taking their memories with them. Formal rating systems cannot completely eliminate the manager's personal biases, however, and they are subject to substantial *halo effect*, the tendency for the evaluator to give the rep consistently high or low ratings on all aspects of performance, rather than considering each criterion objectively.

Among the many characteristics that could be potentially interesting for observation of sales rep's performance, company experience tends to highlight the following: knowledge of products, customers, and competition; degree of customer acceptance; quality of call planning and routing schedules; development of selling skills; personal appearance; understanding and obeying company policies; timely completion of call reports and other reporting requirements; and willingness to accept and act upon the supervisor's suggestions. Whenever possible, objective, observable behavioral chracteristics should be emphasized when the manager gathers data on performance through personal observation. Some companies ask their field sales managers to rate sales representatives on such characteristics as judgment, resourcefulness, imagination, persistence, sociability, cooperativeness, stability, and sensitivity to others. Granted that these are significant and desirable aspects of a rep's performance, they are hard to define, measure, and judge in another person. If such judgments are called for, they should be treated carefully and given secondary emphasis.

Surveys of Customers and Dealers

As part of the sales rep performance appraisal process, some firms gather data from the rep's customers and dealers. Such information can be gathered by the field sales manager on an informal basis during field trips or it can be gathered more systematically through a telephone or mail survey, perhaps guided by a formal questionnaire or interview guide. There are a number of problems with such formal procedures, including the fact that they are time-consuming and expensive to administer. Customers and dealers may not be in a good position to evaluate a sales rep. There is the basic question of whom in the customer or dealer organization to contact, and that person's particular biases with respect to the selling organization and its representatives. The respondent's motivations in providing an evaluation of the rep are likely to be quite complex. While customers, and dealers to some extent, are theoretically the ultimate judges of all marketing and sales activities, that is different from saying that they are the best judges of sales representatives' performance and potential.

The field sales manager is in the best position to observe and solicit, casually, customers' and dealers' opinions about the quality of the sales rep's interactions with them. Assessing the quality of the buyer–seller relationship requires sophisticated and subtle judgments and insightful understanding of the complexities of the buying–selling process. An experienced and well-trained field sales manager can make those judgments based on careful observation. When sales management decides that it needs a formal survey of customer or dealer attitudes to evaluate sales rep performance, it is implicitly concluding that its field sales managers have not been developed and managed properly, and that it is willing to settle for data about the quality of buyer–seller relationships that are relatively "cold."

The Performance Appraisal Session

Most large, well-managed organizations require all supervisors to meet with their subordinates regularly (at least annually and usually more frequently) for the specific purpose of evaluating their performance and setting goals for the subordinate's development and performance during the coming period. Among the many elements of such sessions is the continued gathering of information about performance, especially the rep's perceptions and personal assessment of his or her performance, feelings about its adequacy, causes for deviations from plan, and so on. Objective data, from records and observation, are reviewed with the sales rep, checked for accuracy, and fed back to the rep so that the objective facts about actual performance are understood clearly.

The performance appraisal session, even more than work-with sessions, provides the major opportunity for the sales rep to furnish information about role perceptions and expectations, attitudes toward the job, and other subjective data about performance. It is essential that the performance review session be regarded as a chance to gather such information, not simply as the time when the field sales manager "lays it on the line" for the rep. In other words, the sales supervisor must consciously attempt to elicit such information from the rep and must carefully listen, as part of the appraisal process. A good starting point is always to ask the rep how he or she views the period's performance and results. What were the major satisfactions and disappointments? Were personal goals met? Were there unanticipated developments?

In the performance appraisal session, the field sales manager must also attempt to probe for causes of good and bad performance, as evidenced by deviations from goals and plans.

COMPARING PERFORMANCE
AGAINST STANDARDS

The major reasons for establishing standards for performance were said to be providing direction for field sales effort and setting clear criteria against which performance can be assessed objectively. Prior to meeting with the sales rep to evaluate performance, the field sales manager should complete a thorough review of performance data against quotas and other standards, as well as against goals established for the current period's performance in the previous performance appraisal session. This will insure an efficient session, one focused on specific areas of performance and dealing with solid data and defensible conclusions. Major variations of performance from predetermined standards should be identified and examined carefully.

As a result of field trips, personal observation, discussions with customers and dealers, review of market conditions and competition, and ongoing interaction with the sales representative, the field sales manager should be able to develop some reasonably strong conclusions about the reasons for variances between performance and goals. These reasons should be reviewed and discussed with the rep in the performance review session as a prelude to deciding upon steps to be taken to correct problems and bring performance back into line with standards.

TAKING CORRECTIVE ACTION

Bringing performance into line with objectives and plans is the "payoff" step in the evaluation and control process. To do so, the field sales manager has several areas of activity to consider, several possible courses of action.

As a supervisor, the field sales manager's primary function is that of providing counsel, direction, and support. A first step is to be certain that the sales representative has a complete and accurate set of role perceptions. The field sales manager must be continually alert to areas where role perceptions are inaccurate or ambiguous, and must be sure that the rep understands the job description, current sales and marketing plans and programs, and the manager's own expectations for the rep's performance, especially as formalized in quotas and other targets.

The continued development of the sales rep's abilities, attitudes toward the job, and work motivation is the principal responsibility of the field sales manager. The rep must be provided with ongoing opportunities to develop his or her knowledge of products, customers, markets, and the company, as well as basic skills including selling skills and analytical and decision-making skills. Part of the rep's continued development should be the opportunity to test his or her interest in supervision and management, through exposure to special assignments, and to develop the administrative, supervisory, planning, and analytical abilities relevant for management responsibilities.

Redeployment is a second area to consider in looking for ways to improve sales performance. By changing work assignments and shifting the pattern of territory assignments within the district, the field sales manager has the opportunity to better match the capabilities and potentials of individual reps with the characteristics of customers and market segments. Some reps can handle more work while others might benefit from a reduced assignment. These reassignments of responsibility, of course, should be reflected in adjustments in quotas and other performance objectives and standards.

Another area to examine for corrective action is the resource base, the number of sales reps, the size of the promotional budget, the extent of distribution, and so on. If several reps have not made quota, for example, this could lead to a conclusion that fewer reps are needed and territories should be larger. The first-line field sales manager will need to work with higher levels of sales management to get such changes approved and accomplished, and the need for changing the resource base must be well documented by careful analysis of market and competitive conditions. Plans for executing the desired changes must be worked out in detail and budgeted. Continued development and refinement of the sales organization, and redeployment of resources, is an integral part of the sales manager's responsibility. As sales reps are promoted, reassigned to other areas, or leave the company, their replacements must be recruited, trained, and assigned. Annual turnover in the sales organization of 10% or more is expected in most companies, so the human resource base must be renewed continually, even in a firm experiencing little economic growth.

Even if the size of the resource base is adequate for the work to be done, issues of quality may be identified in evaluation of performance. New training programs may be called for to address problems of sales force efficiency and effectiveness. Additional first-level sales supervisors and sales trainers may allow for significant improvements in sales rep performance.

The final step in taking corrective action is to establish new goals and expectations for the sales rep, which brings us back to the first step in the control process—setting performance standards. The outcome of the performance review process should not be limited to an understanding about quotas and sales performance objectives, however. It also should include specific goals for the sales rep's personal development as well as work assignments related to account and territory development—for example, a specified number of prospects to be developed, number of calls to be made, market studies to be completed, product knowledge to be developed. The most important outcome from this exercise should be the renewed psychological state of the sales rep—a new set of personal goals and aspirations, a clear set of role perceptions, a stronger sense of personal motivation to do the work, and a clear understanding of the linkages between effort and performance and between performance and rewards. For the field sales manager, the outcome should likewise be a deeper and more complete awareness of the needs, goals, aspirations, and capabilities of the sales rep and a renewed commitment to help that individual develop and achieve to the best of his or her abilities.

COMPENSATION: THE REWARD SYSTEM

Sales compensation is perhaps the most controversial area in the study of sales force management. Many strong opinions are held on such issues as fixed *vs* variable (incentive) pay, the proper relationship between income and quota achievement, whether to reward effort or results, and so on.

Traditional treatments of the sales compensation problem have tended to consider it in relative isolation from such other decision areas as deployment, supervision, evaluation, and control. Furthermore, most discussions of sales compensation tend to view the sales representative essentially as an individual contributor, to see sales performance as solely determined by the personal characteristics and behavior of the individual rep. In this context, the purpose of sales compensation is seen primarily as that of stimulating the sales rep to work as hard as possible by linking sales and profit maximization to income maximization.

The central theme of this book has been that sales rep effectiveness and sales results are the product of a complex interaction of many factors including buyer–seller interaction, the field sales manager, territory characteristics, and company marketing and sales policies and programs as well as the sales rep's role perceptions, motivation, and ability. The subject of sales compensation must be examined against the background of this more complex view of the determinants of sales rep effectiveness. The net result is probably to diminish the importance of sales compensation as a cause or explanation for sales performance, or at least to see financial rewards as only one of many factors exerting significant influence on sales force motivation and sales results. As evidenced by the organization of this chapter, I believe it is important to view the compensation system not as an isolated element but as an integral part of sales force planning, deployment, evaluation, and control. The view of sales rep motivation presented in Chapter 6 saw the effect of compensation as mediated by the sales rep's perceptions of the linkages between rewards and performance, linkages between performance and effort, and the rep's role perceptions. Furthermore, those role perceptions have connections back to supervision and sales management policies, and performance reflects ability as well as motivation.

ESTABLISHING COMPENSATION OBJECTIVES

From a theoretical perspective, the objective of the sales compensation system should be to provide a set of rewards with clear linkages to sales results and the sales rep's role performance, so that sales force motivation and the sales results are maximized. The complexity of the sales compensation problem comes partly from the fact that there may be a long time lag, and a weak and hard-to-measure link between effort exerted by the sales rep and actual sales results. That is, the customer's buying decision process may take place over a long period of time and may involve many different people. The selling effort may involve many sales calls at several different buying locations. Multiple marketing influences, including product features, engineering and service support, pricing, and so on, interact with the efforts of one or more sales representatives and field sales managers. This is why the view of the sales rep as an individual contributor, and of a compensation system that causes sales to happen by maximizing sales rep motivation, is inadequate for analyzing the issue of sales force compensation.

The fundamental question in thinking about how to pay the sales reps concerns the relationship between sales effort and sales results. It takes us back to the basic issue of defining the role of the sales representative in the context of overall marketing strategy. The issue is whether to link rewards to effort or results, or more practically speaking, the extent to which pay should be tied to each aspect of performance—work done (effort expended) and results achieved, the latter reflecting many influences in addition to the sales rep's personal efforts.

The point of this discussion is certainly not to absolve the sales rep of all responsibility for sales results. Even when the sales rep's direct influence is hard to trace, it is still the sales rep who has primary responsibility for organizing the other elements of the marketing mix and directing them at the customer's buying problem and the buying situation. We have said that selling is not something that the sales rep does to the customer, and that the outcome of the sales interaction is a function of more than the rep's personal characteristics and behavior. In the more complex view of selling as buyer–seller interaction, with negotiation as the core influence process, the sales rep still carries the burden of responsibility for the entire account relationship.

Compensation is both a stimulus and a reward for effective sales effort. The pay package is a major attraction for people to join the sales organization, a source of incentives to do the job as outlined in the job description and by sales management, and a source of rewards that influence job satisfaction.

At a general level of analysis, any sales compensation system has five objectives:

1. To attract and retain sales representatives with the necessary abilities and background of education and experience.
2. To secure job performance consistent with the job description.
3. To obtain maximum sales results.
4. To reward job performance equitably.
5. To control selling expenses.

Developing more specific objectives for the sales compensation system of a particular company requires, as noted, a careful analysis of the role of the sales representative (i.e., the job description), the nature of the buying decision process and buyer–seller interaction, and a consideration of specific marketing and sales objectives. Thus, specific compensation objectives might include:

1. To obtain new accounts and increase market share.
2. To secure more balanced selling effort across the product line.
3. To focus selling effort on more profitable products (or market segments).
4. To achieve stronger team effort among sales reps and sales districts.

The design of a sales compensation system is a responsibility of top sales and marketing management, but the field sales manager has an important part to play in providing input to compensation system planning and modification, in critical evaluation of the system, and in its ongoing administration. To be an effective administrator of the system, the field manager must understand the system's objectives and its underlying philosophy.

THE SALES COMPENSATION SYSTEM

Designing and administering a sales compensation system calls for two basic decisions—the method by which sales reps will be paid and the level of their compensation. This discussion will be concerned only with the first question—how to pay sales reps. The question of level or "how much?" is a question of administering the system and knowing what market conditions are for sales talent of the caliber needed by the firm.

A sales compensation system has one or more of three types of pay—salary or fixed income; commissions or pay tied directly to the level of sales or quota attainment; and bonus, a variable element tied to some element of sales performance but not in strict relationship to sales results. Each type of compensation has a particular role to play. Two or even all three types of compensation usually are found in a given company's sales compensation system.

Salary

Salary is a fixed wage and can be paid weekly, biweekly, or monthly. It rewards the sales rep for performing the work defined by the job description, including both selling and non-selling functions. There is little incentive value to salary, except that adjustments in salary are likely to be tied to the results of performance appraisal. A sales rep who only minimally meets the manager's expectations and fails to achieve quotas for sales volume, expense control, and activity, and who fails to complete assigned projects would likely receive little or no increase in salary for the coming period. But the salary decided for the period under review would be paid regardless of actual performance.

Straight salary, without commissions or bonus, is most likely to be used where there is only a weak connection between the sales rep's effort and current sales results, and where non-selling activities such as customer service are an important part of the sales rep's total responsibility. This would be the case, for example, with large ticket capital equipment items where the buying decision process takes months or years. The sales rep can focus effort on activities and projects in the best long-term interest of the company rather than scrambling to maximize current period results and income.

Salary compensation gives management maximum control over the activities of the sales force. The sales rep's income will be maximized, over the long run, by doing the best job for management as defined by the job description and marketing and sales plans. When management directs the reps' efforts toward such activities as new account prospecting, new product introduction, market development, gathering market information, and completing written reports, the rep who is paid a salary does not face the conflict of giving up sales volume and therefore income, as would be the case with incentive compensation.

Management control is the major reason for using salary for sales compensation, and the compensation plan may be a critical tool for linking selling effort to long-range marketing strategy.

A major virtue of salary-only plans is that they are easy to understand and to administer. Salary also offers a degree of stability and predictability to selling expense. Management can forecast sales expense with virtual certainty with a salary-only system. The sales rep likewise gains income security and does not face the anxiety of not knowing what income will actually be, which can be a real problem with incentive plans, especially for reps who must support large families or who have other major financial obligations. Salary-only compensation can enhance job loyalty and reduce sales force turnover.

The major issue with salary-only plans is the lack of direct financial incentive to the sales rep to produce current sales results. While a careful performance appraisal process combined with a strong quota system can tie salary income increments to actual sales performance, the link is not a strong as with a commission paid on sales results. Some sales representatives undoubtedly are attracted to sales careers by the opportunity to earn income tied directly to performance, and find challenge and satisfaction in an incentive compensation system. For these people, a salary-only plan would be a negative feature of the sales job. For others, however, who cannot tolerate great uncertainty about income level, salary can enhance the attractiveness of a sales representative's position.

Commissions

Sales commissions are payments tied directly to sales volume. There is an almost infinite variety of commission plans, however. Commissions may be expressed as a percentage of sales revenue or as a dollar amount tied to units sold. They may be based on dollar sales volume, on percentage of quota attainment, or on profit margins. It is not uncommon for a company to pay different commission rates on different products, depending on their profitability or how difficult they are to sell. Commission rates may be *fixed*—constant for the entire range of sales volume; *regressive*—decreasing as sales volume increases (to prevent excessive, windfall payments); or *progressive*—increasing as sales volume increases, on the assumption that each increment in volume is harder to achieve. A fixed rate is easiest to administer and easiest for the sales rep to understand. Income can be calculated at any time by simply multiplying the commission rate times the value of orders written. Variable commission rates are harder to understand and administer, and can weaken the perceived links between effort, results, and income. Commission plans can become very complex.

When commissions are the dominant or only form of sales compensation, the company is most likely to attract the professional "persuasive" sales rep, the supersalesman type. Commission plans are most appropriate when actual selling is the rep's only major duty and where there is a clear link between sales effort and results. Commission plans provide maximum financial incentive for the sales rep. The lack of income security for the rep can be at least partially overcome by adding a *draw*, or drawing account, feature to the commission plan, which will guarantee a minimum regular payment to the rep against which earned sales commissions will be credited. Company practice varies widely in the management of the draw option. In some cases, any deficit in the earned commissions is forgiven at the end of the operating period, giving the commission plan some of the features of a salary plan.

Commission plans have the advantage of tying selling expense directly to sales volume, making selling a completely variable expense item. This can be especially important in industries that experience major fluctuations in sales volume, but it also contributes to high turnover and a reduced sense of company loyalty in the sales force.

Straight commission plans afford management little control over the activities of the sales reps. They are relatively rare in industrial selling organizations. Their use is likely to be accompanied by relatively little attention to training, field supervision, evaluation, and control. Commission reps are free to do whatever they wish to maximize sales volume.

Bonus

Bonus is a term covering a variety of special-purpose types of payments to sales reps. Bonus is always combined with either salary or commission payments, or both. Typically, a bonus is a single lump sum payment earned at the end of the pay period; the amount of the bonus is tied to a specific aspect of performance, such as quota or profitability. The amount of the bonus often is not determined until operating results are finally known, which may be months after the close of the period.

Bonuses are often used to reward team performance, as opposed to individual results. Thus, a bonus may be paid to all reps in a district if the total district achieves quota. Or the bonus may be determined by total company profitability, reflecting the efforts of the total organization to produce sales volume and control expenses. Bonuses are a major tool for encouraging team effort and cooperation and can create a strong sense of common purpose and organizational loyalty. Among the most common uses of bonuses are to encourage expense control, to help introduce new products, to stimulate the development of new accounts, or to encourage special effort to achieve short-term gains in sales performance such as increases in market share or percentage increases in territory sales over previous periods.

A major shortcoming of bonuses in sales compensation has to do with their unpredictability, which can reduce their incentive value because of the weak link between individual effort and reward. Bonuses are best used for special purposes, as described, and for stimulating group effort, not as a reward for individual effort. They can encourage teamwork and cooperation among sales reps, especially valuable when customer buying decisions overlap territory boundaries and where senior sales reps are asked to lend support and help to develop their less-experienced colleagues.

Combination Plans

Compensation plans that combine salary with bonus, commission, or both are the most common, as management seeks to achieve the benefits of each—the control over sales reps' activities afforded by salary, the incentive value of commissions based on sales results, and the teamwork and special efforts encouraged by bonuses. Combination plans may be criticized for being more complex and more difficult to understand, but these concerns are often more than balanced by their benefits in relating compensation more directly to the various parts of the sales rep's total responsibility. They can also offset some of the disadvantages of single-method payment plans, thus providing the incentive lacking in salary-only plans and building the income security and job loyalty that straight commission plans cannot provide. Salary and bonus elements both help to gain management control over sales force activity, and to relate selling effort directly to implementation of marketing programs.

Better integration of marketing planning and sales activities may be reflected in some reported trends in sales compensation. An estimated two thirds of all manufacturing firms now use some type of combination plan. Straight commission plans are least common (roughly 10% of manufacturers), with an estimated 20–30% using straight salary. One study showed straight salary decreasing from 38% of all plans reporting in 1975 to only 31% in 1980, with salary-plus-commission moving from 24% to 25%, and salary-plus-incentive (bonus) increasing from 24% to 34%. Other types of plans, including straight commission and salary plus commission plus incentive (bonus), increased from 20% to 25%.[3] These data might be interpreted to provide evidence that management is moving away from the simple notion of sales representatives as individual contributors and toward a view of them as members of a total marketing team.

Contests and Other Special Incentive Programs

Sales organizations are somewhat notorious for the regular use of special incentive programs to achieve additional sales effort, to stimulate sales force motivation and morale, and to accomplish specific marketing objectives such as new product introduction, expanding distribution, enlisting new accounts, and so on. Sometimes these programs involve bonuses of the kind just described. At other times, they are more in the form of a sales contest with merchandise, travel awards, special recognition, or other forms of reward rather than additional financial compensation. Despite some inherent problems, which we will define and discuss, sales contests and incentive programs play an important role in many sales compensation systems.

The central feature of a sales contest is that earning an award is contingent on a particular outcome—achievement of a specific objective such as selling so many units, finishing first in a rank ordering of sales reps, or obtaining the maximum number of new accounts. Contests tend to cover a brief period of time, such as a month or a quarter. They often are intended to be a general morale booster, as well as

[3]"Compensation: A Cooling Off for Cold Cash," *Sales and Marketing Management,* March 16, 1981, pp. 15–16.

to achieve specific performance objectives, and contest themes are often picked to convey a notion of competition and excitement. The contest theme might feature an exotic travel destination, or use a sports analogy, or commemorate an anniversay in the development of the company.

There are a number of potential inequities in sales contests that can be defined in general terms here, but that must be considered in the context of a specific sales organization when actively designing a special incentive program. Ideally, every rep should have an equal opportunity to win a contest, but that is inherently impossible given differences among reps and territory assignments. It is often argued that sales contests become ineffective with repeated use because they are always won by the same people. One way of coping with this issue is to attempt to set targets that are tailored to each individual's previous sales record, experience, and ability. As a practical matter, that is hard to do fairly.

Another inherent difficulty is to select contest awards that have equal attractiveness (valence, or reward value) for all participants. The perceived value of merchandise or travel awards in particular is highly variable as a function of the rep's interests and personal situation. A fully paid trip to football's Super Bowl may be worth virtually nothing to one rep and highly prized by another. One solution is to offer, at the option of the winner, cash awards of equal value. There is always the issue of whether or not to include the expense of a spouse's travel in any travel award. If it is done, the question arises how to treat an unmarried winner. If it is not, the winner may be forced to spend hundreds or thousands of dollars of his or her own money in order to take advantage of the award won.

One of the most troublesome features of contests is the element of luck. It is highly undesirable to have the final contest outcome determined by chance, as when the names of, say, the five reps who performed best in achieving contest objectives have their names drawn at random to determine the awarding of five differently valued prizes. Such methods are inherently unfair, and destroy the desired linkages among efforts, results, and rewards which are the essential feature of incentive programs.

There is also the nagging question of whether it helps or hinders morale to have sales representatives actually competing with one another. Some argue that the innate competitiveness of sales professionals is well served by pitting them against one another. A stronger argument can be made in favor of having reps competing against a common standard rather than against each another. This criterion would favor a contest, for example, in which all people who exceeded quota by x% received an award, rather than a contest in which the top n reps were rewarded. Taking all these potential issues into account, however, sales contests and other forms of special incentives can effectively supplement the normal sales compensation system if carefully designed to insure that every sales rep has a reasonable opportunity to win.

DESIGNING THE COMPENSATION SYSTEM

How can sales management go about designing a combination of salary, commissions, bonus, and other forms of incentive that will optimally meet the company's unique requirements? A general framework for approaching the task can be outlined briefly. Folllowing that, we will consider a few issues of implementation that are generic to sales compensation programs.

The starting point for designing a sales force compensation system is to list the sales representative's job activities and responsibilities as given by the job description. It is important to make clear the specific performance measurement criterion that is to be used to judge the performance of each activity or responsibility. The importance of each activity/responsibility in terms of the proportion of the rep's time to be spent on it must be judged by the managers doing the compensation analysis, if it is not stated explicitly in the job description. The next judgment called for is whether or not that activity is most appropriately compensated with salary, commission, or bonus, considering the major benefits and limitations of each type of compensation as outlined in the previous section of this chapter. These judgments about the importance of each job element and how it should be compensated can be combined to yield an estimate of the portion of the rep's total compensation that should consist of each element.[4] The re-

---

[4] "For a somewhat different approach to this planning process, which begins with a review of a compensation plan already in place, see Bruce R. Ellig, "Sales Compensation: A Systematic Approach," *Compensation Review*, Vol. 14, No. 1 (First quarter, 1982), pp. 21–45.

sults of this analysis might be combined in a simple framework as follows:

Activity	Compensation Element			
	Salary	Commission	Bonus	Total
1. Making sales calls on assigned customers, to achive quota	30%	20%	0	50%
2. Prospecting for new accounts	10	0	0	10
3. Servicing existing business	10	0	0	10
4. Reporting market information and selling activities	5	0	0	5
5. Controlling expenses	0	0	10%	10
6. Working with new reps	10	0	5	15

These percentages can be multiplied by a target income figure for the sales rep. That target income figure, which should reflect the market value of the rep and his or her value to the firm, is the total income from salary, commissions, and bonus that this particular rep should earn if quota is achieved exactly and if bonus program objectives are met. It is obvious that a sound quota-setting system is absolutely essential as the core around which to build a sound compensation plan. Every new or modified sales compensation system can be tested on paper by using it to recalculate sales reps' incomes using historical data. The test should examine how the new compensation plan would have worked under those historical conditions—how selling expenses would have been affected, how individual incomes would have fared, and whether certain districts or individuals would have been at a disadvantage. Such a test might suggest the need to modify the percentage breakdown among salary, commission, and bonus, or to change the relationship between commission payments and quota attainment. It might also identify sales reps who would have been significantly over- or underpaid. The reasons the new plan produces these results must be analyzed in detail and the necessary modifications made.

The level or amount of a sales representative's compensation must be decided by the first-line manager, usually in consultation with the next level of sales management. Such judgments are always difficult but they must be made and, as noted earlier, must reflect the sales rep's value to the firm and in the marketplace. Seniority by itself is not a reason for a pay increase, but senior sales reps have more experience, which should enhance their value to the firm. There is a complex set of issues concerning the level of sales reps' compensation compared with field sales managers and other executives. It is often true that some superb experienced sales representatives may have total incomes that meet or exceed those of the top levels of company management. That may not necessarily be bad, if the rep turns in outstanding performance and is a critical element in the success of the total organization.

SOME ISSUES OF IMPLEMENTATION

The critical issues in implementation and administration of a sales force compensation system involve maintaining a proper relationship between the quota-setting process and the compensation system, providing consistent and timely appraisal of sales rep performance, and creating levels of compensation that fairly reflect the value of the rep in the market and to the employer. In addition, there are some questions that are peculiar to sales compensation that need to be addressed.

First, there is the issue of when the sale is credited to the rep—when it is written, accepted by the company, scheduled for production, shipped, installed, or paid for by the customer. Most commonly, a sale is assumed to be complete when the company's credit department approves the order and it is entered into the firm's order-processing system. Problems arise when there is a long production and delivery cycle and when order cancellations by customers or dealers are not uncommon. One solution is to pay part of a commission when the order is booked and the remainder when the product is shipped, installed, or paid for. Order cancellations usually are handled by simply deducting the credit from the rep's record, creating a debit in the compensation account against current earnings.

A second issue concerns how to treat *windfalls*—large, unexpected orders that may or may not reflect the efforts of the individual sales rep. Such occurrences may reflect poor market analysis and sales planning. The windfall issue is related to the problem of *house accounts*—large potential accounts or orders that are designated to be a responsibility of management rather than the territory sales rep and thus removed from the incentive compensation system. House accounts may require special pricing authority as well as multiple-level and multiple-location selling, and for all these reasons it may be appropriate to deal with them at the management level.

The territory sales rep may resent having these major earning opportunities taken away, however, especially if he or she is still responsible for providing some of the service to the account. An equitable understanding with the rep may be reached through an agreement that all unanticipated orders above a certain size will be subject to negotiation with sales management concerning how they are to be credited and compensated for. While this does not resolve the issue, it does create a framework for solving it. Without such arrangements, it is possible to face a situation where the rep would be paid much too much if normal commission rates were applied. Not only does this influence selling expense and profitability, but it can be grossly unfair to other members of the sales and marketing team. It may even have significant negative impact on the rep, such as unplanned tax consequences or creating unreasonable expectations about future earnings, which leads to spending habits that cannot be maintained.

A third issue of implementation involves awarding credit for multiple influence sales. A special case, perhaps the most common, concerns the distinction between distributor and direct accounts. Suppose a customer that normally buys direct decides to place a major order through a distributor, perhaps to obtain better delivery or a more favorable price. Should the sales rep, who can argue that the sale actually reflects his or her selling efforts, still get sales credit and earn the commission? It is worth noting that this problem may not reflect a problem with the compensation plan so much as an issue of market segmentation (i.e., which accounts to serve through distribution) and sales force deployment. It is also obvious that such issues as windfalls, house accounts, order cancellations, and the timing of payment are minimized in a compensation system based mostly or exclusively on salary. As a general rule, equity and morale considerations suggest that the sales rep should usually be given the benefit of the doubt when there is a question about whether to give credit for the sale. This may occasionally result in both a rep and a distributor getting credit for the same sale, which may not be all bad. To do otherwise could lead each to view the other as a competitor rather than a partner. These situations can be handled most effectively and equitably if there is a prior understanding in place concerning how they will be resolved.

The final observation to be made about implementing the sales compensation plan relates to the critical importance of sound communication in making the plan function effectively. Reps must know completely and accurately what is expected of them, how they will be evaluated, and how they will be rewarded. The plan itself must be understandable, permitting the rep to predict quite accurately what his or her income will be, based on performance at any point in time. The linkages among effort, results, and rewards must be clear, and the rewards must be perceived as valuable and worthwhile by the reps. Reps' concerns and complaints about the compensation system should be monitored and analyzed continually, and the plan should be modified as required to bring its performance into line with management compensation objectives and marketing plans.

CAREER PLANNING AS PART OF THE REWARD SYSTEM

Few sales reps are motivated only by financial rewards. Observations about the value of recognition and other non-financial incentives are commonplace in the sales management literature, and there can be no question that every sales rep appreciates explicit management recognition for a job well done. On the other hand, that recognition can take forms that make it trivial and even offensive. Wall plaques, mention in the company newsletter, trips to the home office, and so on are often berated as lacking substance.

For the professional, career-minded sales representative, the ultimate recognition is advancement to higher levels of responsibility within the organization. The performance appraisal system, frequently discussed in this chapter, is the key vehicle for helping people set specific, attainable goals for their own development and to monitor their progress toward those goals. Professional development is not only a personal responsibility, however. It is also a major responsibility of the firm to have carefully planned career paths for the development of motivated, knowledgeable, and hard-working sales reps. Such career development is the ultimate reward desired by the best sales representative, whether that person expects to advance in the professional sales ranks or in the management hierarchy. In the former, advancement will take the form of responsibility for larger accounts and more potential, for selling at higher levels of the customer organization, or for more complex parts of the product line. In the latter case, advancement must begin by exposing the person to the nature of management responsibilities and preparation for them. Part of the sales rep's development and career advancement may very well involve assignments in other parts of the business, especially areas such as product planning and engineering, market analysis and market research, applications engineering, brand or product management, or advertising and sales promotion, areas where the field sales experience can be valuable as a base on which to build.

Such career moves cannot be left to chance opportunity but must be carefully planned, including a fairly firm timetable. Lack of timely advancement may cause the best people to be the first to leave. Equally important, company effectiveness ultimately depends on moving good people along, developing human resources as fast as possible.

While financial rewards and recognition are undoubtedly of major importance to virtually every sales rep, they are not enough for the most motivated and able people. As noted in the previous chapter, a sense of personal growth, accomplishment, and promotion are virtually as important. In our discussion of sales rep motivation, these intrinsic rewards were said to be especially important for younger and better-educated people, especially if they had achieved relatively high income levels. The provision of these rewards must not be allowed to happen by chance, but must be specifically designed and planned as part of the reward system. Financial rewards flow one way, from the company to the sales rep. Personal growth and professional advancement are mutually beneficial for the individual and the company; both are better off when they occur and suffer when they don't.

SUMMARY

The central argument of this chapter has been that evaluation, control, and compensation must be viewed as part of a total system for achieving marketing objectives through the allocation of selling effort and for developing the human resources of the sales force. Sales force control was analyzed as a process of setting standards, gathering information, comparing performance with standards, and taking corrective action, where the standards for performance reflect the marketing strategy and the sales rep's job description. Communication was stressed as the central element in this process, especially in terms of assuring that reps understood what was expected of them and how performance was to be measured, evaluated, and rewarded. Compensation planning was approached in the context of our complex view of the determinants of the sales rep's effectiveness, as opposed to the traditional view of the rep as an individual contributor. Plans combining salary, commission, and bonus were said to be favored because of their more complete relationship to the multiple dimensions of the sales rep's responsibility. The ultimate payoff for the most able and motivated people, however, comes from feelings of personal growth and the opportunity for advancement. That, too, must be planned carefully.

EIGHT

The Field Sales Manager of the Future

Sales managers must manage. That simple statement is the whole premise of this text and is the point to be stressed in this concluding chapter. The field sales manager traditionally has been viewed as "first among equals," the best of the sales reps. Management has been viewed in large part as a reward for successful selling. The newly appointed field sales manager has responded all too often to this set of factors by continuing to behave as supersalesman, rather than as a real, full-time manager. In this chapter, the objective is to outline ways in which the responsibilities, activities, and viewpoints of the future field sales manager may differ from those of the past, and to highlight and integrate the central concepts that have guided the development of earlier chapters.

AN OVERVIEW OF THE CENTRAL MODELS

The central model around which our view of field sales management was organized originally was presented in Chapter 1, and now is repeated as Figure 8.1. It is entitled "Determinants of Sales Representative Effectiveness," and ties together the buyer's decision-making process and the seller's marketing strategy as implemented by its sales management program. The central objective of all field sales management activities *is* to maximize the effectiveness of the field sales representatives in their interactions with buyers.

229

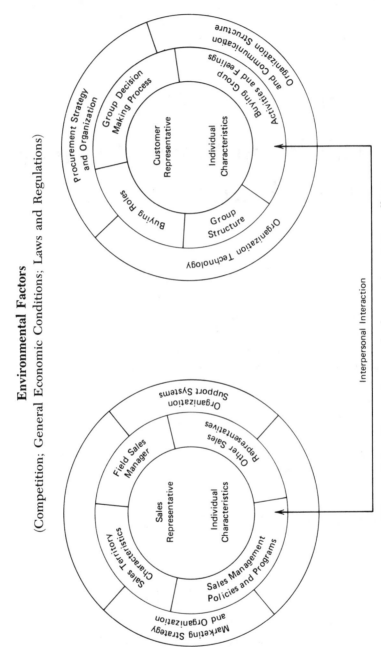

Environmental Factors

(Competition; General Economic Conditions; Laws and Regulations)

Interpersonal Interaction

Figure 8.1. Determinants of sales representative effectiveness.

Three traditional views of sales management have been the target of much of the concern of this text. First, as already noted, we have attacked the idea that the field sales manager is primarily a supersalesman, whose selling duties have precedence over the other responsibilities of supervision, developing the sales organization, administration, and representing the company in the local community. We have focused instead on supervision and organizational development as the two most important duties of the field sales manager.

Second, it has often been asserted in previous chapters that selling must be viewed as interpersonal interaction, a process in which negotiation is the central element, not as something the sales rep does to the buying prospect. Consistent with the philosophy of the modern marketing concept, it has been said that selling is at its core a process of solving customer problems, with the sales rep as the central figure responsible for organizing all of the relevant company resources for finding solutions. At the same time, it was argued strenuously that the selection of customers, and of customer problems to be solved, must not be left to the sales rep's individual judgment. Rather, the deployment of sales reps must be guided by a strong marketing strategy designed to maximize long-term profits by matching company resources with those market opportunities to which it can respond most competently and uniquely, vis-à-vis competition. Sales reps simply cannot make those judgments wisely on their own in the absence of strong corporate strategic marketing direction. The effectiveness of the sales rep must be seen as the critical variable in the implementation of marketing strategy, the infantry pursuing the military objective supported by the deployment of a complex array of organizational resources.

This brings us to the third traditional viewpoint challenged by this text, that of the sales rep as an individual contributor, whose performance is exclusively a matter of personal motivation which is, in turn, almost exclusively a function of financial incentives and rewards. The sales rep has been seen as a member of a sales and marketing team, but also as its tactical leader with the primary responsibility for planning, organizing, and deploying resources against specific accounts. The manager's role, in this context, is to guide and support the rep in these efforts. The sales rep has also been viewed as being influenced by company policies and programs, as well as by the field sales manager, but all of these influences were said to be mediated by the sales rep's own aptitudes, motivations, and role perceptions. As a boundary role person, the sales rep is subject to pressures and expectations from both within and without the organization. Finally, it was asserted that sales reps are motivated not only by financial compensation and management recognition (externally mediated rewards), but also by a sense of personal growth and accomplishment (internally mediated rewards) and by the opportunity for advancement within the organization. We viewed compensation as part of the control process, and career path planning as part of the compensation system.

DEVELOPING HUMAN RESOURCES

The conclusion is inescapable: The primary responsibility of the professional field sales manager of the future will be to develop human resources. Recruitment programs and selection procedures should be upgraded continually to attract people whose backgrounds, interests, and abilities are those specified by the position description. Selling must be viewed and planned as an extension of marketing strategy. Training must be carefully designed to develop the product, company, and market knowledge and selling skills necessary to maximize effectiveness in interactions with customers and to organize company resources to develop solutions to customer problems. Performance criteria must be carefully communicated to the sales reps so that they have clear and accurate role perceptions.

The second major set of obligations of the field sales manager has to do with managing and maintaining the quality of buyer–seller relationships. This does not equate with actually managing accounts. Rather, the field sales manager is responsible for developing the sales representatives, assigning them to accounts that they are equipped to handle, helping the reps plan account strategies, and monitoring, guiding, and supporting them in those endeavors. This includes responsibility for helping the rep manage relationships with other parts of the selling organization and coping with the pressures inherent in the boundary role.

The manager should be concerned ultimately with the quality of the account relationship rather than with short-term sales results exclusively or even primarily. The sales rep should be supervised and evaluated in the context of an account management framework, not just in terms of sales quotas. Top levels of sales management must develop measures of performance for field sales managers and sales reps that are consistent with this longer-term, relationship-management perspective. The manager's objective should not be to manage the account or to solve problems for the rep but rather to maximize the rep's ability to solve problems and to manage accounts.

All of which is to say that the field sales manager's major responsibility is to develop human resources. He or she must be trained for, directed, and evaluated on that basis. The ultimate objective of all supervisory activities is to improve the effectiveness of the sales rep, measured in such terms as overall sales results, increased productivity (the ratio of sales to expenditures) and profitability, and the advancement of sales reps into positions of increased responsibility.

NEW TOOLS FOR THE FIELD SALES MANAGER

The field sales manager of the future will be assisted in his or her responsibilities by three types of resources, or tools, that previously have not been identified closely with field sales management: conceptual knowledge from the behavioral sciences; simple interactive computer models running on small, personal, or time-shared computers; and marketing strategy that has been extended to consider issues of strategic implementation.

Conceptual Knowledge from the Behavioral Sciences

As a first-line supervisor, the field sales manager is directly responsible for managing people. No longer is management ability and ski ll viewed as exclusively an innate ability, although there can be no question that people differ markedly in their basic aptitudes for management. Instead, it has been recognized that management is a set of skills, abilities, attitudes, and knowledge that can be taught and learned, as evidenced by the hundreds of collegiate schools of management, and by the thousands of management seminars and conferences conducted every year. An important part of professional management knowledge and skill is based in the behavioral sciences—those parts of social science, namely psychology, sociology, social psychology, and anthropology, concerned specifically with human behavior. This area of management knowledge is especially significant for field sales managers.

As we have tried to demonstrate throughout this text, many areas of field sales management can be illuminated by casting them into a behavioral science framework. That was done, for example, in the discussions of selling as interpersonal interaction, of the expectancy model of sales rep motivation, of the organizational buying process, of the contingency model of sales rep effectiveness, of role perceptions, of psychological testing, and of supervision. The sales manager of the future will increasingly look to this body of knowledge, not for answers to specific questions but for frameworks and guidelines for thinking about the complexities of sales rep motivation and performance, and for a deeper understanding of the manager's role. Such conceptual knowledge can only be acquired by exposure to it through reading and educational programs, but it comes alive in the actual work environment. The theoretical knowledge can significantly extend the manager's ability to learn from experience, and to interpret and understand that experience. Conceptual knowledge from the behavioral sciences should be part of every field sales manager's professional training.

Computers and Interactive Models

The 1980s are bringing developments in the area of interactive computing that promise to bring the power of computers into the hands of virtually every professional and "knowledge worker," if not every home. Whereas earlier generations of computers were awesome in the view of most line managers, today's computing devices are no more frightening than a typewriter or a calculator. In fact, traditional office functions previously performed by typewriters, calculators, manual filing systems, and traditional bookkeeping methods are being combined into systems of management information and office automation using computers that resemble a typewriter and the common television set much more than they resemble earlier generations of computer technology. Furthermore, the new generation of computing technology is so much easier to use than the earlier versions, that the non-user is rapidly becoming the exception rather than the rule.

In the early days of computers, management science, and management information systems in marketing, the advocates of "scientific" management had a vision of a single, complex mathematical model that would encompass all the entities and interactions in the total marketing system. A statistical data base would describe customers, territories, products, sales reps, distributors, advertising media, and all the other actors in the system. Submodels would examine such critical decision areas as advertising budgets and media allocation, sales force size, sales territory design, sales rep routing patterns, pricing decisions, locations of distribution points, and selection of distribution channels, and calculate optimal or nearly optimal levels of all variables and activities controlled by management.[1] The advent of time-shared computing (several input-output devices permitting multiple users of a computer system at any one time) was seen as a major breakthrough permitting extensive management use for the first time, putting the computer directly into the hands of the manager whenever it was needed. *Interactive modeling*, in which the manager/user provides inputs of data and judgments in response to inquiries and options offered by the computer, was the next step in improving the usability of computers from a management viewpoint. While time-sharing made the computer accessible, interactive modeling made the models themselves accessible and amenable to management judgment.

The management scientist's view of what constitutes a good model also changed significantly, however. The early ideal was a model that was thorough, complex, and provided optimal or nearly optimal solutions (i.e., those that maximized achievement of some goal or criterion such as maximum profit or minimum cost), constrained only by the quality and quantity of data available to the user and by the cost and speed of the necessary computation. When models were criticized for being naive and oversimplified, the modeler was delighted to add more variables and make the model more complex, which was seldom what the manager/user was asking for or what was needed. "Scientific" management was the objective, with "scientific" being es-

---

[1]For one excellent articulation of this viewpoint, and an overview of its elements, see David B. Montgomery and Glen L. Urban, *Management Science in Marketing* (Englewood Cliffs, NJ: Prentice-Hall, 1969).

sentially synonymous with "quantification."[2] This early view encountered a number of problems, including the difficulty of measuring the variables and relationships specified by the models, the cost of developing, testing, maintaining, and refining the models themselves, and, perhaps most importantly, the indifference and resistance of management. The latter was a function of many factors including the manager's lack of training and mathematical sophistication, the fact that managers don't typically look for solutions to global problems, the modeler's unfamiliarity with the manager's perceptions of the problem, and the limited time most managers have to become familiar with models and their uses. The models often were not motivated by the manager's interest in the first place and they were typically not responsive to a real need perceived by the manager. Models were designed to solve problems that a company might consider once every several years, not the daily and monthly decisions faced by line management. These shortcomings were especially evident in the area of sales management.[3]

For these reasons, the early emphasis on sophistication, complexity, quantification, and optimization has been replaced by a view that the best models are simple, easy to use and understand, and accessible. They are not intended to provide final solutions to problems, but rather to assist the manager in finding solutions with which he or she is comfortable. The newer approaches to modeling emphasize accessibility to information and allowing the manager/user to test, easily and economically, a number of different sets of assumptions by asking "what if . . . " questions. The accuracy of measurements in the underlying mathematical model is much less at issue when these can be examined for the impact of changes in their values. Where small changes are seen to produce results of critical significance, the manager quickly sees that additional information and more careful measurement would be worthwhile and can focus attention on those critical areas.

---

[2]Peter F. Drucker, *Management* (New York: Harper & Row, Publishers, 1974), p. 510.

[3]David B. Montgomery and Frederick E. Webster, Jr., "Application of Operations Research to Personal Selling Strategy," *Journal of Marketing*, Vol. 32 (January 1968), pp. 50–57.

In field sales management, published models have focused primarily on the areas of sales force size, territory size and composition (the workload *vs* potential controversy reviewed in Chapter 5), and the whole area of deployment. These areas of analysis and decision making are the province of higher levels of the sales management organization, and are in some ways more appropriate for solution by large, complex analytical models using the large central computing capability that is the domain of the operations researchers. Only the largest sales organizations can afford this degree of expertise.

The first-line field sales manager focuses on a different level and variety of problems. The newer generation of computers and models is bringing its sophistication down to the operating level of the organization, making an attack on these operating problems possible and economical and, at the same time, also making the larger, more sophisticated systems available, at least in part, beyond the operations research department. Both effects are significant in improving the professionalism of the field sales manager. For example, computers and models might help to monitor sales reps' performance *vs* quota on a regular basis, to test the effect of a revision of the compensation system, to keep timely files of information on all key customers, to track new-product introductions or regional media advertising, or to analyze alternative deployment patterns. The major benefit is to provide ready access to important information, to permit easy updating of the information, and to allow the manager to test a number of options quickly and easily, not to find optimal solutions to complex problems. The underlying philosophy is to cope with the inherent complexity of sales force management by using simple methods for studying and dealing with specific aspects of that complexity. The objectives are always the same—to help the field sales manager to manage and to enhance the effectiveness of the sales representatives. The field sales manager's effectiveness is reflected in the performance of the sales reps.

Interactive models can be tremendously helpful in the complex tasks of planning and controlling sales activity at the local level. They allow the field sales manager to make judgments based on a more frequent and up-to-date review of information and a more complete analysis of the data. Used properly, computer-based models allow for a continuous monitoring of performance that permits the manager to maintain close awareness of the progress and development of individual sales reps and the timely identification of problems. They can contribute to closer supervision, highly desirable from the viewpoint of the sales rep, who typically wants to know that his or her progress is being watched and to know the manager's support is there when needed. Such monitoring can also help the manager to allocate work-with time to reps.

Increasingly, the computer has become the handmaiden of managerial judgment rather than a substitute for it. The refinement of time-shared computing and the advent of microcomputers and distributed data processing have made the use of computer power for data file management, data analysis, and modeling of decision problems an accessible reality for first-line field sales managers. The good ones will take advantage of it.

Strategic Interface with Marketing

The organizational and strategic relationship of sales and marketing remains one of the conundrums of marketing management. The marketing concept, as a philosophy of management focused on the satisfaction of customer needs, often has been interpreted as an evolution away from selling. Such is the view expressed by Peter Drucker, for example, when he notes that "selling and marketing are antithetical rather than synonymous or even complementary,"[4] and "consumerism is a clear indication that the right motto for business management should increasingly be 'from selling to marketing'."[5] When Peter Drucker makes a mistake like that, we know how serious the problem is! Drucker is caught in the old trap. He views selling as something the sales rep does to the customer. He does not, unfortunately, see selling as the process of managing customer relationships and creating solutions to customer problems. The latter is completely consistent with the marketing concept, a management philosophy most people attribute to Peter Drucker's own personal creativity. How could Drucker, of all people, make this mistake?

[4]Drucker, *op.cit.*, p. 64.
[5]*Ibid.*, p. 65.

Drucker positioned the marketing concept as having a long-term, strategic orientation, as opposed to a short-term and tactical orientation for selling.[6] Three decades ago, as an articulation of a new management viewpoint about the purpose of a firm, that was useful. The purpose of a business is, fundamentally, to create a satisfied customer (marketing), not to sell whatever the factory produces (selling). But once the factory has decided what to produce (a marketing decision), demand must be generated for it. A commitment to long-term goals doesn't eliminate the need for short-term performance and results. If long-run profit maximization (a measure of the degree to which the firm is satisfying customer needs) is the proper objective of marketing, what is the proper objective of the sales operation with its short-term, strategic, and tactical focus? The issue is primarily one of time horizon, of *when* earnings should be maximized. A recent survey of chief executive officers of manufacturing and service organizations found that the incomplete acceptance of the marketing concept, especially in industrial firms, and the conflict or trade-off between short-term and long-term earnings were two of their central concerns about the marketing function in their businesses.[7]

Drucker's statement of the problem, and top management's concern about the apparent conflict between, or incomplete integration of, sales and marketing, reflect a basic shortcoming of the emphasis on strategic planning that engrossed management's attention in the 1960s and 1970s. Corporate management in the 1980s has recognized part of the problem as an excessive emphasis on short-term (quarterly and annual) profit and return-on-investment as a criterion of management performance, which can conflict in many ways with long-term profit maximization.[8] Interestingly, it can be the case that short-term *sales* maximization *not* short-term *profit* maximization, can lead to long-term profit maximization, especially if sales performance is fo-

---

[6]Peter F. Drucker, *The Practice of Management* (New York: Harper & Row, 1954), pp. 37–41.

[7]Frederick E. Webster, Jr., "Top Management's Concerns about Marketing: Issues for the 1970's," *Journal of Marketing*, Vol. 45 (Summer 1981), pp. 9–16. See also Robert H. Hayes and William J. Abernathy, "Managing Our Way to Economic Decline," *Harvard Business Review*, Vol. 58 (July–August 1980), pp. 66–77.

[8]*Ibid.*

cused on building the customer base and enhancing market share, even at the expense of short-term profitability.[9] The strategic planning process is not complete until management has clearly articulated the connections between long-term marketing goals and short-term sales objectives.

Another problem revealed by the incomplete integration of sales and marketing is the emphasis on strategy *formulation*, which is only one part of the total process of strategic management. In particular, strategy formulation, which must be preceded by strategic analysis of the environment, has to be followed by a detailed plan of strategic *implementation*.[10] Furthermore, a distinction must be made among four levels of strategy:

1. *Enterprise Strategy*. Concerned about the relationship of the firm with society.

2. *Corporate Strategy*. Which answers the question "What business are we in?" and defines the mission of the firm.

3. *Business Strategy*. Which focuses on the product/market intersections to which the firm is committed and defines strategies for competing in those distinct businesses. Product portfolio analyses are used to position each distinct business (product/market combination) in a matrix according to market share relative to competition and some measure of market opportunity such as market growth rate.

4. *Functional Strategy*. Plans for the separate business functions, integrated within, and designated to implement, the business strategy.[11]

As one of the separate business functions, in this more complete view of the strategic planning process, marketing is seen as a vehicle for implementing business strategy, which must be embedded within

[9]For an illustration of a strategic situation where this was believed to be the case, see "Honeywell Information Systems (A)" in Benson P. Shapiro, *Sales Program Management: Formulation and Implementation* (New York: McGraw-Hill Book Co., 1977), pp. 103–18.

[10]Dan E. Schendel and Charles W. Hofer (eds.), *Strategic Management: A New View of Business Policy and Planning* (Boston: Little-Brown, 1979), pp. 14–18.

[11]*Ibid.*, pp. 11–13.

corporate strategy, and so on. But marketing strategy itself is composed of substrategies for product policy, pricing, distribution, advertising and promotion, and sales. Sales management therefore has the ultimate responsibility for implementing marketing, business, corporate, and enterprise strategies. Strategy at each level is guided by and is intended to implement strategy at the next higher level.

Putting this all together brings us back to the central argument of Chapter 5—the sales rep should be thought of as the unit of attack through which a marketing strategy gets implemented. At the core of every effective marketing strategy, it was said, is a clear definition of market segments, targets that are preselected by the strategy for the sales reps' efforts. In the absence of clear strategic direction, sales reps must fill the gap by selecting their own targets, which they will do in a way that will maximize their own income and job satisfaction, which probably means maximizing short-term sales volume. Marketing strategy will be dominated by sales strategy. Short-term goals will override attention to long-term objectives. There is likely to be great inconsistency from sales rep to sales rep, from one territory to another, and this will lead to strategic disarray and weakness in the firm as a whole.

The 1980s are seeing some serious management attention directed to these issues. A broader concern with total strategic management is replacing the narrow emphasis on strategy formulation[12] and management attention is shifting to longer-term performance criteria as opposed to quarterly profit and return-on-investment performance. One major stimulus for these shifts has been the strength of foreign competition, primarily from Japan, with a longer-term emphasis on market dominance and more complete response to customer needs.

If these trends persist, the field sales manager is going to be subject to a much stronger strategic direction from marketing and business strategy. The professional sales manager will welcome this because it should enhance both the effectiveness and efficiency of the field sales reps while also creating a broader range of career opportunities for them within the total marketing organization of the firm.

[12]See Schendel and Hofer, *op. cit.* and a talk entitled "From Strategic Planning to Strategic Management" by Mr. Donald R. Melville, President and Chief Executive Officer of the Norton Company, to the Machinery and Allied Products Institute in Washington, D.C., January 22, 1982.

Better developed career paths within the marketing organization are a highly desirable and highly logical outgrowth of viewing the sales rep as a member of the marketing team, whose overriding responsibility is to manage the interaction between the firm and its customers and to maximize the value of the buyer–seller relationship to both parties.

SUMMARY

Sales management is the critical line function of the marketing organization. With the cost of a single sales call approaching $200 and the average sale requiring close to five calls, improved marketing productivity demands increased attention to enhancing the effectiveness and efficiency of the field sales representative, the key figure in the implementation of marketing strategy in the industrial firm. The field sales manager is the focus of responsibility for enhancing the sales rep's effectiveness.

The sales manager is first and foremost a manager, not a supersalesman. The sales rep is not an individual contributor but a member of a total marketing team, motivated by opportunities for personal growth and advancement within the sales and marketing organization, not just financial rewards and management recognition. The rep is responsible for managing the buyer–seller relationship and maximizing its value to both. Selling is interpersonal interaction, not something the rep does to the customer.

These are the central ideas of this text and imply a professional field sales manager in the future quite different from his or her predecessors. Those future managers will be guided by a strong framework from the behavioral sciences that highlights their responsibility for developing human resources. They will use the computer increasingly as a personalized tool for analysis, planning, and control based on much more detailed attention to an up-to-date file of information on activities and actors in the marketing system. They also will be guided by a much more explicit sense of strategic direction from marketing, as sales strategy is more carefully integrated with marketing strategy and overall business and corporate strategy. The best management talent of any business should hopefully be attracted to, develop in, and grow out of the selling and sales management functions into the top marketing and corporate management positions of the firm. No function is more important to the success of the total enterprise than selling, and the field sales manager is the central element in an effective sales organization.

Index